Revolution in Redline

Revolution

in Redline

The Iterative Journey of the U.S. Constitution

SAM J. MERCHANT

Associate Professor

University of Minnesota Law School

CAROLINA ACADEMIC PRESS

Durham, North Carolina

LIBRARY OF CONGRESS CATALOGING-IN-PUBLICATION DATA

Name: Merchant, Sam J., author.
Title: Revolution in Redline : The Iterative Journey of the U.S. Constitution / Sam J. Merchant.
Description: Durham, North Carolina : Carolina Academic Press, 2025. | Includes bibliographical references and index.
Identifiers: LCCN 2024046894 | ISBN 9781531031756 (paperback) | ISBN 9781531031763 (ebook)
Subjects: LCSH: Constitutional history—United States. | Constitutional law—United States. | Constitutional amendments—United States. | Magna Carta. | United States. Constitution. 1st–10th Amendments.
Classification: LCC KF4541 .M47 2025 | DDC 342.7302/9—dc23/eng/20241008
LC record available at https://lccn.loc.gov/2024046894

CAROLINA ACADEMIC PRESS
700 Kent Street
Durham, North Carolina 27701
(919) 489-7486
www.cap-press.com

Printed in the United States of America

For Ray Ann and Walter Merchant

Contents

Introduction

THE GOAL OF THIS BOOK is for you to learn as much about the U.S. Constitution and Declaration of Independence as quickly as possible. It accomplishes that task by condensing volumes of historical, archival, and scholarly information into one book, and in a medium that is engaging and accessible to the modern reader. In this meticulously crafted guide, you'll see how ancient principles morphed into American democracy. You'll join the drafters as they propose, debate, and approve the final versions of America's founding documents. As you read, links to original sources are provided for virtually every statement and debate, familiarizing you with key historical records and guiding even deeper research.

When making or responding to constitutional arguments, an understanding of the relevant texts, history, tradition, structure, and context is imperative. This kind of understanding is impossible without appreciating *how* and *why* the Framers chose the words that they chose. This book presents that journey in two novel ways: the Constitution's historical journey and its drafting journey.

The historical journey begins with the Magna Carta (1215) and the English Bill of Rights (1689), and then key petitions and declarations that show the road to American independence. But this book not only compiles the full text of all of these documents, it also explains the key connections between them and how they inspired America's founding documents. This interconstitutionalist approach helps unlock a more accurate understanding of the context behind why each provision exists, and the source of certain words, phrases, and concepts.

For example, the book traces how the Constitution's due-process protections, rights to a jury, and representation-based taxation were derived from prior clauses in English documents going all the way back to Magna Carta. Many readers have a sense of this but have not had occasion to analyze the documents and connections themselves. This book also shows where America departed from English traditions. Readers can trace the origins of American self-government in texts like the Articles of Association (1774),[1] see how earlier declarations and petitions informed the grievances in the Declaration of Independence (often verbatim), and easily identify how the Constitution addresses the Articles of Confederation's many shortcomings.

Revolution in Redline then presents and explains the full text of the founding documents, but in a completely unique way that aligns with how we draft documents today. We know that the Framers edited drafts of America's founding documents. We know that they debated and voted on almost every change. If this process occurred in legal circles today, it would almost certainly involve tracking changes or "redlining" drafts, commenting on those drafts, and then engaging in deliberation on the "markup" version. This book reimagines that interactive approach for America's founding documents. It brings the interpretation of these documents into the twenty-first century, presenting them through a modern medium to engage with modern readers. It invites you to step into "the room where it happened," demystifying the process and allowing you to see the drafters revise the founding documents and debate over the proposed changes. The result is hopefully an enlightening and refreshing way to understand these documents and the history that surrounds them—as quickly and efficiently as possible.

This book has a wide array of uses. For non-experts, it is an enjoyable way to read, engage with, and learn much more about the founding documents. For students, lawyers, advocates, or judges, this book will help buttress constitutional arguments in your research, briefing, or court opinions. Care was taken in the selection of specific versions of documents, and changes like the addition of a comma or semicolon have been meticulously tracked because these changes can sometimes change the meaning of a sentence. When interpreting a word or clause, you can refer to this book to see why it exists, why specific words were selected, whether alternatives were debated, whether it existed in earlier documents, and who is responsible for its inclusion.

The eBook version is highly recommended in addition to the print version for this type of research. You can click on *any* image or hyperlink, which will typ-

1. As you'll see, Abraham Lincoln believed that the United States actually started with the Articles of Association, not the Declaration of Independence.

ically take you to the exact page of the original source, making this an invaluable and efficient starting point for further research of the full debate on an issue.[2] For all readers, this is the only book that concisely compiles each of these documents, several drafts, key debates, and then describes the links between the documents and debates.

Should America have five presidents or one? How long should they serve—four years, seven years, or for life? Shouldn't owning property be a requirement for serving in Congress? Perhaps the most controversial topic at the founding, how should we deal with slaves? Are they people, or property? As the tracked changes and debates in this book reveal, each of these topics, and many others, evolved over drafts and amendments to the Constitution. Some options were even proposed at the Constitutional Convention, rejected, and later became amendments (like the popular election of senators). Other edits appear to have been surreptitiously added—sometimes caught and changed back, sometimes not. The importance of understanding this history is reinforced by the fact that Supreme Court justices regularly rely on revisions that are described in this book when deciding cases.[3]

For the Constitution, this book starts with a key draft from the Committee of Detail, a committee comprised of respected delegates who were tasked with

---

2. The eBook version is available on the publisher's website and from major online retailers. *See* cap-press.com/books/isbn/9781531031756/Revolution-in-Redline. For those with only the print version, most sources (other than hyperlinks on images) have been sufficiently identified so that the reader should be able to locate them.

3. *See, e.g.*, *Arizona State Legislature v. Arizona Indep. Redistricting Comm'n*, 576 U.S. 787, 836 (2015) (Roberts, J., dissenting) ("The insertion of 'the legislature' [by the Committee of Detail in Art. I, § 4] indicates that the Framers thought carefully about which entity within the State was to perform congressional districting."); *Adoptive Couple v. Baby Girl*, 570 U.S. 637, 663 (2013) (Thomas, J., concurring) (describing changes in drafts regarding the Indian Commerce Clause in Art. I, § 8, "The Committee [of Detail]'s version, which echoed the Articles of Confederation, was far narrower than Madison's proposal."); *D.C. v. Heller*, 554 U.S. 570, 656 (2008) (Stevens, J., dissenting) (analyzing differences between James Madison's proposal and the final version of the Second Amendment); *Cent. Virginia Cmty. Coll. v. Katz*, 546 U.S. 356, 369 (2006) (describing how two, pre-founding state bankruptcy cases and the need for full faith and credit of bankruptcy discharges among states led to the addition of the Bankruptcy Clause in Art. I, § 8); *Morrison v. Olson*, 487 U.S. 654, 699 (1988) (Scalia, J., dissenting) (noting the difference between the legislative vesting clause, granting powers "herein granted," and the vesting clause for the executive, which has no such qualifier); *324 Liquor Corp. v. Duffy*, 479 U.S. 335, 354 (1987) (O'Connor, J., dissenting) (analyzing the omission of a proposed Section 3 to the Twenty-First Amendment, which would have allowed concurrent federal authority to regulate the sale of liquor); *Powell v. McCormack*, 395 U.S. 486, 539 (1969) (analyzing last-minute changes to Art. I, § 2, concluding that the Committee of Style "had no authority from the Convention to make alterations of substance in the Constitution as voted by the Convention").

drafting a new constitution based on the Framers' preliminary agreements and instructions. By tracking changes between the Committee's final draft and the signed version of the Constitution, we can observe that, time and again, the trusted men of the Committee memorialized many ideas about the Constitution that were later rejected or supplemented. Changes to the Committee of Detail's draft include:

- Rewriting the entire Preamble.
- The Committee draft allowed only *property owners* to serve in the federal government.
- Apportionment for representation in the House changed dramatically.
- Instead of the President, the Committee empowered the *Senate* to make treaties, appoint ambassadors, and appoint Supreme Court Justices.
- The Committee draft required the *states*, not the federal government, to pay salaries and travel for members of Congress.

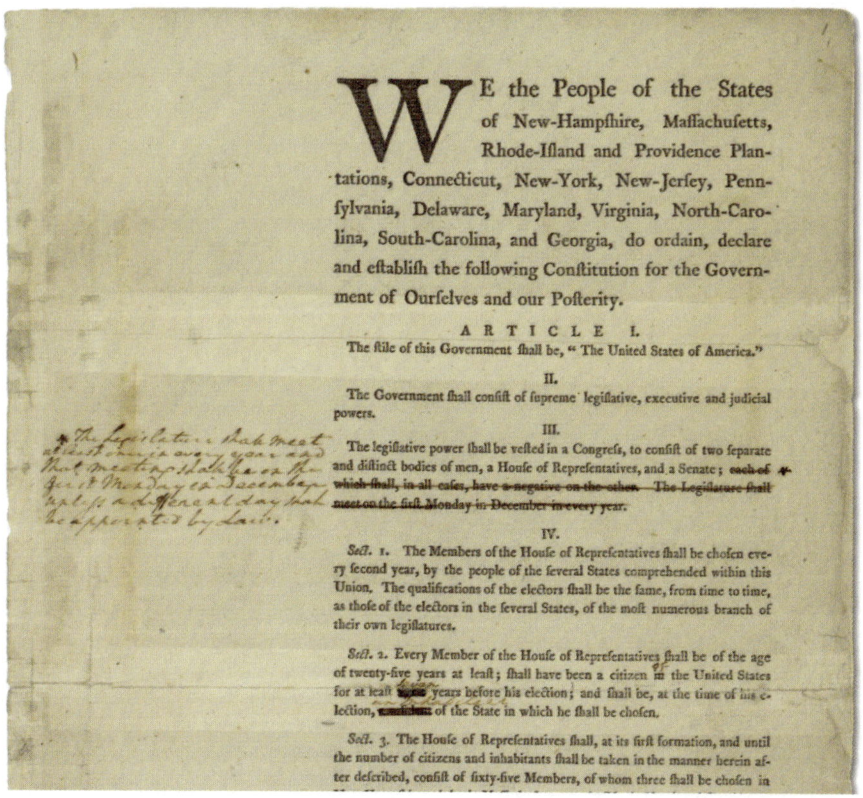

WE the People of the States of New-Hampſhire, Maſſachuſetts, Rhode-Iſland and Providence Plantations, Connecticut, New-York, New-Jerſey, Pennſylvania, Delaware, Maryland, Virginia, North-Carolina, South-Carolina, and Georgia, do ordain, declare and eſtabliſh the following Conſtitution for the Government of Ourſelves and our Poſterity.

ARTICLE I.

The ſtile of this Government ſhall be, "The United States of America."

II.

The Government ſhall conſiſt of ſupreme legiſlative, executive and judicial powers.

III.

The legiſlative power ſhall be veſted in a Congreſs, to conſiſt of two ſeparate and diſtinct bodies of men, a Houſe of Repreſentatives, and a Senate; ~~each of which ſhall, in all caſes, have a negative on the other. The Legiſlature ſhall meet on the firſt Monday in December in every year.~~ *

* The legislature shall meet at least once in every year and that meeting shall be on the first Monday in December unless a different day shall be appointed by Law.

IV.

Sect. 1. The Members of the Houſe of Repreſentatives ſhall be choſen every ſecond year, by the people of the ſeveral States comprehended within this Union. The qualifications of the electors ſhall be the ſame, from time to time, as thoſe of the electors in the ſeveral States, of the moſt numerous branch of their own legiſlatures.

Sect. 2. Every Member of the Houſe of Repreſentatives ſhall be of the age of twenty-five years at leaſt; ſhall have been a citizen of the United States for at leaſt seven years before his election; and ſhall be, at the time of his election, an inhabitant of the State in which he ſhall be choſen.

Sect. 3. The Houſe of Repreſentatives ſhall, at its firſt formation, and until the number of citizens and inhabitants ſhall be taken in the manner herein after deſcribed, conſiſt of ſixty-five Members, of whom three ſhall be choſen in

Excerpt from George Washington's annotated Committee of Detail draft

- The Committee originally gave Congress much more authority on managing the day-to-day aspects of wars.
- The Committee draft called the President "His Excellency," had the legislature elect the President, and limited the presidency to one term of seven years.

These and many other changes jump off the page when reading the Constitution with tracked changes. If a reasonable option was proposed but not ultimately included, one could argue that at least some of the Framers considered the position meritorious. Conversely, one could just as easily argue that if an idea was proposed and expressly rejected, that is the end of the matter. (Justice Stevens and Justice Scalia debated this very issue in ***D.C. v. Heller***, 554 U.S. 570 (2008), regarding James Madison's draft Second Amendment compared to the final version. For the draft and final version, *see* p. 173.) Sometimes the placement of a comma, use of a semicolon, or the sentence structure can have an enormous impact on rights or the government's powers. *See, e.g.*, *Heller* (finding an individual right to bear arms after analyzing the "prefatory clause" and "operative clause" of the Second Amendment).

Some of the changes to the final draft Constitution were made by the "Committee of Style," *after* the full Constitutional Convention had finalized what it wanted in the Constitution. Where we observe changes that the Committee of Style made, is the final text binding (even though it differs from what the Convention approved), or should we enforce the text that the Constitutional Convention approved?[4] Some scholars have even argued that a delegate (Gouverneur Morris) surreptitiously made changes to the final draft that altered the meaning of many provisions and none of the Framers caught the changes before they signed. As you will see, this book serves as a powerful tool to help facilitate a deeper, more nuanced understanding of these documents. By analyzing the iterative process, we can better appreciate what the words or phrases mean (or do not mean).

The Constitution has also undergone a different kind of redlining—formal amendments. Amendments modify, update, or clarify constitutional provisions. Reviewing any constitutional provision requires taking any relevant amendments into account, but with twenty-seven of them—some of which amend other amendments—keeping track of the status of any constitutional provision

4. Justice Stevens and Justice Thomas debated this in ***Utah v. Evans***, 536 U.S. 452 (2002). *See* p. 138.

can be challenging even for Constitution experts. To make that process easier, this book weaves the amendments into the Constitution (as James Madison and others preferred) so that the reader can quickly understand changes between drafts, revisions, and amendments all in one place. As just one example, Art. I, §9, originally provided that Congress can never prohibit the migration or importation of slaves. Section 9 was revised in the final version as a compromise, delaying that prohibition until after 1808 (twenty years). The Thirteenth Amendment abolished slavery altogether in 1865. Rather than piecing all of this history together from multiple documents, the reader can see it clearly and concisely on a single page (page 146).

One final way to better understand the Constitution is by comparing it to the Constitution of the Confederate States of America. (Most people do not even know that the Confederates had a constitution.) The Civil War is a scar on American history but there are lessons it can teach us about the Constitution. The Confederates' constitution is a historically significant piece of constitutional commentary. It represents the culmination of the "states' rights" constitutional tradition that had competed with nationalism since the Founding. The drafters of the CSA constitution saw themselves not as rejecting the American constitutional project, but as restoring it to what they believed was its original, correct interpretation.

The Confederates drafted their own version of the Constitution and copied most of the U.S. Constitution (changing around 38% of it), and therefore had the opportunity to do what many modern scholars only hypothesize: how might we change the Constitution if given the chance, and why?[5] Many, but not all, of the Confederates' changes dealt with slavery. By observing their changes, we can better understand their deepest grievances, observe how they thought the Constitution could be updated and improved almost 100 years after ratification, and analyze their document for strengths, weaknesses, and ideas. The Confederate Constitution departed from the U.S. Constitution in many interesting ways, including adding a single-subject rule for legislation, adding a line-item veto for the President, eliminating diversity jurisdiction in courts, and, of course, protecting domestic slavery.

---

5. Relatedly, the National Constitution Center created the Constitution Drafting Project which brings together scholars of different political and constitutional backgrounds to partake in constitutional conventions to draft their ideal constitutions.

In this book, the Constitution, Declaration of Independence, Articles of Confederation, and Confederate Constitution are redlined with track changes to reveal the iterative processes that went into creating those documents. "Clean" versions of the Constitution, Declaration of Independence, and Articles of Confederation are included at the end of the book for times when the reader only needs to review the final text. Extra space has been intentionally added for your notes.

A brief introduction is provided before each section, and this book includes annotations and debates to give additional context or interesting facts. In the annotations, this book does not present every (or even most) of the views of the Framers or arguments from the state ratifying conventions. Instead, to avoid excessive length, this book concisely identifies notable viewpoints and offers additional resources for further study. Relatedly, the founding documents went through multiple drafts, and this book only tracks changes between the final version and a key draft. Interesting changes might exist between other versions of the documents, which are simply beyond the scope of this book.

An early step in analyzing any constitutional provision is to see whether the language has changed—through amendment or otherwise. Comparing a clause and its revisions with other early documents helps understand how we arrived at where we are today. This book facilitates this analysis, which will lead to a deeper understanding and exciting new conversations. By analyzing the iterative process, we can better appreciate these foundational documents and their significance in the world.

How to Use This Book

THIS BOOK COMPARES the final versions of some of America's most significant documents to an important draft of the document. It also provides many of the key documents that led to America's founding. Unless otherwise indicated, the final versions that are used are the documents located at the National Archives in Washington, D.C. Comparator drafts are typically the latest draft from which the drafters made substantive changes. In each case, the specific documents that were compared are identified on page 291.

Changes between drafts are indicated in modified "tracked changes" or "redline": if there is no change between the draft and the final version, the text appears normally (in black with no added formatting). If content appeared in the draft but was omitted from the final version, it is shown in ~~*italics and stricken through*~~. If the drafters added new language to a draft, it is shown in red and underlined. Commentary from this book's author, generally providing context or interesting facts, is in the footnotes and margins. Any content in brackets *[ ]* was added by this book's author or the document's transcriber. In the redlined documents, bracketed numbering links the drafter's margin commentary to specific parts of the text, and traditional footnotes provide annotations and connections. To help frame the material, bracketed headings are included in most sections that summarize the respective content.

It is often difficult for readers of the Constitution to remember whether and how any amendments changed certain provisions. As you will see, James Madison and others thought that amendments should be explicitly included in modified provisions, weaving them into the existing Constitution. This proposal was rejected, but a version of that serves as a valuable way to quickly read and understand the Constitution. This makes particular sense in a book like this—we can compare drafts, the final version, and amendments next to each other to appreciate the evolution of certain provisions and principles. In this book, the constitutional amendments are appended to the end of the Constitution as is traditionally done, but they are also included in footnotes next to the relevant constitutional provisions. To flag to the reader that an amendment changed a provision of the Constitution, constitutional language that an amendment directly impacted appears with a border around the text.

This book serves as an opportunity to engage with the Framers, including with some of their thoughts and debates. Commentary from the Framers or those responsible for a provision is included in the margins of the founding documents. Additionally, different readers will undoubtedly make different observations and conclusions while reading this book, so extra space is included for reader notes.

Capitalization and formatting changes are typically not tracked in redline, and the long "*s*" (which looks like an "*ſ*": **of New-Hampſhire, Maſſachuſetts,**) that was prevalent when many of these documents were drafted has been converted to an "s." Because punctuation differences can arguably impact the resulting meaning, punctuation changes are tracked.

The combination of the print version and eBook is highly recommended. The print version is intended to be your go-to desktop reference for founding documents.[1] When further research is needed, you can use the eBook version to follow the trail of hyperlinks. Every image is hyperlinked (from those in the introductory sections to profile photos of each drafter), taking you to the original source of the referenced material on government-maintained websites. Text in blue is also hyperlinked, taking you to the source of the referenced material.

As explained in more detail in subsequent sections, there is some debate over which version is the "official" version of the Constitution—the engrossed (written) version or later, printed versions (all of which have minor variations). Because this book focuses on the minds of the Framers and their changes to drafts (not the mind of subsequent printers who may have made changes), the redlined Constitution tracks the changes between the Committee of Detail draft and the engrossed version that the Framers signed. But the engrossed version is not the version that the states ratified—that version is the September 28, 1787, printed version, so that is the version that is included as the "clean" version. *See* p. 131.

1. Headers help quickly identify the document you are viewing. You might also consider tabbing chapters that are referenced often, like the clean version of the Constitution and Declaration of Independence.

It was not always possible to show changes in a manner that is readable because the drafters rearranged some drafts and moved content between sections or paragraphs. This was particularly true with the Articles of Confederation and Article I of the Constitution, where the drafters included most of the content from the drafts in the final versions but heavily reorganized clauses. In these cases, this book identifies the additions or deletions but does not identify reorganization. If the relocation of a sentence or clause matters for your use (which is not inconceivable), all of the transcriptions that were used are identified at the end of the book so that you can engage in additional research if needed.

The documents in this book are in chronological order. Simply reading this list offers a telling summary of how we arrived at the Constitution we know today:

- Magna Carta (1215)
- English Declaration of Rights (1689)
- Declaration of Rights and Grievances (1765)
- Declaratory Act (1766)
- Declaration of Resolves of the First Continental Congress (1774)
- Articles of Association (1774)
- Petition to King George III (1774)
- Olive Branch Petition to King George III (1774)
- Declaration on the Causes and Necessity of Taking Up Arms (1775)
- King George III's Proclamation for Suppressing Rebellion (1775)
- Declaration of Independence (1776) (redlined)
- Article of Confederation (1777) (redlined)
- Northwest Ordinance (1787)
- Constitution of the United States (1787) (redlined)
- Constitution of the United States compared to the Constitution of the Confederate States of America (1861)
- Declaration of Independence (1776) (clean)
- Articles of Confederation (1777) (clean)
- Constitution of the United States (1787) (clean)

Revolution in Redline

Magna Carta

JUNE 15, 1215

Introduction

In 1215, a group of rebellious English barons (nobles) were embattled with the unpopular King John, and Magna Carta arose as a peace treaty. The barons were outraged at arbitrary arrests, crippling fines, and the King's failures in foreign policy. From the barons' perspectives, the treaty attempted to protect their rights and property against the tyrannical King. Despite the King's initial reluctance, he affixed his royal seal to the document and copies were disseminated widely across England.

The 1215 Magna Carta consisted of 63 clauses that were largely focused on regulating feudal customs and the administration of justice, not foundational legal principles. Clauses 39 and 40, however, laid early groundwork for significant legal concepts and outlined the framework for the right to due process, trial by jury, and habeas corpus (challenging detention and imprisonment). Clause 39 explicitly stated that no free man would be imprisoned, dispossessed, deprived of his standing, or exiled without lawful judgment by his peers or by the law of the land.[1] This idea of "law of the land" evolved into the due-process provisions of later

1. Of course, by "peers" Magna Carta meant other barons, not all citizens. This and other critiques of the traditional story suggest that later legal scholars like Edward Coke and William Blackstone overstated the significance of the document. Under this "myth of Magna Carta" perspective, the American Framers were actually influenced by powerful reinterpretations of Magna Carta, not the document itself.

1215 Magna Carta

constitutions. Clause 40 promised that justice would not be delayed or denied, and indirectly underscored the modern presumption of innocence.

Clause 14 outlined the important principle that taxation should only occur with proper representation, requiring the King to consult his great council of barons before levying new taxes, an early form of consent-based governance. Other clauses addressed commercial regulations, including weights and measures for commodities like grain, wine, beer, and cloth, to prevent exploitation through inconsistent pricing. (The U.S. Constitution has similar provisions, *see* p. 144.) Magna Carta also outlined free navigation of rivers and established a council of barons to monitor the King's adherence to the treaty, acting as a precursor to the English Parliament.

The most enduring legacy of the Magna Carta is the notion that no one, not even a king, stands above the law. Despite this principle, successive monarchs often ignored the document's constraints, with King John himself appealing to Pope Innocent III to nullify the charter shortly after its creation. Magna Carta would, however, be reaffirmed multiple times by later kings and gained renewed prominence during the English Civil War when Charles I's disregard for its principles partly led to his execution. Over time, Magna Carta's legacy firmly established it as a cornerstone for constitutional law, influencing future democratic institutions and legal frameworks worldwide.

Clauses in the text below marked (+) were repeated in the charter of 1225 and are still in effect today, but with minor changes. Clauses marked *(*) and in italics* were omitted in all later reissues of the charter. Numbering of clauses added by the British Library.

Magna Carta

JOHN, by the grace of God King of England, Lord of Ireland, Duke of Normandy and Aquitaine, and Count of Anjou, to his archbishops, bishops, abbots, earls, barons, justices, foresters, sheriffs, stewards, servants, and to all his officials and loyal subjects, Greeting.

KNOW THAT BEFORE GOD, for the health of our soul and those of our ancestors and heirs, to the honour of God, the exaltation of the holy Church, and the better ordering of our kingdom, at the advice of our reverend fathers Stephen, archbishop of Canterbury, primate of all England, and cardinal of the holy Roman Church, Henry archbishop of Dublin, William bishop of London, Peter bishop of Winchester, Jocelin bishop of Bath and Glastonbury, Hugh bishop of Lincoln, Walter bishop of Worcester, William bishop of Coventry, Benedict bishop of Rochester, Master Pandulf subdeacon and member of the papal household, Brother Aymeric master of the knighthood of the Temple in England, William Marshal earl of Pembroke, William earl of Salisbury, William earl of Warren, William earl of Arundel, Alan of Galloway constable of Scotland, Warin fitz Gerald, Peter fitz Herbert,

Hubert de Burgh seneschal of Poitou, Hugh de Neville, Matthew fitz Herbert, Thomas Basset, Alan Basset, Philip Daubeny, Robert de Roppeley, John Marshal, John fitz Hugh, and other loyal subjects:

+[1] FIRST, THAT WE HAVE GRANTED TO GOD, and by this present charter have confirmed for us and our heirs in perpetuity, that the English Church shall be free, and shall have its rights undiminished, and its liberties unimpaired. That we wish this so to be observed, appears from the fact that of our own free will, before the outbreak of the present dispute between us and our barons, we granted and confirmed by charter the freedom of the Church's elections—a right reckoned to be of the greatest necessity and importance to it—and caused this to be confirmed by Pope Innocent III. This freedom we shall observe ourselves, and desire to be observed in good faith by our heirs in perpetuity. TO ALL FREE MEN OF OUR KINGDOM we have also granted, for us and our heirs for ever, all the liberties written out below, to have and to keep for them and their heirs, of us and our heirs:

[2] If any earl, baron, or other person that holds lands directly of the Crown, for military service, shall die, and at his death his heir shall be of full age and owe a 'relief', the heir shall have his inheritance on payment of the ancient scale of 'relief'. That is to say, the heir or heirs of an earl shall pay £100 for the entire earl's barony, the heir or heirs of a knight 100s. at most for the entire knight's 'fee', and any man that owes less shall pay less, in accordance with the ancient usage of 'fees'.

[3] But if the heir of such a person is under age and a ward, when he comes of age he shall have his inheritance without 'relief' or fine.

[4] The guardian of the land of an heir who is under age shall take from it only reasonable revenues, customary dues, and feudal services. He shall do this without destruction or damage to men or property. If we have given the guardianship of the land to a sheriff, or to any person answerable to us for the revenues, and he commits destruction or damage, we will exact compensation from him, and the land shall be entrusted to two worthy and prudent men of the same 'fee', who shall be answerable to us for the revenues, or to the person to whom we have assigned them. If we have given or sold to anyone the guardianship of such land, and he causes destruction or damage, he shall lose the guardianship of it, and it shall be handed over to two worthy and prudent men of the same 'fee', who shall be similarly answerable to us.

[5] For so long as a guardian has guardianship of such land, he shall maintain the houses, parks, fish preserves, ponds, mills, and everything else pertaining to it,

from the revenues of the land itself. When the heir comes of age, he shall restore the whole land to him, stocked with plough teams and such implements of husbandry as the season demands and the revenues from the land can reasonably bear.

[6] Heirs may be given in marriage, but not to someone of lower social standing. Before a marriage takes place, it shall be made known to the heir's next-of-kin.

[7] At her husband's death, a widow may have her marriage portion and inheritance at once and without trouble. She shall pay nothing for her dower, marriage portion, or any inheritance that she and her husband held jointly on the day of his death. She may remain in her husband's house for forty days after his death, and within this period her dower shall be assigned to her.

[8] No widow shall be compelled to marry, so long as she wishes to remain without a husband. But she must give security that she will not marry without royal consent, if she holds her lands of the Crown, or without the consent of whatever other lord she may hold them of.

[9] Neither we nor our officials will seize any land or rent in payment of a debt, so long as the debtor has movable goods sufficient to discharge the debt. A debtor's sureties shall not be distrained upon so long as the debtor himself can discharge his debt. If, for lack of means, the debtor is unable to discharge his debt, his sureties shall be answerable for it. If they so desire, they may have the debtor's lands and rents until they have received satisfaction for the debt that they paid for him, unless the debtor can show that he has settled his obligations to them.

**[10] If anyone who has borrowed a sum of money from Jews dies before the debt has been repaid, his heir shall pay no interest on the debt for so long as he remains under age, irrespective of whom he holds his lands. If such a debt falls into the hands of the Crown, it will take nothing except the principal sum specified in the bond.*[2]

**[11] If a man dies owing money to Jews, his wife may have her dower and pay nothing towards the debt from it. If he leaves children that are under age, their needs may also be provided for on a scale appropriate to the size of his holding of lands. The debt is to be paid out of the residue, reserving the service due to his feudal lords. Debts owed to persons other than Jews are to be dealt with similarly.*

2. The Church prohibited Christians from lending money to one another with interest, and the Old Testament forbade Jews the same regarding fellow Jews ("usury"), but the free flow of credit was needed in a commercialized society. Interfaith loans were not prohibited, so Jewish bankers filled the void with the support of the Crown (which also benefitted). Magna Carta reflects the reactionary public discontent with this practice.

**[12] No 'scutage' or 'aid' may be levied in our kingdom without its general consent, unless it is for the ransom of our person, to make our eldest son a knight, and [once] to marry our eldest daughter. For these purposes only a reasonable 'aid' may be levied. 'Aids' from the city of London are to be treated similarly.*

**[13] The city of London shall enjoy all its ancient liberties and free customs, both by land and by water. We also will and grant that all other cities, boroughs, towns, and ports shall enjoy all their liberties and free customs.*

**[14] To obtain the general consent of the realm for the assessment of an 'aid'—except in the three cases specified above—or a 'scutage', we will cause the archbishops, bishops, abbots, earls, and greater barons to be summoned individually by letter. To those who hold lands directly of us we will cause a general summons to be issued, through the sheriffs and other officials, to come together on a fixed day [of which at least forty days notice shall be given] and at a fixed place. In all letters of summons, the cause of the summons will be stated. When a summons has been issued, the business appointed for the day shall go forward in accordance with the resolution of those present, even if not all those who were summoned have appeared.*

**[15] In future we will allow no one to levy an 'aid' from his free men, except to ransom his person, to make his eldest son a knight, and [once] to marry his eldest daughter. For these purposes only a reasonable 'aid' may be levied.*

[16] No man shall be forced to perform more service for a knight's 'fee', or other free holding of land, than is due from it.

[17] Ordinary lawsuits shall not follow the royal court around, but shall be held in a fixed place.

[18] Inquests of novel disseisin, mort d'ancestor, and darrein presentment shall be taken only in their proper county court. We ourselves, or in our absence abroad our chief justice, will send two justices to each county four times a year, and these justices, with four knights of the county elected by the county itself, shall hold the assizes in the county court, on the day and in the place where the court meets.

[19] If any assizes cannot be taken on the day of the county court, as many knights and freeholders shall afterwards remain behind, of those who have attended the court, as will suffice for the administration of justice, having regard to the volume of business to be done.

[20] For a trivial offence, a free man shall be fined only in proportion to the degree of his offence, and for a serious offence correspondingly, but not so heavily as to deprive him of his livelihood. In the same way, a merchant shall be spared his merchandise, and a villein the implements of his husbandry, if they fall upon

the mercy of a royal court. None of these fines shall be imposed except by the assessment on oath of reputable men of the neighbourhood.

[21] Earls and barons shall be fined only by their equals, and in proportion to the gravity of their offence.

[22] A fine imposed upon the lay property of a clerk in holy orders shall be assessed upon the same principles, without reference to the value of his ecclesiastical benefice.

[23] No town or person shall be forced to build bridges over rivers except those with an ancient obligation to do so.

[24] No sheriff, constable, coroners, or other royal officials are to hold lawsuits that should be held by the royal justices.

**[25] Every county, hundred, wapentake, and tithing shall remain at its ancient rent, without increase, except the royal demesne manors.*

[26] If at the death of a man who holds a lay 'fee' of the Crown, a sheriff or royal official produces royal letters patent of summons for a debt due to the Crown, it shall be lawful for them to seize and list movable goods found in the lay 'fee' of the dead man to the value of the debt, as assessed by worthy men. Nothing shall be removed until the whole debt is paid, when the residue shall be given over to the executors to carry out the dead man's will. If no debt is due to the Crown, all the movable goods shall be regarded as the property of the dead man, except the reasonable shares of his wife and children.

**[27] If a free man dies intestate, his movable goods are to be distributed by his next-of-kin and friends, under the supervision of the Church. The rights of his debtors are to be preserved.*

[28] No constable or other royal official shall take corn or other movable goods from any man without immediate payment, unless the seller voluntarily offers postponement of this.

[29] No constable may compel a knight to pay money for castle-guard if the knight is willing to undertake the guard in person, or with reasonable excuse to supply some other fit man to do it. A knight taken or sent on military service shall be excused from castle-guard for the period of this service.

[30] No sheriff, royal official, or other person shall take horses or carts for transport from any free man, without his consent.

[31] Neither we nor any royal official will take wood for our castle, or for any other purpose, without the consent of the owner.

[32] We will not keep the lands of people convicted of felony in our hand for longer than a year and a day, after which they shall be returned to the lords of the 'fees' concerned.

[33] All fish-weirs shall be removed from the Thames, the Medway, and throughout the whole of England, except on the sea coast.[3]

[34] The writ called precipe shall not in future be issued to anyone in respect of any holding of land, if a free man could thereby be deprived of the right of trial in his own lord's court.

[35] There shall be standard measures of wine, ale, and corn [the London quarter], throughout the kingdom. There shall also be a standard width of dyed cloth, russet, and haberject, namely two ells within the selvedges. Weights are to be standardised similarly.[4]

[36] In future nothing shall be paid or accepted for the issue of a writ of inquisition of life or limbs. It shall be given gratis, and not refused.

[37] If a man holds land of the Crown by 'fee-farm', 'socage', or 'burgage', and also holds land of someone else for knight's service, we will not have guardianship of his heir, nor of the land that belongs to the other person's 'fee', by virtue of the 'fee-farm', 'socage', or 'burgage', unless the 'fee-farm' owes knight's service. We will not have the guardianship of a man's heir, or of land that he holds of someone else, by reason of any small property that he may hold of the Crown for a service of knives, arrows, or the like.

[38] In future no official shall place a man on trial upon his own unsupported statement, without producing credible witnesses to the truth of it.

+[39] No free man shall be seized or imprisoned, or stripped of his rights or possessions, or outlawed or exiled, or deprived of his standing in any way, nor will

---

3. Clause 33 attempted to allow free navigation in English rivers. Navigation disputes have existed throughout history, and the Constitution addresses the issue in Article I, §§ 8 and 10. *See* pp. 144, 147. Navigation disputes were a significant contributor to the need for a U.S. Constitution. Disputes between Maryland and Virginia over water rights to the Potomac River led to the Annapolis Convention, which set the framework for the Constitutional Convention. Shay's Rebellion coincided with the Annapolis Convention, further highlighting the precarious infighting among the states that existed under the Articles of Confederation.

4. Clause 35 standardizes the weights and measures of certain commodities. Similar provisions are included in American founding documents, as varying weights and measures impede the free flow of commerce. *See* pp. 111, 144.

we proceed with force against him, or send others to do so, except by the lawful judgment of his equals or by the law of the land.[5]

+ [40] To no one will we sell, to no one deny or delay right or justice.

[41] All merchants may enter or leave England unharmed and without fear, and may stay or travel within it, by land or water, for purposes of trade, free from all illegal exactions, in accordance with ancient and lawful customs. This, however, does not apply in time of war to merchants from a country that is at war with us. Any such merchants found in our country at the outbreak of war shall be detained without injury to their persons or property, until we or our chief justice have discovered how our own merchants are being treated in the country at war with us. If our own merchants are safe they shall be safe too.

** [42] In future it shall be lawful for any man to leave and return to our kingdom unharmed and without fear, by land or water, preserving his allegiance to us, except in time of war, for some short period, for the common benefit of the realm. People that have been imprisoned or outlawed in accordance with the law of the land, people from a country that is at war with us, and merchants—who shall be dealt with as stated above—are excepted from this provision.*

[43] If a man holds lands of any 'escheat' such as the 'honour' of Wallingford, Nottingham, Boulogne, Lancaster, or of other 'escheats' in our hand that are baronies, at his death his heir shall give us only the 'relief' and service that he would have made to the baron, had the barony been in the baron's hand. We will hold the 'escheat' in the same manner as the baron held it.

[44] People who live outside the forest need not in future appear before the royal justices of the forest in answer to general summonses, unless they are actually involved in proceedings or are sureties for someone who has been seized for a forest offence.

** [45] We will appoint as justices, constables, sheriffs, or other officials, only men that know the law of the realm and are minded to keep it well.*

5. Clauses 39 and 40 are likely the most important and lasting provisions for the purposes of the American founding. They set the stage for rights to due process, jury trials, and habeas corpus. *See* pp. 146, 153, 154, 176, 178, 181, and 197.

Some scholars go back even further, to at least the Assize of Clarendon (1166), in which Henry II set forth early due-process procedures in criminal matters including a trial by evidence (instead of by combat) and grand-jury presentment of charges against an accused.

[46] All barons who have founded abbeys, and have charters of English kings or ancient tenure as evidence of this, may have guardianship of them when there is no abbot, as is their due.

[47] All forests that have been created in our reign shall at once be disafforested. River-banks that have been enclosed in our reign shall be treated similarly.

***** *[48] All evil customs relating to forests and warrens, foresters, warreners, sheriffs and their servants, or river-banks and their wardens, are at once to be investigated in every county by twelve sworn knights of the county, and within forty days of their enquiry the evil customs are to be abolished completely and irrevocably. But we, or our chief justice if we are not in England, are first to be informed.*

* *[49] We will at once return all hostages and charters delivered up to us by Englishmen as security for peace or for loyal service.*[6]

* *[50] We will remove completely from their offices the kinsmen of Gerard de Athée, and in future they shall hold no offices in England. The people in question are Engelard de Cigogné, Peter, Guy, and Andrew de Chanceaux, Guy de Cigogné, Geoffrey de Martigny and his brothers, Philip Marc and his brothers, with Geoffrey his nephew, and all their followers.*

* *[51] As soon as peace is restored, we will remove from the kingdom all the foreign knights, bowmen, their attendants, and the mercenaries that have come to it, to its harm, with horses and arms.*

* *[52] To any man whom we have deprived or dispossessed of lands, castles, liberties, or rights, without the lawful judgment of his equals, we will at once restore these. In cases of dispute the matter shall be resolved by the judgment of the twenty-five barons referred to below in the clause for securing the peace [§ 61]. In cases, however, where a man was deprived or dispossessed of something without the lawful judgment of his equals by our father King Henry or our brother King Richard, and it remains in our hands or is held by others under our warranty, we shall have respite for the period commonly allowed to Crusaders, unless a lawsuit had been begun, or an enquiry had been made at our order, before we took the Cross as a Crusader. On our return from the Crusade, or if we abandon it, we will at once render justice in full.*

* *[53] We shall have similar respite in rendering justice in connexion with forests that are to be disafforested, or to remain forests, when these were first afforested by our father Henry or our brother Richard; with the guardianship of lands in another person's 'fee', when we have hitherto had this by virtue of a 'fee' held of us for*

---

6. As a peace treaty, Magna Carta addressed existing hostages, occupation, land seizures, etc.

knight's service by a third party; and with abbeys founded in another person's 'fee', in which the lord of the 'fee' claims to own a right. On our return from the Crusade, or if we abandon it, we will at once do full justice to complaints about these matters.

[54] No one shall be arrested or imprisoned on the appeal of a woman for the death of any person except her husband.

**[55] All fines that have been given to us unjustly and against the law of the land, and all fines that we have exacted unjustly, shall be entirely remitted or the matter decided by a majority judgment of the twenty-five barons referred to below in the clause for securing the peace [§ 61] together with Stephen, archbishop of Canterbury, if he can be present, and such others as he wishes to bring with him. If the archbishop cannot be present, proceedings shall continue without him, provided that if any of the twenty-five barons has been involved in a similar suit himself, his judgment shall be set aside, and someone else chosen and sworn in his place, as a substitute for the single occasion, by the rest of the twenty-five.*

[56] If we have deprived or dispossessed any Welshmen of land, liberties, or anything else in England or in Wales, without the lawful judgment of their equals, these are at once to be returned to them. A dispute on this point shall be determined in the Marches by the judgment of equals. English law shall apply to holdings of land in England, Welsh law to those in Wales, and the law of the Marches to those in the Marches. The Welsh shall treat us and ours in the same way.

**[57] In cases where a Welshman was deprived or dispossessed of anything, without the lawful judgment of his equals, by our father King Henry or our brother King Richard, and it remains in our hands or is held by others under our warranty, we shall have respite for the period commonly allowed to Crusaders, unless a lawsuit had been begun, or an enquiry had been made at our order, before we took the Cross as a Crusader. But on our return from the Crusade, or if we abandon it, we will at once do full justice according to the laws of Wales and the said regions.*

**[58] We will at once return the son of Llywelyn, all Welsh hostages, and the charters delivered to us as security for the peace.*

**[59] With regard to the return of the sisters and hostages of Alexander, king of Scotland, his liberties and his rights, we will treat him in the same way as our other barons of England, unless it appears from the charters that we hold from his father William, formerly king of Scotland, that he should be treated otherwise. This matter shall be resolved by the judgment of his equals in our court.*

[60] All these customs and liberties that we have granted shall be observed in our kingdom in so far as concerns our own relations with our subjects. Let all

men of our kingdom, whether clergy or laymen, observe them similarly in their relations with their own men.

**[61] SINCE WE HAVE GRANTED ALL THESE THINGS for God, for the better ordering of our kingdom, and to allay the discord that has arisen between us and our barons, and since we desire that they shall be enjoyed in their entirety, with lasting strength, for ever, we give and grant to the barons the following security:*

The barons shall elect twenty-five of their number to keep, and cause to be observed with all their might, the peace and liberties granted and confirmed to them by this charter.

If we, our chief justice, our officials, or any of our servants offend in any respect against any man, or transgress any of the articles of the peace or of this security, and the offence is made known to four of the said twenty-five barons, they shall come to us—or in our absence from the kingdom to the chief justice—to declare it and claim immediate redress. If we, or in our absence abroad the chief justice, make no redress within forty days, reckoning from the day on which the offence was declared to us or to him, the four barons shall refer the matter to the rest of the twenty-five barons, who may distrain upon and assail us in every way possible, with the support of the whole community of the land, by seizing our castles, lands, possessions, or anything else saving only our own person and those of the queen and our children, until they have secured such redress as they have determined upon. Having secured the redress, they may then resume their normal obedience to us.

Any man who so desires may take an oath to obey the commands of the twenty-five barons for the achievement of these ends, and to join with them in assailing us to the utmost of his power. We give public and free permission to take this oath to any man who so desires, and at no time will we prohibit any man from taking it. Indeed, we will compel any of our subjects who are unwilling to take it to swear it at our command.

If one of the twenty-five barons dies or leaves the country, or is prevented in any other way from discharging his duties, the rest of them shall choose another baron in his place, at their discretion, who shall be duly sworn in as they were.

In the event of disagreement among the twenty-five barons on any matter referred to them for decision, the verdict of the majority present shall have the same validity as a unanimous verdict of the whole twenty-five, whether these were all present or some of those summoned were unwilling or unable to appear.

The twenty-five barons shall swear to obey all the above articles faithfully, and shall cause them to be obeyed by others to the best of their power.

We will not seek to procure from anyone, either by our own efforts or those of a third party, anything by which any part of these concessions or liberties might be revoked or diminished. Should such a thing be procured, it shall be null and void and we will at no time make use of it, either ourselves or through a third party.

**[62] We have remitted and pardoned fully to all men any ill-will, hurt, or grudges that have arisen between us and our subjects, whether clergy or laymen, since the beginning of the dispute. We have in addition remitted fully, and for our own part have also pardoned, to all clergy and laymen any offences committed as a result of the said dispute between Easter in the sixteenth year of our reign [i.e. 1215] and the restoration of peace.*

In addition we have caused letters patent to be made for the barons, bearing witness to this security and to the concessions set out above, over the seals of Stephen archbishop of Canterbury, Henry archbishop of Dublin, the other bishops named above, and Master Pandulf.

**[63] IT IS ACCORDINGLY OUR WISH AND COMMAND that the English Church shall be free, and that men in our kingdom shall have and keep all these liberties, rights, and concessions, well and peaceably in their fullness and entirety for them and their heirs, of us and our heirs, in all things and all places for ever.*

Both we and the barons have sworn that all this shall be observed in good faith and without deceit. Witness the abovementioned people and many others.

Given by our hand in the meadow that is called Runnymede, between Windsor and Staines, on the fifteenth day of June in the seventeenth year of our reign [i.e. 1215: the new regnal year began on 28 May][7]

---

7. Beyond inspiring subsequent English and American tradition, rights and protections are regularly traced back to Magna Carta in Supreme Court decisions. *See, e.g.*, *Consumer Fin. Prot. Bureau v. Cmty. Fin. Servs. Ass'n of Am.*, 601 U.S. 416, 428 (2024) (citing Magna Carta and explaining that "[e]xtraordinary revenues were financed through various forms of taxation and therefore required parliamentary authorization."); *Obergefell v. Hodges*, 576 U.S. 644, 723 (2015) (Thomas, J., dissenting) ("Both of the Constitution's Due Process Clauses reach back to Magna Carta."); *McDonald v. City of Chicago*, 561 U.S. 742, 815 (2010) (Thomas, J., concurring) (The tradition of privileges and immunities "begins with our country's English roots. Parliament declared the basic liberties of English citizens in a series of documents ranging from the Magna Carta to the Petition of Right and the English Bill of Rights."); *Hamdi v. Rumsfeld*, 542 U.S. 507, 552 (2004) (Souter, J. concurring) ("we are heirs to a tradition given voice 800 years ago by Magna Carta, which, on the barons' insistence, confined executive power by 'the law of the land'"); *Washington v. Glucksberg*, 521 U.S. 702 (1997) (Souter, J. concurring) (noting Magna Carta's "guarantee of 'the law of the land'").

1689 English Declaration of Rights (Bill of Rights)

DECEMBER 16, 1689

Introduction

Magna Carta of 1215 underwent several revisions before fading from public discourse over the centuries. Throughout this period, Parliament made several attempts to enshrine the principle that some laws should also bind the Crown, like in the Petition of Right in 1628 (following King Charles I's extra-parliamentary taxation and the unlawful imprisonment of five knights in the *Five Knights Case* in 1627) and the Habeas Corpus Acts of 1640 and 1679. However, the Crown consistently circumvented the explicit text or spirit of these measures, evading accountability until the English Revolution of 1688–1689, also known as the Glorious Revolution.

Magna Carta received renewed interest and significance during this period. After a crisis caused by the policies and purported abdication of King James II, the Houses of Lords and Commons organized a convention to resolve the emergency. Part of resolving the dispute involved compiling all of the major resolutions that the assembly had passed over the years and drafting a "declaration of rights," declaring the rights of the people and certain expectations of rulers. The final version of the 1689 English Declaration of Rights was presented to Prince William and Princess Mary of Orange in early 1689, which the Prince and Princess accepted and agreed to follow. The Declaration was enshrined as the English Bill of Rights, which is considered to be part of the English Constitution.

The Declaration enumerated thirteen of King James II's transgressions, recites other grievances, and then lists thirteen clauses limiting the power of the Crown. (Many of the grievances in the English Declaration of Rights appear almost verbatim in subsequent American documents like the Declaration of Independence.) It claimed "ancient and indubitable rights and liberties" (a reference to Magna Carta), justified the removal of King James II for his abdication, and placed new restrictions on the powers of the monarchy.

Many of its clauses and themes appear in American founding documents, including references to free speech and free elections; controls on spending; speech and debate immunity; opposing a standing army in peacetime without consent; protections for the ability to bear arms; and protections against unfair jury trials, excessive bail and fines, cruel and illegal punishments, and illegal seizures and forfeitures. The Declaration expands on Magna Carta's early version of separa-

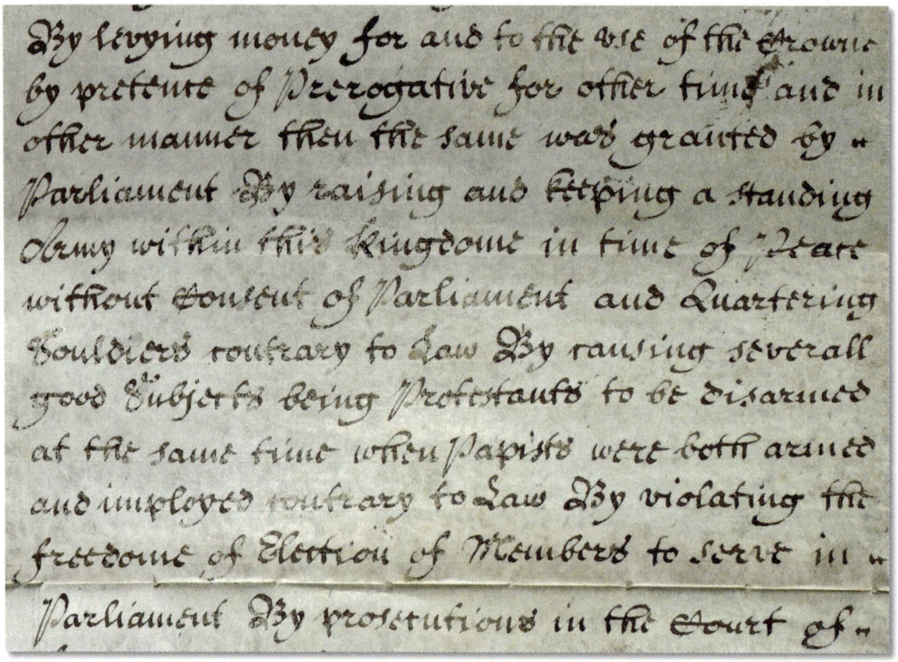
By levying money for and to the use of the Crowne
by pretence of Prerogative for other time and in
other manner then the same was granted by
Parliament By raising and keeping a Standing
Army within this Kingdome in time of Peace
without Consent of Parliament and Quartering
Souldiers contrary to Law By causing severall
good Subjects being Protestants to be disarmed
at the same time when Papists were both armed
and imployed contrary to Law By violating the
freedome of Election of Members to serve in
Parliament By prosecutions in the Court of

Excerpt from English Bill of Rights

tion of powers—requiring Parliament's approval for taxing and new laws. Most colonists were deeply familiar with the rights and protections outlined in the English Bill of Rights, which informed their understanding of governance and civil liberties.

An Act Declaring the Rights and Liberties of the Subject and Settling the Succession of the Crown

[Preamble]

Whereas the Lords Spiritual and Temporal and Commons assembled at Westminster, lawfully, fully and freely representing all the estates of the people of this realm, did upon the thirteenth day of February in the year of our Lord one thousand six hundred eighty-eight[1] present unto their Majesties, then called and known by the names and style of William and Mary, prince and princess of Orange, being present in their proper persons, a certain declaration in writing made by the said Lords and Commons in the words following, viz.:

Whereas the late King James the Second, by the assistance of divers evil counsellors, judges and ministers employed by him, did endeavour to subvert and extirpate the Protestant religion and the laws and liberties of this kingdom;

[Grievances][2]

[1.] By assuming and exercising a power of dispensing with and suspending of laws and the execution of laws without consent of Parliament;[3]

[2.] By committing and prosecuting divers worthy prelates for humbly petitioning to be excused from concurring to the said assumed power;

1. Under the "old style" calendar of the 17th century, the new year began on March 25, not January 1.

2. Many of these grievances reappear almost verbatim in later American declarations, petitions, and constitutional protections.

3. King James II suspended laws without involving Parliament, inspiring America's separation of powers. He also prosecuted people for speaking against him, which was part of the inspiration behind the First Amendment.

[3.] By issuing and causing to be executed a commission under the great seal for erecting a court called the Court of Commissioners for Ecclesiastical Causes;[4]

[4.] By levying money for and to the use of the Crown by pretence of prerogative for other time and in other manner than the same was granted by Parliament;

[5.] By raising and keeping a standing army within this kingdom in time of peace without consent of Parliament, and quartering soldiers contrary to law;[5]

[6.] By causing several good subjects being Protestants to be disarmed at the same time when papists were both armed and employed contrary to law;

[7.] By violating the freedom of election of members to serve in Parliament;

[8.] By prosecutions in the Court of King's Bench for matters and causes cognizable only in Parliament, and by divers other arbitrary and illegal courses;

[9.] And whereas of late years partial corrupt and unqualified persons have been returned and served on juries in trials, and particularly divers jurors in trials for high treason which were not freeholders;

[10.] And excessive bail hath been required of persons committed in criminal cases to elude the benefit of the laws made for the liberty of the subjects;

[11.] And excessive fines have been imposed;

[12.] And illegal and cruel punishments inflicted;

[13.] And several grants and promises made of fines and forfeitures before any conviction or judgment against the persons upon whom the same were to be levied;

---

4. Early English courts were a patchwork of different courts with jurisdiction over different matters. The third grievance references the King's association with the Catholic Church (many of his subjects were loyal to the Church of England) and elevating church courts over lay courts.

5. Standing armies were largely unknown in England until the 17th century. Militias were more common. Early Americans also generally opposed standing armies, unless the relevant legislature consented. Thomas Jefferson said in 1789 that "there are instruments so dangerous to the rights of the nation, and which place them so totally at the mercy of their governors, that those governors, whether legislative or executive, should be restrained from keeping such instruments on foot but in well-defined cases. Such an instrument is a standing army."

All which are utterly and directly contrary to the known laws and statutes and freedom of this realm;

And whereas the said late King James the Second having abdicated the government and the throne being thereby vacant, his Highness the prince of Orange (whom it hath pleased Almighty God to make the glorious instrument of delivering this kingdom from popery and arbitrary power) did (by the advice of the Lords Spiritual and Temporal and divers principal persons of the Commons) cause letters to be written to the Lords Spiritual and Temporal being Protestants, and other letters to the several counties, cities, universities, boroughs and cinque ports, for the choosing of such persons to represent them as were of right to be sent to Parliament, to meet and sit at Westminster upon the two and twentieth day of January in this year one thousand six hundred eighty and eight [old style date], in order to such an establishment as that their religion, laws and liberties might not again be in danger of being subverted, upon which letters elections having been accordingly made;

And thereupon the said Lords Spiritual and Temporal and Commons, pursuant to their respective letters and elections, being now assembled in a full and free representative of this nation, taking into their most serious consideration the best means for attaining the ends aforesaid, do in the first place (as their ancestors in like case have usually done) for the vindicating and asserting their ancient rights and liberties declare

[Declaration of Rights][6]

[1.] That the pretended power of suspending the laws or the execution of laws by regal authority without consent of Parliament is illegal;

[2.] That the pretended power of dispensing with laws or the execution of laws by regal authority, as it hath been assumed and exercised of late, is illegal;

[3.] That the commission for erecting the late Court of Commissioners for Ecclesiastical Causes, and all other commissions and courts of like nature, are illegal and pernicious;

[4.] That levying money for or to the use of the Crown by pretence of prerogative, without grant of Parliament, for longer time, or in other manner than the same is or shall be granted, is illegal;

6. Many of these clauses limit the Crown's authority to act without Parliament (clarifying the sovereignty of Parliament).

[5.] That it is the right of the subjects to petition the king, and all commitments and prosecutions for such petitioning are illegal;

[6.] That the raising or keeping a standing army within the kingdom in time of peace, unless it be with consent of Parliament, is against law;[7]

[7.] That the subjects which are Protestants may have arms for their defence suitable to their conditions and as allowed by law;[8]

[8.] That election of members of Parliament ought to be free;

[9.] That the freedom of speech and debates or proceedings in Parliament ought not to be impeached or questioned in any court or place out of Parliament;

[10.] That excessive bail ought not to be required, nor excessive fines imposed, nor cruel and unusual punishments inflicted;

[11.] That jurors ought to be duly impanelled and returned, and jurors which pass upon men in trials for high treason ought to be freeholders;

[12.] That all grants and promises of fines and forfeitures of particular persons before conviction are illegal and void;

[13.] And that for redress of all grievances, and for the amending, strengthening and preserving of the laws, Parliaments ought to be held frequently.

And they do claim, demand and insist upon all and singular the premises as their undoubted rights and liberties, and that no declarations, judgments, doings or proceedings to the prejudice of the people in any of the said premises ought in any wise to be drawn hereafter into consequence or example; to which demand

7. Interestingly, quartering of soldiers is included in the grievances above [5] but is omitted from these rights.

8. Arms bearing has a long and complicated history in England, including during the Thirty Years War (1618–1648), which made citizens cautious of both arms prohibitions and standing armies. Later, Parliament passed the City of London Militia Act of 1662 to disarm a Protestant sect that was attempting to take over London. The Act was then used to disarm Catholics. King James II then disarmed Protestants and armed Catholics (as referenced throughout this Declaration). This clause is in response to these struggles for the right to bear arms, and America constitutionalized the right in the Second Amendment. *See* p. 173.

At this time, the right to bear arms was closely connected with militia service. The House of Lords also added a qualifier to the draft version of this clause (adding "suitable to their conditions and allowed by law") to limit the right to the Protestant upper classes. This was consistent with existing laws regulating gun ownership. (For example, no one having an annual income of under £100 was permitted to keep arms.)

of their rights they are particularly encouraged by the declaration of his Highness the prince of Orange as being the only means for obtaining a full redress and remedy therein.

[Succession]

Having therefore an entire confidence that his said Highness the prince of Orange will perfect the deliverance so far advanced by him, and will still preserve them from the violation of their rights which they have here asserted, and from all other attempts upon their religion, rights and liberties, the said Lords Spiritual and Temporal and Commons assembled at Westminster do resolve that William and Mary, prince and princess of Orange, be and be declared king and queen of England, France and Ireland and the dominions thereunto belonging, to hold the crown and royal dignity of the said kingdoms and dominions to them, the said prince and princess, during their lives and the life of the survivor to them, and that the sole and full exercise of the regal power be only in and executed by the said prince of Orange in the names of the said prince and princess during their joint lives, and after their deceases the said crown and royal dignity of the same kingdoms and dominions to be to the heirs of the body of the said princess, and for default of such issue to the Princess Anne of Denmark and the heirs of her body, and for default of such issue to the heirs of the body of the said prince of Orange. And the Lords Spiritual and Temporal and Commons do pray the said prince and princess to accept the same accordingly.

And that the oaths hereafter mentioned be taken by all persons of whom the oaths have allegiance and supremacy might be required by law, instead of them; and that the said oaths of allegiance and supremacy be abrogated.

I, A.B., do sincerely promise and swear that I will be faithful and bear true allegiance to their Majesties King William and Queen Mary. So help me God.

I, A.B., do swear that I do from my heart abhor, detest and abjure as impious and heretical this damnable doctrine and position, that princes excommunicated or deprived by the Pope or any authority of the see of Rome may be deposed or murdered by their subjects or any other whatsoever. And I do declare that no foreign prince, person, prelate, state or potentate hath or ought to have any jurisdiction, power, superiority, pre-eminence or authority, ecclesiastical or spiritual, within this realm. So help me God.

Upon which their said Majesties did accept the crown and royal dignity of the kingdoms of England, France and Ireland, and the dominions thereunto belonging, according to the resolution and desire of the said Lords and Commons contained in the said declaration. And thereupon their Majesties were pleased that the said Lords Spiritual and Temporal and Commons, being the two Houses of Parliament, should continue to sit, and with their Majesties' royal concurrence make effectual provision for the settlement of the religion, laws and liberties of this kingdom, so that the same for the future might not be in danger again of being subverted, to which the said Lords Spiritual and Temporal and Commons did agree, and proceed to act accordingly.

Now in pursuance of the premises the said Lords Spiritual and Temporal and Commons in Parliament assembled, for the ratifying, confirming and establishing the said declaration and the articles, clauses, matters and things therein contained by the force of law made in due form by authority of Parliament, do pray that it may be declared and enacted that all and singular the rights and liberties asserted and claimed in the said declaration are the true, ancient and indubitable rights and liberties of the people of this kingdom, and so shall be esteemed, allowed, adjudged, deemed and taken to be; and that all and every the particulars aforesaid shall be firmly and strictly holden and observed as they are expressed in the said declaration, and all officers and ministers whatsoever shall serve their Majesties and their successors according to the same in all time to come.

And the said Lords Spiritual and Temporal and Commons, seriously considering how it hath pleased Almighty God in his marvellous providence and merciful goodness to this nation to provide and preserve their said Majesties' royal persons most happily to reign over us upon the throne of their ancestors, for which they render unto him from the bottom of their hearts their humblest thanks and praises, do truly, firmly, assuredly and in the sincerity of their hearts think, and do hereby recognize, acknowledge and declare, that King James the Second having abdicated the government, and their Majesties having accepted the crown and royal dignity as aforesaid, their said Majesties did become, were, are and of right ought to be by the laws of this realm our sovereign liege lord and lady, king and queen of England, France and Ireland and the dominions thereunto belonging, in and to whose princely persons the royal state, crown and dignity of the said realms with all honours, styles, titles, regalities, prerogatives, powers, jurisdictions and authorities to the same belonging and appertaining are most fully, rightfully and entirely invested and incorporated, united and annexed.

And for preventing all questions and divisions in this realm by reason of any pretended titles to the crown, and for preserving a certainty in the succession thereof, in and upon which the unity, peace, tranquility and safety of this nation doth under God wholly consist and depend, the said Lords Spiritual and Temporal and Commons do beseech their Majesties that it may be enacted, established and declared, that the crown and regal government of the said kingdoms and dominions, with all and singular the premises thereunto belonging and appertaining, shall be and continue to their said Majesties and the survivor of them during their lives and the life of the survivor of them, and that the entire, perfect and full exercise of the regal power and government be only in and executed by his Majesty in the names of both their Majesties during their joint lives; and after their deceases the said crown and premises shall be and remain to the heirs of the body of her Majesty, and for default of such issue to her Royal Highness the Princess Anne of Denmark and the heirs of the body of his said Majesty; and thereunto the said Lords Spiritual and Temporal and Commons do in the name of all the people aforesaid most humbly and faithfully submit themselves, their heirs and posterities for ever, and do faithfully promise that they will stand to, maintain and defend their said Majesties, and also the limitation and succession of the crown herein specified and contained, to the utmost of their powers with their lives and estates against all persons whatsoever that shall attempt anything to the contrary.

And whereas it hath been found by experience that it is inconsistent with the safety and welfare of this Protestant kingdom to be governed by a popish prince, or by any king or queen marrying a papist, the said Lords Spiritual and Temporal and Commons do further pray that it may be enacted, that all and every person and persons that is, are or shall be reconciled to or shall hold communion with the see or Church of Rome, or shall profess the popish religion, or shall marry a papist, shall be excluded and be for ever incapable to inherit, possess or enjoy the crown and government of this realm and Ireland and the dominions thereunto belonging or any part of the same, or to have, use or exercise any regal power, authority or jurisdiction within the same; and in all and every such case or cases the people of these realms shall be and are hereby absolved of their allegiance; and the said crown and government shall from time to time descend to and be enjoyed by such person or persons being Protestants as should have inherited and enjoyed the same in case the said person or persons so reconciled, holding communion or professing or marrying as aforesaid were naturally dead; and that every king and queen of this realm who at any time hereafter shall come to and succeed in the imperial crown of this kingdom shall on the first day of the meeting of the first Parliament next after his or her coming to the crown, sitting in his or her throne in the House of Peers in the presence of the Lords and Commons therein assembled, or at his or her coronation before such person or persons who shall administer the coronation oath to him or her at the time of his or her taking the said oath (which shall first happen), make, subscribe and audibly repeat the declaration mentioned in the statute made in the thirtieth year of the reign of King Charles the Second entitled, An Act for the more effectual preserving the king's person and government by disabling papists from sitting in either House of Parliament.

But if it shall happen that such king or queen upon his or her succession to the crown of this realm shall be under the age of twelve years, then every such king or queen shall make, subscribe and audibly repeat the same declaration at his or her coronation or the first day of the meeting of the first Parliament as aforesaid which shall first happen after such king or queen shall have attained the said age of twelve years.

All which their Majesties are contented and pleased shall be declared, enacted and established by authority of this present Parliament, and shall stand, remain and be the law of this realm for ever; and the same are by their said Majesties, by and with the advice and consent of the Lords Spiritual and Temporal and Commons in Parliament assembled and by the authority of the same, declared, enacted and established accordingly.

II. And be it further declared and enacted by the authority aforesaid, that from and after this present session of Parliament no dispensation by non obstante of or to any statute or any part thereof shall be allowed, but that the same shall be held void and of no effect, except a dispensation be allowed of in such statute, and except in such cases as shall be specially provided for by one or more bill or bills to be passed during this present session of Parliament.

III. Provided that no charter or grant or pardon granted before the three and twentieth day of October in the year of our Lord one thousand six hundred eighty-nine shall be any ways impeached or invalidated by this Act, but that the same shall be and remain of the same force and effect in law and no other than as if this Act had never been made.

1765 Declaration of Rights and Grievances

(OCTOBER 14, 1765)

Introduction

Around seventy-five years later and across the Atlantic Ocean, tensions were growing between the colonies and the British largely over taxation, self-governance, and whether colonists could expand westward. Between 1754 and 1765, the North American colonies fought a war against the French, with various Native American tribes taking a side (the French and Indian War, a part of the Seven Years' War). England supported its colonies and the colonies ultimately prevailed, but at great expense to the British (it doubled the British debt). The economic theory of mercantilism and the desire to control liquid resources would also contribute to England's desire to use the colonies as a funneling mechanism to get resources back to Britain. But defending the colonies against ongoing threats from the French, Spanish, and various Native American tribes would require significant future expenses.

To address these financial burdens, Parliament introduced the Stamp Act in 1765, taxing all paper goods from contracts and newspapers to stationery and playing cards. These items were required to bear an official stamp and had to be produced on paper manufactured in London. The colonists were outraged,

1p Stamp Act Stamp (1765 proof)

particularly due to their lack of representation in the decision-making process. Adding to their frustrations, the British also imposed restrictions on westward expansion of the colonies (an attempt to prevent conflicts with tribes).

In response, nine colonies assembled the Stamp Act Congress to draft formal petitions to Parliament in opposition. This was the first organized American body that challenged British authority. The Stamp Act Congress approved the Declaration of Rights and Grievances of 1765 (the "1765 Declaration") on October 14, 1765. John Dickinson was the chief drafter. (As you will see, Dickinson is known as the "Penman of the Revolution," penning key drafts of multiple important documents.) The 1765 Declaration raised several grievances but did not purport to declare independence or establish a new national government. Colonists complained about equality with British subjects, taxation without representation, and rights to jury trials.

A well-established part of English law at the time was the right to be taxed only by one's elected representatives, and colonists claimed that they lacked adequate representation in Parliament. There are parallels between this and the earlier British

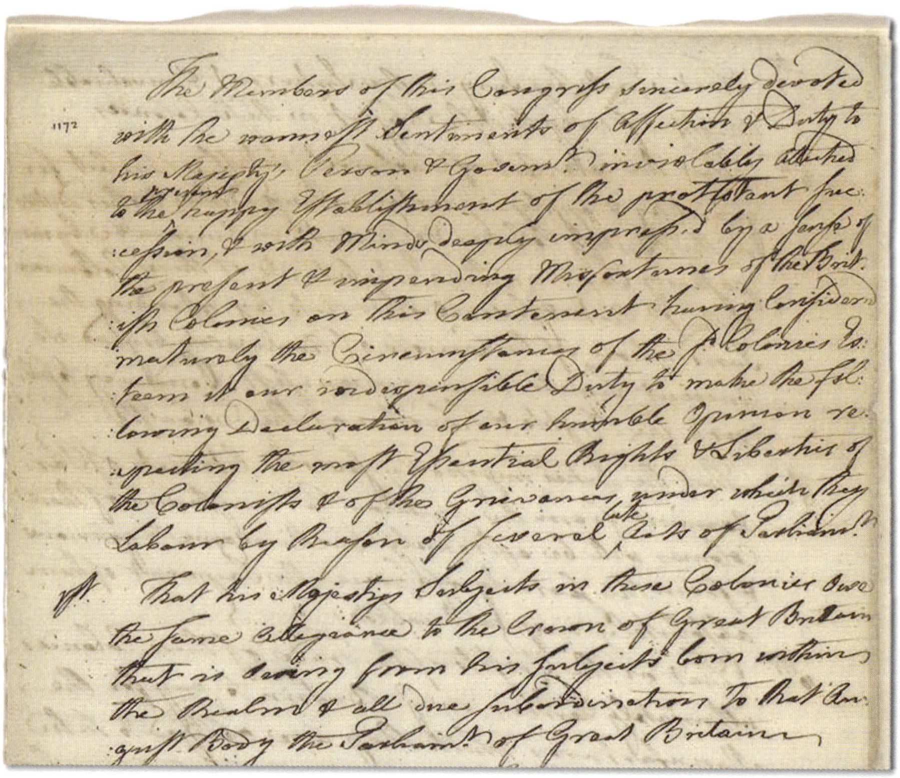
1172

The Members of this Congress sincerely devoted with the warmest Sentiments of Affection & Duty to his Majesty's Person & Governmt. inviolably attached to the present happy Establishment of the protestant Succession, & with Minds deeply impressed by a Sense of the present & impending Misfortunes of the British Colonies on this Continent having considered maturely the Circumstances of the sd. Colonies esteem it our indispensible Duty to make the following Declaration of our humble Opinion respecting the most Essential Rights & Liberties of the Colonists & of the Grievances under which they labour by Reason of several late Acts of Parliamt.

1st. That his Majestys Subjects in these Colonies owe the same Allegiance to the Crown of Great Britain that is owing from his Subjects born within the Realm & all due Subordination to that August Body the Parliamt. of Great Britain

Excerpt from William Samuel Johnson's written Declaration of Rights and Grievances, October 19, 1765

outrage at various kings taxing them without going through Parliament. (Colonists rejected the British concept of "virtual" representation, the view that elected members of Parliament represented the whole British empire—including the colonies—not specific areas.)

Interestingly, colonists voiced many grievances that echoed those outlined in the 1689 English Declaration of Rights. (Indeed, many seem to be direct copies.) Many other grievances were based on the colonists' belief that they were not enjoying the same rights that other British subjects enjoyed in Britain. Put another way, they believed that they were being treated as subjects of British subjects. In many of the grievances, we see themes that will resurface in the Declaration of Independence and in the Constitution. The 1765 Declaration represents a significant intellectual starting point for seriously considering independence.

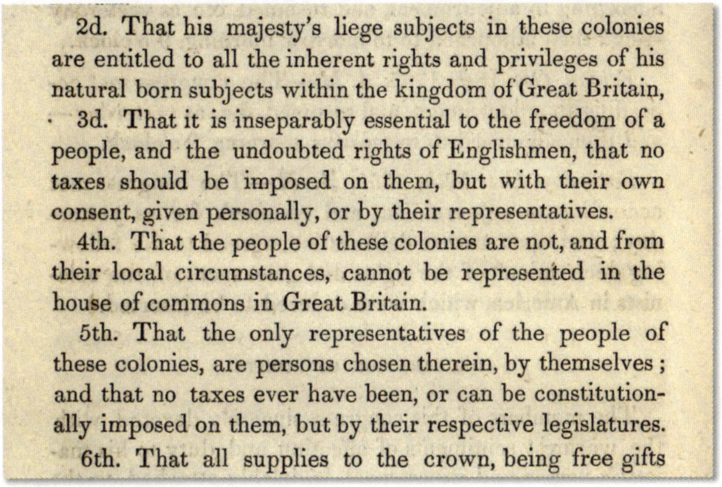

2d. That his majesty's liege subjects in these colonies are entitled to all the inherent rights and privileges of his natural born subjects within the kingdom of Great Britain,

3d. That it is inseparably essential to the freedom of a people, and the undoubted rights of Englishmen, that no taxes should be imposed on them, but with their own consent, given personally, or by their representatives.

4th. That the people of these colonies are not, and from their local circumstances, cannot be represented in the house of commons in Great Britain.

5th. That the only representatives of the people of these colonies, are persons chosen therein, by themselves; and that no taxes ever have been, or can be constitutionally imposed on them, but by their respective legislatures.

6th. That all supplies to the crown, being free gifts

Excerpt from Journals of the Stamp Act Congress

Declaration of Rights and Grievances (1765)

The members of this congress, sincerely devoted, with the warmest sentiments of affection and duty to his majesty's person and government, inviolably attached to the present happy establishment of the protestant succession, and with minds deeply impressed by a sense of the present and impending misfortunes of the British colonies on this continent; having considered as maturely as time would permit, the circumstances of said colonies, esteem it our indispensable duty to make the following declarations, of our humble opinions, respecting the most essential rights and liberties of the colonists, and of the grievances under which they labor, by reason of several late acts of parliament.[1]

1st. That his majesty's subjects in these colonies, owe the same allegiance to the crown of Great Britain, that is owing from his subjects born within the realm, and all due subordination to that august body, the parliament of Great Britain.

1. The 1765 Declaration echoes common grievances throughout this era of taxation without representation and infringing on the colonists' right to participate in governance.

2d. That his majesty's liege subjects in these colonies are entitled to all the inherent rights and privileges of his natural born subjects within the kingdom of Great Britain.

3d. That it is inseparably essential to the freedom of a people, and the undoubted rights of Englishmen, that no taxes should be imposed on them, but with their own consent, given personally, or by their representatives.

4th. That the people of these colonies are not, and from their local circumstances, cannot be represented in the house of commons in Great Britain.

5th. That the only representatives of the people of these colonies, are persons chosen therein, by themselves; and that no taxes ever have been, or can be constitutionally imposed on them, but by their respective legislatures.

6th. That all supplies to the crown, being free gifts of the people, it is unreasonable and inconsistent with the principles and spirit of the British constitution, for the people of Great Britain to grant to his majesty the property of the colonists.

7th. That trial by jury is the inherent and invaluable right of every British subject in these colonies.[2]

8th. That the late act of parliament entitled, an act for granting and applying certain stamp duties, and other duties in the British colonies and plantations in America, &c, by imposing taxes on the inhabitants of these colonies, and the said act, and several other acts, by extending the jurisdiction of the courts of admiralty beyond its ancient limits,[3] have a manifest tendency to subvert the rights and liberties of the colonists.

9th. That the duties imposed by several late acts of parliament, from the peculiar circumstances of these colonies, will be extremely buthensome and grievous, and from the scarcity of specie, the payment of them absolutely impracticable.[4]

10th. That as the profits of the trade of these colonies ultimately centre in Great Britain, to pay for the manufactures which they are obliged to take from

---

2. The 1765 Declaration proclaims the importance of trial by jury (enjoyed by British subjects, but sometimes denied colonists).

3. Colonists accused of violating the Stamp Act faced trial in vice admiralty courts, which lacked juries.

4. Specie is currency made from precious metals. (This word is edited to "gold" in Article I, Section 10 of the Constitution. *See* p. 147.) Britain prohibited colonists from coining money, making commerce incredibly difficult and ultimately leading to the creation of colonial paper money as a creative workaround.

thence, they eventually contribute very largely to all supplies granted there to the crown.

11th. That the restrictions imposed by several late acts of parliament, on the trade of these colonies, will render them unable to purchase the manufactures of Great Britain.

12th. That the increase, prosperity, and happiness of these colonies, depend on the full and free enjoyment of their rights and liberties, and an intercourse, with Great Britain, mutually affectionate and advantageous.

13th. That it is the right of the British subjects in these colonies, to petition the king or either house of parliament.

Lastly, That it is the indispensable duty of these colonies to the best of sovereigns, to the mother country, and to themselves, to endeavor, by a loyal and dutiful address to his majesty, and humble application to both houses of parliament, to procure the repeal of the act for granting and applying certain stamp duties, of all clauses of any other acts of parliament, whereby the jurisdiction of the admiralty is extended as aforesaid, and of the other late acts for the restriction of the American commerce.

Declaratory Act

(MARCH 18, 1766)

Parliament responded to the 1765 Declaration by repealing the Stamp Act and the colonies abandoned their ban on imported British goods. One can perhaps see now why the colonists continued to submit declarations and petitions to the King until independence—at least one of their declarations seemed to actually work. But accompanying the repeal of the Stamp Act was the 1766 Declaratory Act. Many in the public were so pleased with the repeal of the Stamp Act that the Declaratory Act did not receive much immediate attention. In time, however, the colonists became infuriated with the Declaratory Act, as shown throughout this book. The Act essentially asserted that the King and Parliament held the same power over the American colonies as it did over the rest of the British Empire. This short Act reasserted Britain's control over its colonies and declared that any laws or resolutions passed by the colonial assemblies that contradicted this principle were null and void:

An act for the better securing the dependency of his majesty's dominions in America upon the crown and parliament of Great Britain.

Whereas several of the houses of representatives in his Majesty's colonies and plantations in America, have of late against law, claimed to themselves, or to the general assemblies of the same, the sole and exclusive right of imposing duties and taxes upon his majesty's subjects in the said colonies and plantations; and have in pursuance of such claim, passed certain votes, resolutions, and orders derogatory to the legislative authority of parliament, and inconsistent with the dependency Of the said colonies and plantations upon the crown of Great Britain: may it therefore please your most excellent Majesty, that it may be declared; and be it declared by the King's most excellent majesty, by and with the advice and consent of the lords spiritual and temporal, and commons, in this present parliament assembled,[1] and by the authority of the same, That the said colonies and plantations in America have been, are, and of right ought to be, subordinate unto, and dependent upon the imperial crown and parliament of Great Britain;[2] and that the King's majesty, by and with the advice and consent of the lords spiritual and temporal, and commons of Great Britain, in parliament assembled, had, hath, and of right ought to have, full power and authority to make laws and statutes of sufficient force and validity to bind the colonies and people of America, subjects of the crown of Great Britain, in all cases whatsoever.[3]

II. And be it further declared and enacted by the authority aforesaid, That all resolutions, votes, orders, and proceedings, in any of the said colonies or plantations, whereby the power and authority of the parliament of Great Britain, to make laws and statutes as aforesaid, is denied, or drawn into question, arc, and are hereby declared to be, utterly null and void to all in purposes whatsoever.

---

1. Congress borrowed "in Congress assembled" (seen in many later documents) from the English tradition. *See, e.g.*, pp. 98, 104, 122, 143, and 163.

2. This language (the colonies "have been, are, and of right ought to be, subordinate unto, and dependent upon the imperial crown and parliament of Great Britain") resurfaces (as modified) in the Declaration of Independence, in what might be considered colonial trolling. *See* p. 98.

3. Colonists repeatedly complained about this language "in all cases whatsoever" in subsequent documents. Interestingly, the language is used in the Constitution to describe Congress's authority over Washington, D.C. *See* p. 145.

1774 Declaration and Resolves

(OCTOBER 14, 1774)

Introduction

The British taxed the colonies throughout the 1760s and 1770s, which the colonists forcefully opposed. The British repealed some of these taxes, only to replace them with other unfavorable acts. Each act was met with organized protests and unrest in the colonies. Matters escalated after Britain's passage of the Tea Act—an effort to help the financially troubled British East India Company sell 17,000,000 pounds of tea stored in England. Tea was shipped to colonists and sold at a discount, but this was seen as undercutting local merchants and as a maneuver to buy support for the legitimacy of existing taxes. In December 1773, Bostonians dumped 342 chests of British tea into Boston Harbor.

The British promptly passed the "Intolerable Acts" (known in Britain as the "Coercive Acts") in an attempt to restore order in Massachusetts following the Boston Tea Party:

- The Boston Port Act closed the port of Boston to all colonists until damages from the Boston Tea Party were paid.
- The Massachusetts Government Act gave the British government total control of town meetings, taking all decisions out of the hands of the colonists.

- The **Administration of Justice Act** made British officials immune to criminal prosecution in America.
- The **Quartering Act** required colonists to house and provide provisions for British troops on demand.

As tensions escalated, the colonial political discourse increasingly featured ideas of self-governance and resistance to British interference. Influential pamphlets like Thomas Paine's ***Common Sense*** and the widespread circulation of letters and essays discussing liberty and rights fanned the flames of revolution.

In response to the Intolerable Acts, the colonies called to order the First Continental Congress in Philadelphia on September 5, 1774. Georgia was the only colony that did not send representatives. (Georgia was a younger colony that was more dependent on Britain, and the Intolerable Acts had less of an effect there.) Virginia's representative (and Thomas Jefferson's cousin) Peyton Randolph was elected President of the First Continental Congress. Each colony was allotted a single, secret ballot for voting.

Representatives disagreed on the level of severity of their response to the Intolerable Acts. Joseph Galloway proposed a plan of union with Britain that offered a peaceful reconciliation, which the Congress rejected. On September 9, 1774, the First Continental Congress instead accepted the **Suffolk Resolves**, which encouraged Massachusetts to protest the Intolerable Acts by stockpiling military supplies, operating an independent government, boycotting British goods, and announcing no allegiance to Britain.

The First Continental Congress also agreed to a Declaration and Resolves of the First Continental Congress (the "1774 Declaration"), outlining rights like those to life, liberty, property, and the right to establish their own taxes within the colonies (or at least have taxes approved by their own provincial legislatures). Like the Declaration of Independence, the 1774 Declaration also outlined justifications for a possible rebellion, including the Intolerable Acts. Several localities had similar documents, including the popular **Fairfax County Resolves** (July 17, 1774) drafted by George Mason and George Washington. The 1774 Declaration was also likely heavily inspired by Jefferson's ***A Summary View of the Rights of British America***, drafted in July 1774 and circulated thereafter. *A Summary View* complains of many of the same grievances described in the 1765 Declaration, but adds many others.

Ultimately, the 1774 Declaration constituted a formal declaration from Congress that the actions of the British must cease or a revolution would result.

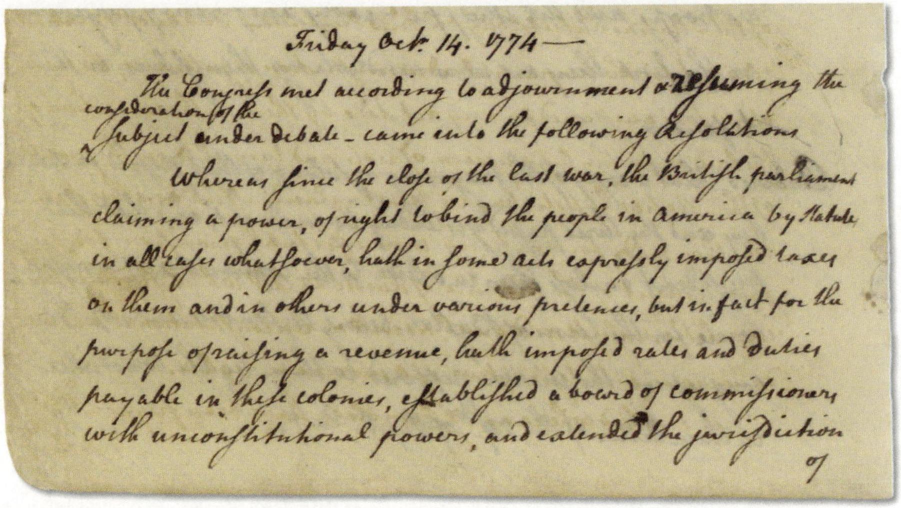
Friday Oct. 14. 1774—
The Congress met according to adjournment & resuming the consideration of the Subject under debate – came into the following Resolutions
Whereas since the close of the last war, the British parliament claiming a power, of right to bind the people in America by statute in all cases whatsoever, hath in some acts expressly imposed taxes on them and in others under various pretences, but in fact for the purpose of raising a revenue, hath imposed rates and duties payable in these colonies, established a board of commissioners, with unconstitutional powers, and extended the jurisdiction of

Excerpt from Papers of the Continental Congress, October 14, 1774

Declaration and Resolves of the First Continental Congress

Whereas, since the close of the last war, the British parliament, claiming a power, of right, to bind the people of America by statutes in all cases whatsoever,[1] hath, in some acts, expressly imposed taxes on them, and in others, under various presences, but in fact for the purpose of raising a revenue, hath imposed rates and duties payable in these colonies, established a board of commissioners, with unconstitutional powers, and extended the jurisdiction of courts of admiralty, not only for collecting the said duties, but for the trial of causes merely arising within the body of a county:

And whereas, in consequence of other statutes, judges, who before held only estates at will in their offices, have been made dependant on the crown alone for their salaries, and standing armies kept in times of peace: And whereas it has lately been resolved in parliament, that by force of a statute, made in the thirty-fifth year of the reign of King Henry the Eighth, colonists may be transported

1. This reference to "all cases whatsoever," which appears in many of these early documents (including the Declaration of Independence), refers to the British 1766 Declaratory Act. *See* p. 34. That Act accompanied the repeal of the Stamp Act but in effect proclaimed a more expanded view of Parliament's authority over the colonies; instead of authority for certain matters, the British had authority "in all cases whatsoever."

to England, and tried there upon accusations for treasons and misprisions, or concealments of treasons committed in the colonies, and by a late statute, such trials have been directed in cases therein mentioned:

And whereas, in the last session of parliament, three statutes were made; one entitled, "An act to discontinue, in such manner and for such time as are therein mentioned, the landing and discharging, lading, or shipping of goods, wares and merchandise, at the town, and within the harbour of Boston, in the province of Massachusetts-Bay in New England;" another entitled, "An act for the better regulating the government of the province of Massachusetts-Bay in New England;" and another entitled, "An act for the impartial administration of justice, in the cases of persons questioned for any act done by them in the execution of the law, or for the suppression of riots and tumults, in the province of the Massachusetts-Bay in New England;" and another statute was then made, "for making more effectual provision for the government of the province of Quebec, etc." All which statutes are impolitic, unjust, and cruel, as well as unconstitutional, and most dangerous and destructive of American rights:

And whereas, assemblies have been frequently dissolved, contrary to the rights of the people, when they attempted to deliberate on grievances; and their dutiful, humble, loyal, and reasonable petitions to the crown for redress, have been repeatedly treated with contempt, by his Majesty's ministers of state:

The good people of the several[2] colonies of New-Hampshire, Massachusetts-Bay, Rhode Island and Providence Plantations, Connecticut, New-York, New-Jersey, Pennsylvania, Newcastle, Kent, and Sussex on Delaware, Maryland, Virginia, North-Carolina and South-Carolina, justly alarmed at these arbitrary proceedings of parliament and administration, have severally elected, constituted, and appointed deputies to meet, and sit in general Congress, in the city of Philadelphia, in order to obtain such establishment, as that their religion, laws, and liberties, may not be subverted: Whereupon the deputies so appointed being now assembled, in a full and free representation of these colonies, taking into their most serious consideration, the best means of attaining the ends aforesaid, do, in the first place, as Englishmen, their ancestors in like cases have usually done, for asserting and vindicating their rights and liberties, DECLARE,

---

2. The 1774 Declaration identifies each of the "several colonies," a trend that continues until revisions to the Preamble to the Constitution (through Gouverneur Morris and the Committee of Style) struck these references and instead refers to one nation, the "United States," to convey unity and to accommodate the addition of new states. *See* p. 136.

That the inhabitants of the English colonies in North-America, by the immutable laws of nature, the principles of the English constitution, and the several charters or compacts, have the following RIGHTS:[3]

Resolved, N.C.D.[4] 1. That they are entitled to life, liberty and property: and they have never ceded to any foreign power whatever, a right to dispose of either without their consent.[5]

Resolved, N.C.D. 2. That our ancestors, who first settled these colonies, were at the time of their emigration from the mother country, entitled to all the rights, liberties, and immunities of free and natural-born subjects, within the realm of England.

Resolved, N.C.D. 3. That by such emigration they by no means forfeited, surrendered, or lost any of those rights, but that they were, and their descendants now are, entitled to the exercise and enjoyment of all such of them, as their local and other circumstances enable them to exercise and enjoy.

Resolved, 4. That the foundation of English liberty, and of all free government, is a right in the people to participate in their legislative council: and as the English colonists are not represented, and from their local and other circumstances, cannot properly be represented in the British parliament, they are entitled to a free and exclusive power of legislation in their several provincial legislatures, where their right of representation can alone be preserved, in all cases of taxation and internal polity, subject only to the negative of their sovereign, in such manner as has been heretofore used and accustomed: But, from the necessity of the case, and a regard to the mutual interest of both countries, we cheerfully consent to the operation of such acts of the British parliament, as are bonfide, restrained to the regulation of our external commerce, for the purpose of securing the commercial advantages of the whole empire to the mother country, and the commercial benefits of its respective members; excluding every idea of taxation internal or external, for raising a revenue on the subjects, in America, without their consent.

3. The drafting committee struggled to agree on how to convey the source of these rights: natural law, statutes, or the British constitution. The committee decided to declare that colonists had rights pursuant to each.

4. N.C.D. refers to "*nemine contradicente*," which is a Latin term meaning "no one dissenting" or "unanimously."

5. We see this evolve into inalienable rights to life, liberty, and the pursuit of happiness in the Declaration of Independence. *See* p. 92.

Resolved, N.C.D. 5. That the respective colonies are entitled to the common law of England, and more especially to the great and inestimable privilege of being tried by their peers of the vicinage, according to the course of that law.

Resolved, N.C.D. 6. That they are entitled to the benefit of such of the English statutes, as existed at the time of their colonization; and which they have, by experience, respectively found to be applicable to their several local and other circumstances.

Resolved, N.C.D. 7. That these, his Majesty's colonies, are likewise entitled to all the immunities and privileges granted and confirmed to them by royal charters, or secured by their several codes of provincial laws.[6]

Resolved, N.C.D. 8. That they have a right peaceably to assemble, consider of their grievances, and petition the king; and that all prosecutions, prohibitory proclamations, and commitments for the same, are illegal.

Resolved, N.C.D. 9. That the keeping a standing army in these colonies, in times of peace, without the consent of the legislature of that colony, in which such army is kept, is against law.

Resolved, N.C.D. 10. It is indispensably necessary to good government, and rendered essential by the English constitution, that the constituent branches of the legislature be independent of each other; that, therefore, the exercise of legislative power in several colonies, by a council appointed, during pleasure, by the crown, is unconstitutional, dangerous and destructive to the freedom of American legislation.

All and each of which the aforesaid deputies, in behalf of themselves, and their constituents, do claim, demand, and insist on, as their indubitable rights and liberties, which cannot be legally taken from them, altered or abridged by any power whatever, without their own consent, by their representatives in their several provincial legislature.

In the course of our inquiry, we find many infringements and violations of the foregoing rights, which, from an ardent desire, that harmony and mutual intercourse of affection and interest may be restored, we pass over for the present,

---

6. Just as citizens of different *states* are entitled to privileges and immunities in the Constitution, colonists claimed immunities and privileges that British citizens enjoyed.

and proceed to state such acts and measures as have been adopted since the last war, which demonstrate a system formed to enslave America.[7]

Resolved, N.C.D. That the following acts of parliament are infringements and violations of the rights of the colonists; and that the repeal of them is essentially necessary, in order to restore harmony between Great Britain and the American colonies, viz.

The several acts of Geo. III. ch. 15, and ch. 34.-5 Geo. III. ch.25.-6 Geo. ch. 52.-7 Geo.III. ch. 41 and ch. 46.-8 Geo. III. ch. 22. which impose duties for the purpose of raising a revenue in America, extend the power of the admiralty courts beyond their ancient limits, deprive the American subject of trial by jury, authorize the judges certificate to indemnify the prosecutor from damages, that he might otherwise be liable to, requiring oppressive security from a claimant of ships and goods seized, before he shall be allowed to defend his property, and are subversive of American rights.

Also 12 Geo. III. ch. 24, intituled, "An act for the better securing his majesty's dockyards, magazines, ships, ammunition, and stores," which declares a new offence in America, and deprives the American subject of a constitutional trial by jury of the vicinage, by authorizing the trial of any person, charged with the committing any offence described in the said act, out of the realm, to be indicted and tried for the same in any shire or county within the realm.

Also the three acts passed in the last session of parliament, for stopping the port and blocking up the harbour of Boston, for altering the charter and government of Massachusetts-Bay, and that which is entitled, "An act for the better administration of justice, etc."

Also the act passed in the same session for establishing the Roman Catholic[8] religion, in the province of Quebec, abolishing the equitable system of English laws, and erecting a tyranny there, to the great danger (from so total a dissimilarity of religion, law and government) of the neighboring British colonies, by the assistance of whose blood and treasure the said country was conquered from France.

---

7. This Declaration and later petitions compare the treatment of colonists to slavery or servitude. Pauline Maier and other scholars have argued that such references demonstrate that the Framers appreciated the immorality of slavery.

8. Among colonial grievances was Britain's recognition of the Roman Catholic religion in neighboring Canada, which the British had acquired from France through victories in the French and Indian War.

Also the act passed in the same session, for the better providing suitable quarters for officers and soldiers in his majesty's service, in North-America.

Also, that the keeping a standing army in several of these colonies, in time of peace, without the consent of the legislature of that colony, in which such army is kept, is against law.

To these grievous acts and measures, Americans cannot submit, but in hopes their fellow subjects in Great Britain will, on a revision of them, restore us to that state, in which both countries found happiness and prosperity, we have for the present, only resolved to pursue the following peaceable measures: 1. To enter into a non-importation, non-consumption, and non-exportation agreement or association.[9] 2. To prepare an address to the people of Great Britain, and a memorial to the inhabitants of British America: and 3. To prepare a loyal address to his majesty, agreeable to resolutions already entered into.

9. This first measure was achieved through the Articles of Association, provided in the next chapter.

Articles of Association

(October 20, 1774)

Introduction

A week after approving the 1774 Declaration of Resolves, the First Continental Congress took a significant step toward independence by ratifying the Articles of Association on October 20, 1774. This document established the Continental Association, which functioned somewhat like a modern international agreement in which each colony agreed to certain terms but retained full sovereignty. The Articles mandated a comprehensive embargo on all trade between America and Great Britain, covering virtually all goods, wares, or merchandise. The colonists hoped that this economic pressure would compel Britain to repeal the Intolerable Acts. The First Continental Congress also declared the Intolerable Acts unconstitutional. The British responded by further restricting trade by passing the New England Restraining Act, which specifically targeted New England because of its pivotal role in the unrest.

Abraham Lincoln later recognized the profound significance of the Continental Association, crediting it as the foundation of the Union (not just the Declaration of Independence or the Constitution). He stated, "The Union is much older than the Constitution. It was formed, in fact, by the Articles of Association in 1774. It was matured and continued by the Declaration of Independence in 1776. It was further matured, and the faith of all the then thirteen States expressly plighted and engaged that it should be perpetual, by the Articles of Confederation in 1778. And finally, in 1787, one of the declared objects for ordaining and establishing the Constitution was 'to form a more perfect Union.'" Lincoln powerfully used this argument to refute secessionists' legal positions. The Articles created a single, perpetual nation; later documents merely developed a "more perfect Union." Therefore, there is no constitutionally legitimate basis for states to secede from the Union. Joining the Union is voluntary, but once a state is in, there is no lawful mechanism for leaving.

The urgency of unity among the colonies in 1774 was captured by the famous rallying cry "unite or die." The disparate colonies understood that their individual capacities would be insufficient against Britain in the event of war. Moreover, if any single state were to defect or be overtaken, it could serve as a gateway for British forces to infiltrate and dominate the remaining colonies. It was more important than ever to unite.

Benjamin Franklin's famous "Unite or Die" political cartoon. This was a repurposed version of his 1754 cartoon, "Join or Die," galvanizing colonial support for the French and Indian War.

The Articles of Association drastically decreased the value of British goods and drew the colonies closer together for a common cause. Interestingly, Section 2 of the Articles bans the importation of slaves (though not domestic slavery as an institution) in an attempt to harm the British economy. These collective (other than Georgia, which was still not participating) economic and political measures marked critical early steps toward forming a unified front that would eventually lead to independence and a new nation. As far as Great Britain was concerned, the Continental Congress was an illegal body with no right to meet or to pass such agreements.

The *Association* entered into by the *American Continental Congress* on Behalf of all the Colonies

[Preamble; Pledge of Loyalty; Grievances]

We his Majesty's most dutiful and loyal Subjects, the Delegates of the several[1] Colonies of New Hampshire, Massachusetts Bay, Rhode Island, Connecticut, New York, New Jersey, Pennsylvania, the Three Lower Counties of Newcastle,

1. Although the colonies are working together, they are still "several" (or separate) under the Continental Association.

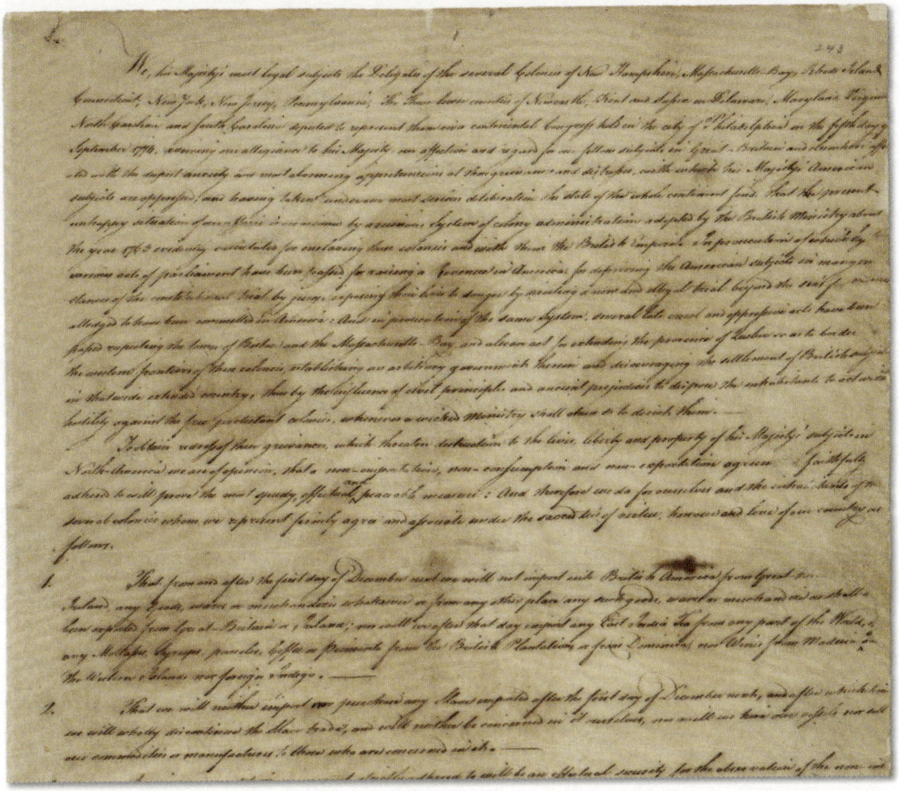

Excerpt of Engrossed Articles of Association (1774)

Kent, and Sussex, on Delaware, Maryland, Virginia, North Carolina, and South Carolina, deputed to represent them in a Continental Congress, held in the City of Philadelphia on the 5th Day of September 1774, avowing our Allegiance to his Majesty, our Affection and Regard for our Fellow Subjects in Great Britain and elsewhere, affected with the deepest Anxiety, and most alarming Apprehensions at those Grievances and Distresses with which his Majesty's American Subjects are oppressed, and having taken under our most serious Deliberation the State of the whole Continent, find that the present unhappy Situation of our Affairs is occasioned by a ruinous System of Colony Administration, adopted by the British Ministry about the Year 1763, evidently calculated for enslaving these Colonies, and, with them, the British Empire: In Prosecution of which System, various Acts of Parliament have been passed for raising a Revenue in America, for depriving the American Subjects, in many Instances, of the constitutional Trial by Jury, exposing their Lives to Danger, by directing a new and illegal Trial beyond the Seas, for Crimes alledged to have been committed in America; and, in Prosecution of the same System, several late, cruel, and oppressive Acts, have been passed respecting the Town of Boston and the Massachusetts Bay, and also an Act for extending the Province of Quebeck, so as to border on the western Frontiers of these Colonies, establishing an arbitrary Government therein, and discouraging the Settlement of British Subjects in that wide-extended Country; thus, by the Influence of civil Principles, and ancient Prejudices, to dispose the Inhabitants to act with Hostility against the free Protestant Colonies, whenever a wicked Ministry shall choose so to direct them.

To obtain Redress of these Grievances, which threaten Destruction to the Lives, Liberty, and Property, of his Majesty's Subjects in North America, we are of Opinion that a Non-importation, Non-consumption, and Non-exportation Agreement, faithfully adhered to, will prove the most speedy, effectual, and peaceable Measure; and therefore we do, for ourselves and the Inhabitants of the several Colonies whom we represent, firmly agree and associate, under the sacred Ties of Virtue, Honour, and Love of our Country, as follows:

[Section 1: Boycott of Importation of British Goods]

First. That from and after the first Day of December next we will not import into British America, from Great Britain or Ireland, any Goods, Wares, or Merchandise whatsoever, or from any other Place, any such Goods, Wares, or Merchandise, as shall have been exported from Great Britain or Ireland; nor will we, after that Day, import any East India Tea from any Part of the World, nor any Molosses, Syrups, Paneles, Coffee, or Pimenta, from the British Plantations, or from Dominica, nor Wines from Madeira, or the Western Islands, nor foreign Indigo.

[Section 2: Prohibition on Importation of Slaves and Slave Trade][2]

Second. That we will neither import nor purchase any Slave imported after the first Day of December next, after which Time we will wholly discontinue the Slave Trade, and will neither be concerned in it ourselves, nor will we hire our Vessels, nor sell our Commodities or Manufactures, to those who are concerned in it.

---

2. Some colonists had moral objections to slavery, but the primary purpose of this clause was to prohibit the slave trade because it had become lucrative for British merchants. (The Constitution does almost the opposite—as a compromise with Southern states, it protected the slave trade for at least 20 years after ratification.) Some Framers (including Adams, Franklin, and Gouverneur Morris) worked actively to abolish slavery. Jefferson and others hoped that slavery would naturally wither away over time, first by ending importation, then by limiting its expansion westward. *See, e.g.*, the

[Section 3: Boycott of East India Tea]

Third. As a Non-consumption Agreement, strictly adhered to, will be an effectual Security for the Observation of the Non-importation, we, as above, solemnly agree and associate, that, from this Day, we will not purchase or use any Tea imported on Account of the East India Company, or any on which a Duty hath been or shall be paid; and, from and after the first Day of March next, we will not purchase or use any East India Tea whatever: Nor will we, nor shall any Person for or under us, purchase or use any of those Goods, Wares, or Merchandise, we have agreed not to import, which we shall know, or have Cause to suspect, were imported after the first Day of December, except such as come under the Rules and Directions of the tenth Article, hereafter mentioned.

[Section 4: Boycott of Exports to Great Britain, Ireland, and the West Indies (in one year)]

Fourth. The earnest Desire we have not to injure our Fellow Subjects in Great Britain, Ireland, or the West Indies, induces us to suspend a Non-exportation until the tenth Day of September 1775; at which Time, if the said Acts, and Parts of Acts of the British Parliament herein after mentioned, are not repealed, we will not, directly or indirectly, export any Merchandise, or Commodity whatsoever, to Great Britain, Ireland, or the West Indies, except Rice,[3] to Europe.

[Section 5: Boycott of Any Merchant Who Violates the Articles]

Fifth. Such as are Merchants, and use the British and Irish Trade, will give Orders, as soon as possible, to their Factors, Agents, and Correspondents, in Great Britain and Ireland, not to ship any Goods to them, on any Pretence whatsoever, as they cannot be received in America; and if any Merchant residing in Great Britain or Ireland shall, directly or indirectly, ship any Goods, Wares, or Merchandise, for America, in Order to break the said Non-importation Agreement,

---

Northwest Ordinance, p.119. He also supported the idea of "colonization" or deporting slaves to other countries in Central America or Africa. He believed that they were entitled to freedom and liberty but he could not envision a fully integrated American society.

In 1808, British abolitionist Thomas Clarkson made a **visual representation** of the scope of slavery and its progress toward abolition, representing the slave trade on a map with "springs or rivulets" that would ultimately sweep away slavery.

3. South Carolina succeeded in getting rice excluded from the boycott, fearing that its economy would be ruined otherwise.

or in any Manner contravene the same, on such unworthy Conduct being well attested, it ought to be made publick; and, on the same being so done, we will not, from thenceforth, have any commercial Connexion with such Merchant.

[Section 6: Boycott Applies to Ship Owners]

Sixth. That such as are Owners of Vessels will give positive Orders to their Captains, or Masters, not to receive on Board their Vessels any Goods prohibited by the said Non-importation Agreement, on Pain of immediate Dismission from their Service.

[Section 7: Preservation of Sheep][4]

Seventh. We will use our utmost Endeavours to improve the Breed of Sheep, and increase their Number to the greatest Extent; and to that End we will kill them as sparingly as may be, especially those of the most profitable Kind: Nor will we export any to the West Indies, or elsewhere. And those of us who are or may become overstocked with, or can conveniently spare any Sheep, will dispose of them to our Neighbours, especially to the poorer Sort, on moderate Terms.

[Section 8: Frugality and Extravagance Commitment]

Eighth. That we will, in our several Stations, encourage Frugality Economy, and Industry; and promote Agriculture, Arts, and the Manufactures of this Country,[5] especially that of Wool; and will discountenance and discourage every Species of Extravagance and Dissipation, especially all Horse-racing, and all Kinds of Gaming, Cock-fighting, Exhibitions of Shows, Plays, and other expensive Diversions and Entertainments; and on the Death of any Relation, or Friend, none of us, or any of our Families, will go into any farther Mourning Dress than a black Crape or Riband on the Arm or Hat for Gentlemen, and a black Riband and Necklace for Ladies, and we will discontinue the giving of Gloves and Scarfs at Funerals.

---

4. Wool was important and scarce in the colonies. Sections 7 and 8 aim to reduce dependence on British wool (and to reduce extravagance in general).

5. The colonies agreed to promote manufacturing and industry, which was a direct violation of many of the trade acts that the British had imposed. England wanted its American colonies to remain agrarian to provide food and goods to Britain, but not to innovate in technology and manufacturing, which would threaten Britain's supremacy. *See also* Art. I, § 8 of the U.S. Constitution, p. 144 (patent and trademark protection, encouraging innovation).

[Section 9: Price-Gauging Prohibition: Vendors]

Ninth. That such as are Venders of Goods or Merchandise will not take Advantage of the Scarcity of Goods that may be occasioned by this Association, but will sell the same at the Rates we have been respectively accustomed to do for twelve Months last past; and if any Venders of Goods or Merchandise shall sell any such Goods on higher Terms, or shall in any Manner, or by any Device whatsoever, violate or depart from this Agreement, no Person ought, nor will any of us deal with any such Person, or his or her Factor or Agent, at any Time thereafter, for any Commodity whatever.

[Section 10: Dispute Resolution for Interim Shipments]

Tenth. In Case any Merchant, Trader, or other Persons, shall import any Goods or Merchandise after the first Day of December, and before the first Day of February next, the same ought forthwith, at the Election of the Owner, to be either reshipped or delivered up to the Committee of the County or Town wherein they shall be imported, to be stored at the Risk of the Importer, until the Non-importation Agreement shall cease, or be sold under the Direction of the Committee aforesaid: And, in the last mentioned Case, the Owner or owners of such goods shall be reimbursed (out of the Sales) the first cost and charges, the profit, if any, to be applied towards relieving and employing such poor inhabitants of the Town of Boston as are immediate sufferers by the Boston Port Bill, and a particular Account of all goods so returned, stored, or sold, to be inserted in the publick Papers. And if any goods or merchandizes shall be imported after the said first Day of February the same ought forthwith to be sent back again, without breaking any of the packages thereof.

[Section 11: Local Oversight Committees][6]

Eleventh. That a Committee be chosen in every County, City, and Town, by those who are qualified to vote for representatives in the Legislature, whose Business it shall be attentively to observe the conduct of all Persons touching this Association; and when it shall be made to appear, to the Satisfaction of a Majority of any such Committee that any Person within the Limits of their Appointment

6. Local committees were responsible for ensuring compliance with the boycott; punishments included tar-and-feathering.

has violated this association, that such Majority do forthwith cause the truth of the case to be published in the Gazette, to the End that all such foes to the rights of British America may be publickly known and universally contemned as the Enemies of American Liberty; and thence forth we respectively will break off all Dealings with him, or her.

[Section 12: Oversight Committee Duties]

Twelfth. That the Committee of Correspondence, in the respective Colonies do frequently inspect the Entries of their Custom Houses, and inform each other, from Time to Time, of the true state thereof and of every other material Circumstance that may occur relative to this association.

[Section 13: Price-Gauging Prohibition: Manufacturers]

Thirteenth. That all Manufactures of this country be sold at reasonable Prices, so that no undue Advantage be taken of a future scarcity of Goods.

[Section 14: Boycott Colonies Not Parties to Articles]

Fourteenth. And we do farther agree and resolve, that we will have no Trade, Commerce, Dealings, or intercourse whatsoever, with any Colony or Province in North America, which shall not accede to, or which shall hereafter violate, this association, but will hold them as unworthy of the Rights of Freemen, and as inimical to the liberties of their Country.[7]

[Effective Until Intolerable Acts Repealed]

And we do solemnly bind ourselves and our Constituents under the Ties aforesaid, to adhere to this Association until such parts of the several Acts of Parliament, passed since the Close of the last War as impose or continue Duties on Tea, Wine, Molosses, Syrups, paneles, Coffee, Sugar, Pimenta, Indigo, foreign Paper, glass and Painters Colours, imported into America, and extend the Powers

7. As you can see with the signatories on the next page, Georgia is still not participating. One theme throughout this period is the coercive power of being left out of an association when the rest of the colonies are united. For example, New York had to be coaxed into agreeing to declaring independence, agreeing only after others had agreed and left New York as an outlier.

of the Admiralty Courts beyond their ancient Limits, deprive the American Subject of Trial by Jury, authorise the Judge's Certificate to indemnify the Prosecutor from Damages that he might otherwise be liable to from a Trial by his Peers, require oppressive Security from a Claimant of Ships or Goods seized before he shall be allowed to defend his Property, are repealed; and until that Part of the Act of the 12th of George III. Chapter 24th, entitled "An Act for the better securing his Majesty's Dockyards, Magazines, Ships, Ammunition, and Stores," by which any Persons charged with committing any of the Offences therein described in America may be tried in any Shire or County within the Realm, is repealed; and until the four Acts passed in the last Session of Parliament, viz. that for stopping the Port and blocking up the Harbour of Boston, that for altering the Charter and Government of Massachusetts Bay; and that which is entitled "An Act for the better Administration of Justice, &c." and that "For extending the Limits of Quebeck, &c." are repealed. And we recommend it to the Provincial Conventions, and to the Committees in the respective Colonies, to establish such farther Regulations as they may think proper, for carrying into Execution this Association.

The foregoing Association being determined upon by the Congress, was ordered to be subscribed by the several Members thereof; and thereupon, we have hereunto set our respective Names accordingly. IN CONGRESS, PHILADELPHIA, OCTOBER 20, 1774.

Signed, *Peyton Randolph*, President.

CONNECTICUT
Eliphalet Dyer,
Roger Sherman,
Silas Deane

THE LOWER COUNTIES [DELAWARE]
Caesar Rodney,
Thomas McKean,
George Read

MARYLAND
Matthew Tilghman,
Thomas Johnson, Jr.,
William Paca,
Samuel Chase

MASSACHUSETTS BAY
Thomas Cushing,
Samuel Adams,
John Adams,
Robert Treat Paine

NEW HAMPSHIRE
John Sullivan,
Nathaniel Folsom

NEW JERSEY
James Kinsey,
William Livingston,
Stephen Crane,
Richard Smith,
John De Hart

NEW YORK
Isaac Low,
John Alsop,
John Jay,
James Duane,
Philip Livingston,
William Floyd,
Henry Wisner,
Simon Boerum

NORTH CAROLINA
William Hooper,
Joseph Hewes,
Richard Caswell

PENNSYLVANIA
Joseph Galloway,
John Dickinson,
Charles Humphreys,
Thomas Mifflin,
Edward Biddle,
John Morton,
George Ross

RHODE ISLAND
Stephen Hopkins,
Samuel Ward

SOUTH CAROLINA
Henry Middleton,
Thomas Lynch,
Christopher Gadsden,
John Rutledge,
Edward Rutledge

VIRGINIA
Richard Henry Lee,
George Washington,
Patrick Henry,
Richard Bland,
Benjamin Harrison,
Edmund Pendleton

Petition to King George III

(OCTOBER 26, 1774)

Introduction

Soon after approving the 1774 Declaration of Resolves and Articles of Association, Congress sent a petition to King George III setting forth key grievances and calling for the repeal of the Intolerable Acts. The petition bypassed Parliament and was a direct appeal to King George III. Colonists believed (or at least claimed) that Parliament and the King's *agents* were responsible for many of the punitive measures enacted against them, not necessarily the King. The document expressed loyalty to the Crown and emphasized the colonists' desire to remain British subjects, while protesting Parliament's interference in their local affairs.

Many of these grievances resurface (sometimes almost verbatim) in the Declaration of Independence and later served as the basis for many constitutional protections. The Petition's grievances include a lack of adequate political representation; the presence of a standing army without consent; military power that is superior to the civil power; creating new and expensive offices; ignoring prior petitions; dissolving assemblies; unlawful searches, seizures, and takings; and failure to protect jury-trial rights. The Petition was couched in respectful and conciliatory language, aiming to persuade the King that the colonies remained loyal but were driven to action by necessity and the protection of their rights as British subjects. The strategy was to appeal to the King's reputed sense of justice and his power to override or influence Parliamentary decisions.

The Petition (drafted by John Dickinson) was sent to colony agents (including Benjamin Franklin) to present in England. It was delivered to Parliament in January 1775, but according to Benjamin Franklin, was intermingled with many other documents, resulting in little to no attention being given to it. More likely than Franklin's account is that the King was convinced that the colonies were in

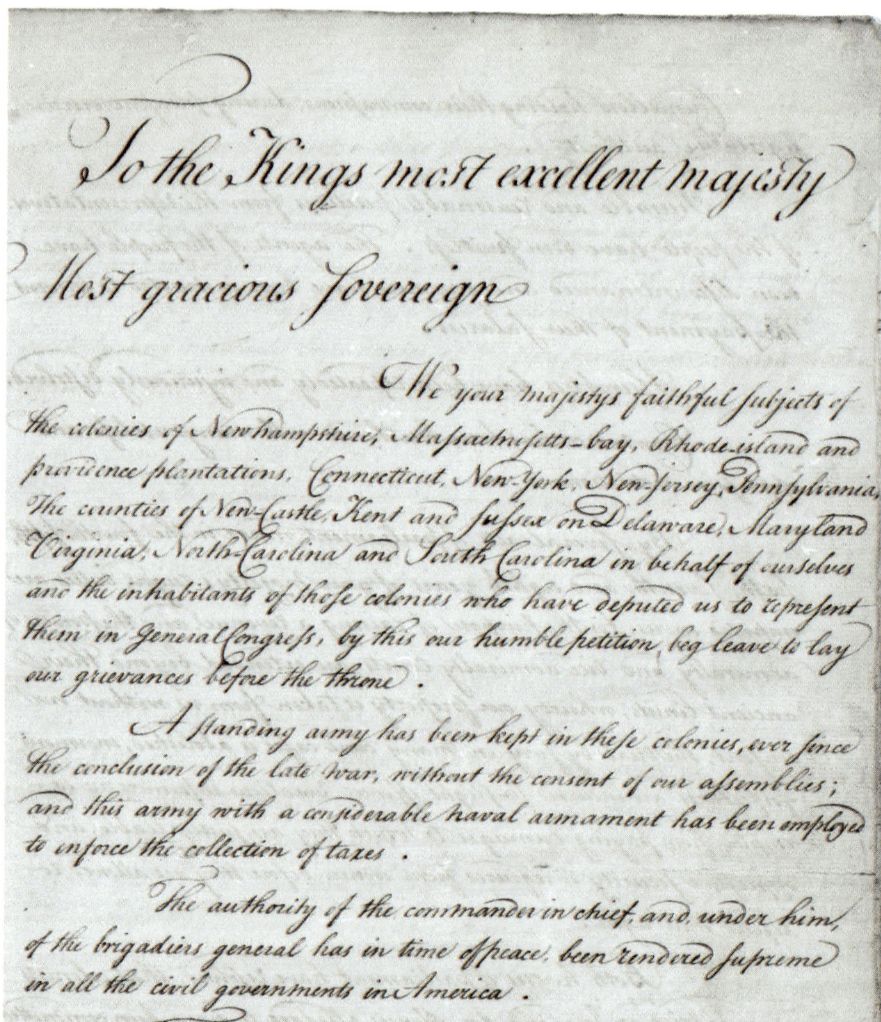
To the Kings most excellent majesty

Most gracious Sovereign

We your majestys faithful subjects of the colonies of New hampshire, Massachusetts-bay, Rhode-island and providence plantations, Connecticut, New-York, New-Jersey, Pennsylvania, The counties of New-Castle Kent and Sussex on Delaware, Maryland Virginia, North-Carolina and South Carolina in behalf of ourselves and the inhabitants of those colonies who have deputed us to represent them in General Congress, by this our humble petition, beg leave to lay our grievances before the throne.

A standing army has been kept in these colonies, ever since the conclusion of the late war, without the consent of our assemblies; and this army with a considerable naval armament has been employed to enforce the collection of taxes.

The authority of the commander in chief, and, under him, of the brigadiers general has in time of peace, been rendered supreme in all the civil governments in America.

Excerpt from engrossed version of Petition to King George III (from the Papers of Benjamin Franklin)

a state of rebellion, and he felt insulted by the direct appeal that seemed to undermine his Parliament. In any event, the King never issued a formal reply, which further frustrated the colonists and set the stage for the escalation of conflict. When subsequent documents reference ignoring the colonists' petitions, the 1774 Petition is an example.

Petition to King George III

The Petition of Congress.[1]

To the Kings most excellent majesty

Most gracious Sovereign

We your majestys faithful subjects of the colonies of Newhampshire, Massachusetts-bay, Rhode-island and Providence Plantations, Connecticut, New-York, New-Jersey, Pennsylvania, the counties of New-Castle Kent and Sussex on Delaware, Maryland, Virginia, North-Carolina, and South Carolina, in behalf of ourselves and the inhabitants of these colonies who have deputed us to represent them in General Congress, by this our humble petition, beg leave to lay our grievances before the throne.

A standing army has been kept in these colonies, ever since the conclusion of the late war, without the consent of our assemblies; and this army with a considerable naval armament has been employed to enforce the collection of taxes.

The Authority of the commander in chief, and, under him, of the brigadiers general has in time of peace, been rendered supreme in all the civil governments in America.

The commander in chief of all your majesty's forces in North-America has, in time of peace, been appointed governor of a colony.

The charges of usual offices have been greatly increased; and, new, expensive and oppressive offices have been multiplied.

The judges of admiralty and vice-admiralty courts are empowered to receive their salaries and fees from the effects condemned by themselves. The officers of

1. The Petition is structured like prior British petitions, including an introduction, list of grievances, bases for action, and conclusion. Notice the same structure in America's Declaration of Independence.

the customs are empowered to break open and enter houses without the authority of any civil magistrate founded on legal information.

The judges of courts of common law have been made entirely dependant on one part of the legislature for their salaries, as well as for the duration of their commissions.

Councellors holding their commissions, during pleasure, exercise legislative authority.

Humble and reasonable petitions from the representatives of the people have been fruitless.

The agents of the people have been discountenanced and governors have been instructed to prevent the payment of their salaries.

Assemblies have been repeatedly and injuriously dissolved.

Commerce has been burthened with many useless and oppressive restrictions.

By several acts of parliament made in the fourth, fifth, sixth, seventh, and eighth years of your majestys reign, duties are imposed on us, for the purpose of raising a revenue, and the powers of admiralty and vice-admiralty courts are extended beyond their ancient limits, whereby our property is taken from us without our consent, the trial by jury in many civil cases is abolished, enormous forfeitures are incurred for slight offences, vexatious informers are exempted from paying damages, to which they are justly liable, and oppressive security is required from owners before they are allowed to defend their right.

Both houses of parliament have resolved that colonists may be tried in England, for offences alledged to have been committed in America, by virtue of a statute passed in the thirty fifth year of Henry the eighth; and in consequence thereof, attempts have been made to enforce that statute. A statute was passed in the twelfth year of your majesty's reign, directing, that persons charged with committing any offence therein described, in any place out of the realm, may be indicted and tried for the same, in any shire or county within the realm, whereby inhabitants of these colonies may, in sundry cases by that statute made capital, be deprived of a trial by their peers of the vicinage.

In the last sessions of parliament, an act was passed for blocking up the harbour of Boston; another, empowering the governor of the Massachusetts-bay to send persons indicted for murder in that province to another colony or even to Great Britain for trial whereby such offenders may escape legal punishment; a third, for altering the chartered constitution of government in that province; and a fourth for extending the limits of Quebec, abolishing the English and restoring the French laws, whereby great numbers of British freemen are subjected to the latter, and establishing an absolute government and the Roman Catholick religion throughout those vast regions, that border on the westerly and northerly boundaries of the free protestant English settlements; and a fifth for the better providing suitable quarters for officers and soldiers in his majesty's service in North America.

To a sovereign, who "glories in the name of Briton" the bare recital of these acts must we presume, justify the loyal subjects, who fly to the foot of his throne and implore his clemency for protection against them.

From this destructive system of colony administration adopted since the conclusion of the last war, have flowed those distresses, dangers, fears and jealousies, that overwhelm your majesty's dutiful colonists with affliction; and we defy our most subtle and inveterate enemies, to trace the unhappy differences between Great-Britain and these colonies, from an earlier period or from other causes than we have assigned. Had they proceeded on our part from a restless levity of temper, unjust impulses of ambition, or artful suggestions of seditious persons, we should merit the opprobrious terms frequently bestowed upon us, by those we revere. But so far from promoting innovations, we have only opposed them; and can be charged with no offence, unless it be one, to receive injuries and be sensible of them.

Had our creator been pleased to give us existence in a land of slavery, the sense of our condition might have been mitigated by ignorance and habit. But thanks be to his adoreable goodness, we were born the heirs of freedom, and ever enjoyed our right under the auspices of your royal ancestors, whose family was seated on the British throne, to rescue and secure a pious and gallant nation from the popery and despotism of a superstitious and inexorable tyrant.[2] Your majesty, we are confident, justly rejoices, that your title to the crown is thus founded on the title of your people to liberty; and therefore we doubt not, but your royal wisdom must approve the sensibility, that teaches your subjects anxiously to guard the blessings, they received from divine providence, and thereby to prove the performance of that compact, which elevated the illustrious house of Brunswick to the imperial dignity it now possesses.

---

2. This is a reference to King James II, a Roman Catholic who was deposed in 1688 during the Glorious Revolution and replaced by William III of the House of Brunswick. *See* p. 17.

The apprehension of being degraded into a state of servitude from the pre-eminent rank of English freemen, while our minds retain the strongest love of liberty, and clearly foresee the miseries preparing for us and our posterity, excites emotions in our breasts, which though we cannot describe, we should not wish to conceal. Feeling as men, and thinking as subjects, in the manner we do, silence would be disloyalty. By giving this faithful information, we do all in our power, to promote the great objects of your royal cares, the tranquillity of your government, and the welfare of your people.

Duty to your majesty and regard for the preservation of ourselves and our posterity, the primary obligations of nature and society command us to entreat your royal attention; and as your majesty enjoys the signal distinction of reigning over freemen, we apprehend the language of freemen can not be displeasing. Your royal indignation, we hope, will rather fall on those designing and dangerous men, who daringly interposing themselves between your royal person and your faithful subjects,[3] and for several years past incessantly employed to dissolve the bonds of society,[4] by abusing your majesty's authority, misrepresenting your American subjects and prosecuting the most desperate and irritating projects of oppression, have at length compelled us, by the force of accumulated injuries too severe to be any longer tolerable, to disturb your majesty's repose by our complaints.

These sentiments are extorted from hearts, that much more willingly would bleed in your majesty's service. Yet so greatly have we been misrepresented, that a necessity has been alledged of taking our property from us without our consent "to defray the charge of the administration of justice, the support of civil government, and the defence protection and security of the colonies."[5] But we beg leave to assure your majesty, that such provision has been and will be made for defraying the two first articles, as has been and shall be judged, by the legislatures of the several colonies, just and suitable to their respective circumstances: And for the defence protection and security of the colonies, their militias, if prop-

3. Congress placed the blame not directly on the King, but on his agents and Parliament. And for understandable reasons—countering the King could be considered treason, punishable by death at the time. Directing grievances at the King's agents or Parliament is a safer way to express dissatisfaction. This is also in stark contrast to the Declaration of Independence, which (treasonously) aims its charges and grievances directly at the King.

4. Because we already know what happens in 1776, this reference to "dissolving the bonds of society" (borrowed from John Locke) might be considered foreshadowing. *See* p. 91.

5. This is a reference to taxes imposed by the June 1767 Townshend Acts, taxing imports of glass, lead, paint, paper, and tea. It also created an enforcement mechanism and additional vice-admiralty courts (which did not have juries).

erly regulated, as they earnestly desire may immediately be done, would be fully sufficient, at least in times of peace; and in case of war, your faithful colonists will be ready and willing, as they ever have been when constitutionally required, to demonstrate their loyalty to your majesty, by exerting their most strenuous efforts in granting supplies and raising forces. Yielding to no British subjects, in affectionate attachment to your majesty's person, family and government, we too dearly prize the privilege of expressing that attachment by those proofs, that are honourable to the prince who receives them, and to the people who give them, ever to resign it to any body of men upon earth.

Had we been permitted to enjoy in quiet the inheritance left us by our forefathers, we should at this time have been peaceably, cheerfully and usefully employed in recommending ourselves by every testimony of devotion to your majesty, and of veneration to the state, from which we derive our origin. But though now exposed to unexpected and unnatural scenes of distress by a contention with that nation, in whose parental guidance on all important affairs we have hitherto with filial reverence constantly trusted, and therefore can derive no instruction in our present unhappy and perplexing circumstances from any former experience, yet we doubt not, the purity of our intention and the integrity of our conduct will justify us at that grand tribunal, before which all mankind must submit to judgment.

We ask but for peace, liberty, and safety. We wish not a diminution of the prerogative, nor do we solicit the grant of any new right in our favour. Your royal authority over us and our connexion with Great-Britain, we shall always carefully and zealously endeavour to support and maintain.

Filled with sentiments of duty to your majesty, and of affection to our parent state, deeply impressed by our education and strongly confirmed by our reason, and anxious to evince the sincerity of these dispositions, we present this petition only to obtain redress of grievances and relief from fears and jealousies occasioned by the system of statutes and regulations adopted since the close of the late war, for raising a revenue in America—extending the powers of courts of admiralty and vice-admiralty—trying persons in Great Britain for offences alledged to be committed in America—affecting the province of Massachusetts-bay, and altering the government and extending the limits of Quebec; by the abolition of which system, the harmony between Great-Britain and these colonies so necessary to the happiness of both and so ardently desired by the latter, and the usual intercourses will be immediately restored. In the magnanimity and justice of your majesty and parliament we confide, for a redress of our other grievances, trusting, that when the causes of our apprehensions are removed, our future conduct will prove us not unworthy of the regard, we have been accustomed, in our happier days, to enjoy. For appealing to that being who searches thoroughly the hearts of his creatures, we solemnly profess, that our councils have been influenced by no other motive, than a dread of impending destruction.

Permit us then, most gracious sovereign, in the name of all your faithful people in America, with the utmost humility to implore you, for the honour of Almighty God, whose pure religion our enemies are undermining; for your glory, which can be advanced only by rendering your subjects happy and keeping them united; for the interests of your family depending on an adherence to the principles that enthroned it; for the safety and welfare of your kingdoms and dominions threatened with almost unavoidable dangers and distresses; that your majesty, as the loving father of your whole people, connected by the same bands of law, loyalty, faith and blood, though dwelling in various countries, will not suffer the transcendant relation formed by these ties to be farther violated, in uncertain expectation of effects, that, if attained, never can compensate for the calamities, through which they must be gained.

We therefore most earnestly beseech your majesty, that your royal authority and interposition may be used for our relief; and that a gracious answer may be given to this petition.

That your majesty may enjoy every felicity through a long and glorious reign over loyal and happy subjects, and that your descendants may inherit your prosperity and dominions 'til time shall be no more, is and always will be our sincere and fervent prayer.

PRESIDENT:
Henry Middleton

NEW-HAMPSHIRE:
Jno Sullivan,
Nathl Folsom

MASSACHUSETTS BAY:
Thomas Cushing,
Samuel Adams,
John Adams,
Robt. Treat Paine

RHODE-ISLAND:
Step Hopkins,
Sam: Ward

CONNECTICUT:
Elipht Dyer,
Roger Sherman,
Silas Deane

NEW-YORK:
Phil. Livingston,
John Alsop,
Isaac Low,
Jas. Duane,
John Jay,
Wm. Floyd,
Henry Wisner,
S: Boerum

NEW-JERSEY:
Wil: Livingston,
John De Hart,
Stepn. Crane,
Richd. Smith

PENNSYLVANIA:
E Biddle,
J: Galloway,
John Dickinson,
John Morton,
Thomas Mifflin,
George Ross,
Chas Humphreys

DELAWARE:
Cæsar Rodney,
Thos M: Kean,
Geo: Read

MARYLAND:
Mat. Tilghman,
Ths. Johnson Junr,
Wm. Paca,
Samuel Chase

VIRGINIA:
Richard Henry Lee,
Patrick Henry,
Go. Washington,
Edmund Pendleton,
Richd. Bland,
Benjn Harrison

NORTH CAROLINA:
Will Hooper,
Joseph Hewes,
Rd. Caswell

SOUTH CAROLINA:
Tho Lynch,
Christ Gadsden,
J. Rutledge,
Edward Rutledge

Agents to whom the Address to King is to be sent for

NEW HAMPSHIRE:
Paul Wentworth Esqr.

MASSACHUSETTS BAY:
William Bollan Esqr,
Doctr. Benj: Franklin,
Doctr. Arthur Lee.

RHODE ISLAND:
none

CONNECTICUT:
Thomas Life, Esqr.

NEW JERSEY:
Doctr Benj. Franklin

PENSYLVANIA:
. . . ditto

NEW YORK:
Edmund Burke

DELAWARE,
MARYLAND,
VIRGINIA,
N. CAROLINA:
none

SOUTH CAROLINA:
Charles Garth, Esqr.

Olive Branch Petition to King George III

(JULY 5, 1775)

Introduction

For the colonists, the Olive Branch Petition was a final attempt to avoid a war with Britain. The Boston Massacre (March 5, 1770), Lexington and Concord (April 19, 1775), and various skirmishes had already occurred. John Dickinson pushed for a final request to reconcile with the King (perhaps inspired by his nonviolent, Quaker roots), claiming that the colonies had no hidden ambitions for independence and merely wanted adequate representation and reasonable taxes. The Petition emphasized the colonists' loyalty to the Crown and emphasized their rights as British citizens. In a somewhat contradictory move, Congress approved a declaration to take up arms the next day (the next document in this book). Similarly, Congress had already approved an invasion of Canada (controlled by the British) over a week before. (General Richard Montgomery was killed and Benedict Arnold was injured in the failed invasion.) The King and others in Britain viewed pleas for peace as disingenuous. Adam Smith contended in the *Wealth of Nations* (1776) that the colonies were not worth the time, effort, and expense that Britain put into them.

Both Thomas Jefferson and John Dickinson worked on drafts of the Petition, and Dickinson's less inflammatory version was selected. The Second Continental Congress approved the Petition on July 5, 1775, and signed it on July 8. It reached Britain in late August. After receiving conflicting information regarding the colonists' sincerity, the King ignored the Petition and considered the colonies to be in rebellion.

The Crown's rejection of the Petition galvanized support for independence within the colonies. It marked a turning point in the American revolutionary struggle. It effectively ended any hope of a peaceful resolution and positioned the conflict as an inevitable move towards American independence. The Petition's failure led directly to the drafting of the Declaration of Independence in 1776, formally severing political ties between the colonies and Great Britain.

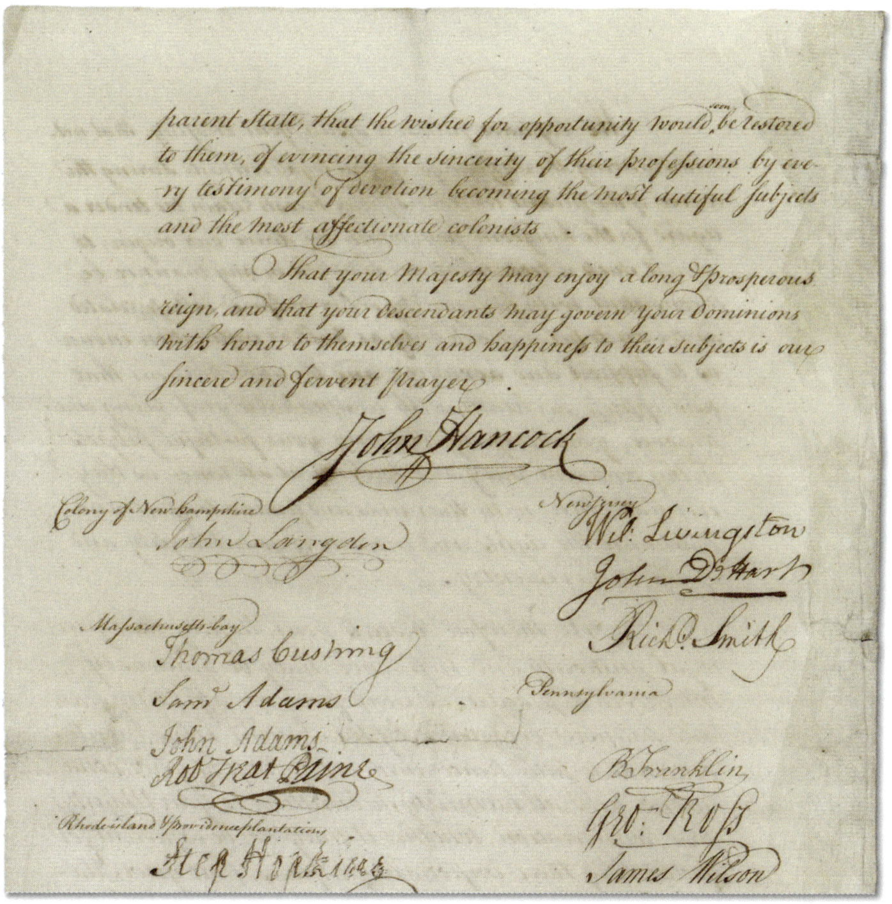

parent State, that the wished for opportunity would soon be restored to them, of evincing the sincerity of their professions by every testimony of devotion becoming the most dutiful subjects and the most affectionate colonists.

That your Majesty may enjoy a long & prosperous reign, and that your descendants may govern your dominions with honor to themselves and happiness to their subjects is our sincere and fervent prayer.

John Hancock

Colony of New Hampshire
John Langdon

Massachusetts-bay
Thomas Cushing
Saml Adams
John Adams
Robt Treat Paine

Rhode island & providence plantations
Step Hopkins

New Jersey
Wil: Livingston
John De Hart
Richd Smith

Pennsylvania
B Franklin
Geo: Ross
James Wilson

Excerpt from Olive Branch Petition to King George III

Olive Branch Petition to King George III

To the king's most excellent Majesty:

Most gracious sovereign,

We, your Majesty's faithful subjects of the colonies of new Hampshire, Massachusetts bay, Rhode island and Providence Plantations, Connecticut, New York, New Jersey, Pennsylvania, the counties of New Castle, Kent, and Sussex, on Delaware, Maryland, Virginia, North Carolina, and South Carolina, in behalf of ourselves, and the inhabitants of these colonies, who have deputed us to represent them in general Congress, entreat your Majesty's gracious attention to this our humble petition.

The union between our Mother country and these colonies, and the energy of mild and just government, produced benefits so remarkably important, and afforded such an assurance of their permanency and increase, that the wonder and envy of other Nations were excited, while they beheld Great Britain riseing to a power the most extraordinary the world had ever known.

Her rivals, observing that there was no probability of this happy connexion being broken by civil dissensions, and apprehending its future effects, if left any longer undisturbed, resolved to prevent her receiving such continual and formidable accessions of wealth and strength, by checking the growth of these settlements from which they were to be derived.

In the prosecution of this attempt, events so unfavourable to the design took place, that every friend to the interests of Great Britain and these colonies, entertained pleasing and reasonable expectations of seeing an additional force and extension immediately given to the operations of the union hitherto experienced, by an enlargement of the dominions of the Crown, and the removal of ancient and warlike enemies to a greater distance.

At the conclusion, therefore, of the late war, the most glorious and advantageous that ever had been carried on by British arms, your loyal colonists having contributed to its success, by such repeated and strenuous exertions, as frequently procured them the distinguished approbation of your Majesty, of the late king, and of parliament, doubted not but that they should be permitted, with the rest of the empire, to share in the blessings of peace, and the emoluments of victory and conquest. While these recent and honorable acknowledgments of their merits remained on record in the journals and acts of that august legislature, the Parliament, undefaced by the imputation or even the suspicion of any offence, they were alarmed by a new system of statutes and regulations adopted for the administration of the colonies, that filled their minds with the most painful fears and jealousies; and, to their inexpressible astonishment, perceived the dangers of a foreign quarrel quickly succeeded by domestic dangers, in their judgment, of a more dreadful kind.

Nor were their anxieties alleviated by any tendency in this system to promote the welfare of the Mother country. For tho' its effects were more immediately felt by them, yet its influence appeared to be injurious to the commerce and prosperity of Great Britain.

We shall decline the ungrateful task of describing the irksome variety of artifices, practised by many of your Majesty's Ministers, the delusive pretences, fruitless terrors, and unavailing severities, that have, from time to time, been dealt out by them, in their attempts to execute this impolitic plan, or of traceing, thro' a series of years past, the progress of the unhappy differences between Great Britain and these colonies, which have flowed from this fatal source.

Your Majesty's Ministers, persevering in their measures, and proceeding to open hostilities for enforcing them, have compelled us to arm in our own defence, and have engaged us in a controversy so peculiarly abhorrent to the affections of your still faithful colonists, that when we consider whom we must oppose in this contest, and if it continues, what may be the consequences, our own particular misfortunes are accounted by us only as parts of our distress.

Knowing to what violent resentments and incurable animosities, civil discords are apt to exasperate and inflame the contending parties, we think ourselves required by indispensable obligations to Almighty God, to your Majesty, to our fellow subjects, and to ourselves, immediately to use all the means in our power, not incompatible with our safety, for stopping the further effusion of blood, and for averting the impending calamities that threaten the British Empire.

Thus called upon to address your Majesty on affairs of such moment to America, and probably to all your dominions, we are earnestly desirous of performing this office, with the utmost deference for your Majesty; and we therefore pray, that your royal magnanimity and benevolence may make the most favourable construction of our expressions on so uncommon an occasion. Could we represent in their full force, the sentiments that agitate the minds of us your dutiful subjects, we are persuaded your Majesty would ascribe any seeming deviation from reverence in our language, and even in our conduct, not to any reprehensible intention, but to the impossibility of reconciling the usual appearances of respect, with a just attention to our own preservation against those artful and cruel enemies, who abuse your royal confidence and authority, for the purpose of effecting our destruction.[1]

Attached to your Majesty's person, family, and government, with all devotion that principle and affection can inspire, connected with Great Britain by the strongest ties that can unite societies, and deploring every event that tends in any degree to weaken them, we solemnly assure your Majesty, that we not only most ardently desire the former harmony between her and these colonies may be restored, but that a concord may be established between them upon so firm a basis as to perpetuate its blessings, uninterrupted by any future dissentions, to succeeding generations in both countries, and to transmit your Majesty's Name to posterity, adorned with that signal and lasting glory, that has attended the memory of those illustrious personages, whose virtues and abilities have extricated states from dangerous convulsions, and, by securing happiness to others, have erected the most noble and durable monuments to their own fame.

We beg leave further to assure your Majesty, that notwithstanding the sufferings of your loyal colonists, during the course of the present controversy, our breasts retain too tender a regard for the kingdom from which we derive our origin, to request such a reconciliation as might in any manner be inconsistent with her dignity or her welfare. These, related as we are to her, honor and duty, as well as inclination, induce us to support and advance; and the apprehensions that now oppress our hearts with unspeakable grief, being once removed, your Majesty will find your faithful subjects on this continent ready and willing at all times, as they ever have been, with their lives and fortunes, to assert and maintain the rights and interests of your Majesty, and of our Mother country.

We, therefore, beseech your Majesty, that your royal authority and influence may be graciously interposed to procure us relief from our afflicting fears and jealousies, occasioned by the system before mentioned, and to settle peace through every part of your dominions, with all humility submitting to your Majesty's wise consideration whether it may not be expedient for facilitating those important purposes, that your Majesty be pleased to direct some mode, by which the united applications of your faithful colonists to the throne, in pursuance of their common councils, may be improved into a happy and permanent recon-

1. In this paragraph, we see again that the colonists (1) blame the King's agents and (2) assert that colonists are merely defending themselves.

ciliation; and that, in the mean time, measures may be taken for preventing the further destruction of the lives of your Majesty's subjects; and that such statutes as more immediately distress any of your Majesty's colonies may be repealed.

For by such arrangements as your Majesty's wisdom can form, for collecting the united sense of your American people, we are convinced your Majesty would receive such satisfactory proofs of the disposition of the colonists towards their sovereign and parent state, that the wished for opportunity would soon be restored to them, of evincing the sincerity of their professions, by every testimony of devotion becoming the most dutiful subjects, and the most affectionate colonists.

That your Majesty may enjoy a long and prosperous reign, and that your descendants may govern your dominions with honor to themselves and happiness to their subjects, is our sincere and fervent prayer.

Signers:

John Hancock

COLONY OF NEW HAMPSHIRE
John Langdon

COLONY OF MASSACHUSETTS BAY
Thomas Cushing,
Saml Adams,
John Adams,[2]
Robt Treat Paine

COLONY OF CONNECTICUT
Elipht Dyer,
Roger Sherman,
Silas Deane

COLONY OF NEW YORK
Phil. Livingston,
Jas Duane,
John Alsop,
Frans. Lewis,
John Jay,
Robt R Livingston junr,
Lewis Morris,
Wm Floyd,
Henry Wisner

NEW JERSEY
Wil: Livingston,
John De Hart,
Richd Smith

PENNSYLVANIA
John Dickinson,
B Franklin,
Geo: Ross,
James Wilson,
Chas Humphreys,
Edwd Biddle

COUNTIES OF NEW CASTLE KENT AND SUSSEX ON DELAWAR
Cæsar Rodney,
Thos Mc. Kean,
Geo: Read

2. John Adams signed this Petition, but considered it a waste of time, "like childrens play at marbles or push pin, or rather like misses in their teens emulating each other in their pearls, their braceletts their Diamond Pins and brussells lace."

COLONY OF RHODE ISLAND AND PROVIDENCE PLANTATIONS:

Step Hopkins,
Sam: Ward

MARYLAND

Mat. Tilghman,
Ths Johnson Junr,
Wm Paca,
Samuel Chase,
Thos Stone

COLONY OF VIRGINIA

P. Henry Jr,
Richard Henry Lee,
Edmund Pendleton,
Benja Harrison,
Th: Jefferson

NORTH CAROLINA

Will Hooper,
Joseph Hewes

SOUTH CAROLINA

Henry Middleton,
Tho Lynch,
Christ Gadsden,
J. Rutledge,
Edward Rutledge

Declaration on the Causes and Necessity of Taking Up Arms

(JULY 6, 1775)

Introduction

On July 6, 1775, the Second Continental Congress set forth the causes and necessity of taking up arms against British authority in the American colonies. Notably, this was one day after restating loyalty to King George III and wishing him "a long and prosperous reign" in the Olive Branch Petition. (Recall that many petitions and declarations impugned Parliament, not the King.) Written by John Dickinson and Thomas Jefferson (Congress rejected an earlier draft by John Rutledge), the Declaration laid out the reasons for taking up arms and for starting a violent revolution against British rule of the colonies. Jefferson's draft, written in fiery language, was tempered by Dickinson to ensure the tone remained conciliatory but firm.

The Declaration on the Causes and Necessity of Taking Up Arms begins with a preamble similar to that of the Declaration of Independence. (The preamble appears to be **John Dickinson's**.) It proceeds with a concise and quite interesting

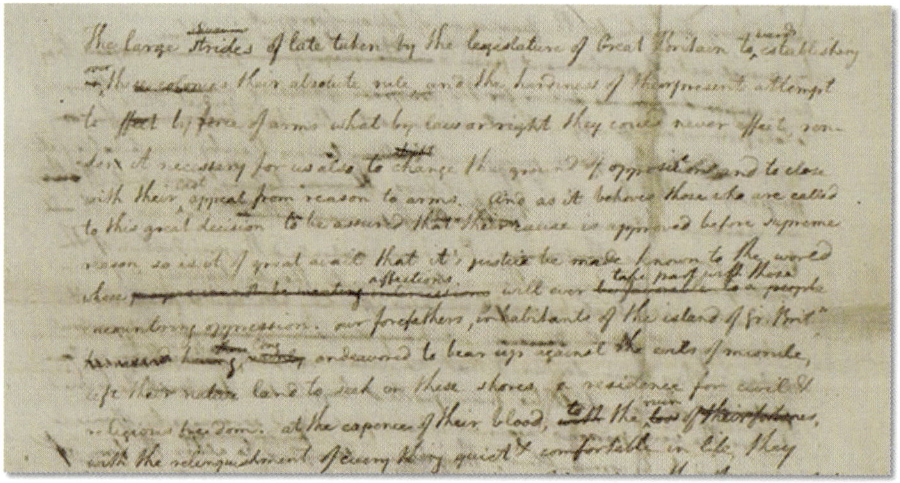

Excerpt from Thomas Jefferson's draft Declaration on the Causes and Necessity of Taking Up Arms

overview of colonial relations between European powers and the colonies. It continues with grievances that justify taking up arms in defense and then threatens war and foreign alliances. The document stresses that taking up arms was a last resort, necessary for the defense of liberties. It emphasizes that the colonies have tried every peaceful means of redress, such as petitions to the Crown, but these efforts were ignored or rejected. The Continental Congress published the Declaration and sent copies to the King, hoping that when presented with this history, justification, and threats, the King would rectify the colonists' grievances. When the King sided with Parliament, the Declaration of Independence soon followed.

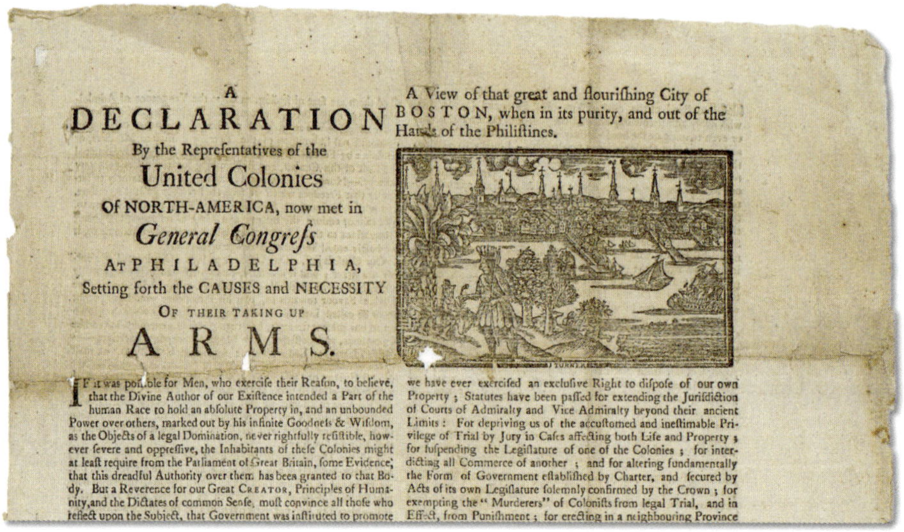

A
DECLARATION
By the Repreſentatives of the
United Colonies
Of NORTH-AMERICA, now met in
General Congreſs
AT PHILADELPHIA,
Setting forth the CAUSES and NECESSITY
OF THEIR TAKING UP
ARMS.

IF it was poſſible for Men, who exerciſe their Reaſon, to believe, that the Divine Author of our Exiſtence intended a Part of the human Race to hold an abſolute Property in, and an unbounded Power over others, marked out by his infinite Goodneſs & Wiſdom, as the Objects of a legal Domination, never rightfully reſiſtible, however ſevere and oppreſſive, the Inhabitants of theſe Colonies might at leaſt require from the Parliament of Great Britain, ſome Evidence, that this dreadful Authority over them has been granted to that Body. But a Reverence for our Great CREATOR, Principles of Humanity, and the Dictates of common Senſe, muſt convince all thoſe who reflect upon the Subject, that Government was inſtituted to promote

A View of that great and flouriſhing City of BOSTON, when in its purity, and out of the Hands of the Philiſtines.

we have ever exercifed an excluſive Right to diſpoſe of our own Property ; Statutes have been paſſed for extending the Juriſdiction of Courts of Admiralty and Vice Admiralty beyond their ancient Limits : For depriving us of the accuſtomed and ineſtimable Privilege of Trial by Jury in Caſes affecting both Life and Property ; for ſuſpending the Legiſlature of one of the Colonies ; for interdicting all Commerce of another ; and for altering fundamentally the Form of Government eſtabliſhed by Charter, and ſecured by Acts of its own Legiſlature ſolemnly confirmed by the Crown ; for exempting the "Murderers" of Coloniſts from legal Trial, and in Effect, from Puniſhment ; for erecting in a neighbouring Province

Portsmouth, Pennsylvania, broadside printing of Declaration on the Causes and Necessity of Taking Up Arms (1775)

A Declaration By the Representatives of the United Colonies[1] Of North-America, now met in General Congress At Philadelphia, Setting Forth the Causes and Necessity Of Their Taking Up Arms.

If it was possible for Men, who exercise their Reason to believe, that the Divine Author of our Existence intended a Part of the human Race to hold an absolute Property in, and an unbounded Power over others, marked out by his infinite Goodness and Wisdom, as the Objects of a legal Domination never rightfully resistible, however severe and oppressive, the Inhabitants of these Colonies might at least require from the Parliament of Great-Britain some Evidence, that this dreadful Authority over them has been granted to that Body. But a Reverence for our great Creator, Principles of Humanity, and the Dictates of Common Sense,[2] must convince all those who reflect upon the Subject, that Government was instituted to promote the Welfare of Mankind, and ought to be administered for the Attainment of that End. The Legislature of Great-Britain, however, stimulated by an inordinate Passion for a Power not only unjustifiable, but which they know to be peculiarly reprobated by the very Constitution of that Kingdom, and desperate of Success in any Mode of Contest, where Regard should be had to Truth, Law, or Right, have at Length, deserting those, attempted to effect their cruel and impolitic Purpose of enslaving[3] these Colonies by Violence, and have thereby rendered it necessary for us to close with their last Appeal from Reason to Arms. Yet, however blinded that Assembly may be, by their intemperate Rage

1. Notice that the colonies are now presenting as the "United Colonies." Congress formally approved the use of "United States of America" on September 9, 1776, soon after approving the Declaration of Independence.

2. This important theme resurfaces in the later founding documents: religion, humanism, and common sense all confirm that the purpose of government is to advance the welfare of mankind, and governments "ought to be administered for the attainment of that end."

3. One irony cannot be ignored: as with prior documents, this Declaration has several references to Britain effectively enslaving the colonists. (Interestingly, here arguing that enslavement justifies the colonists taking up arms instead of appealing to reason). The Declaration later proclaims the signers' preference "to die free men rather than live as slaves." As Samuel Johnson pointed out in a British response to calls for independence, "how is it that we hear the loudest yelps for liberty among the drivers of negroes?"

for unlimited Domination, so to Slight Justice and the Opinion of Mankind, we esteem ourselves bound by Obligations of Respect to the Rest of the World, to make known the Justice of our Cause.

Our Forefathers, Inhabitants of the Island of Great-Britain, left their Native Land, to seek on these Shores a Residence for civil and religious Freedom. At the Expence of their Blood, at the Hazard of their Fortunes, without the least Charge to the Country from which they removed, by unceasing Labour and an unconquerable Spirit, they effected Settlements in the distant and inhospitable Wilds of America, then filled with numerous and warlike Nations of Barbarians. Societies or Governments, vested with perfect Legislatures, were formed under Charters from the Crown, and an harmonious Intercourse was established between the Colonies and the Kingdom from which they derived their Origin. The mutual Benefits of this Union became in a short Time so extraordinary, as to excite Astonishment. It is universally confessed, that the amazing Increase of the Wealth, Strength, and Navigation of the Realm, arose from this Source; and the Minister, who so wisely and successfully directed the Measures of Great-Britain in the late War, publicly declared, that these Colonies enabled her to triumph over her Enemies. Towards the Conclusion of that War, it pleased our Sovereign to make a Change in his Counsels. From that fatal Moment, the Affairs of the British Empire began to fail into Confusion, and gradually sliding from the Summit of glorious Prosperity to which they had been advanced by the Virtues and Abilities of one Man, are at length distracted by the Convulsions, that now shake it to its deepest Foundations. The new Ministry finding the brave Foes of Britain, though frequently defeated, yet still contending, took up the unfortunate Idea of granting them a hasty Peace, and of then subduing her faithful Friends.

These devoted Colonies were judged to be in such a State, as to present Victories without Bloodshed, and all the easy Emoluments of statuteable Plunder. The uninterrupted Tenor of their peaceable and respectful Behaviour from the Beginning of Colonization, their dutiful, zealous, and useful Services during the War, though so recently and amply acknowledged in the most honourable Manner by his Majesty, by the late King, and by Parliament, could not save them from the meditated Innovations. Parliament was influenced to adopt the pernicious Project, and assuming a new Power over them, have in the Course of eleven Years given such decisive Specimens of the Spirit and Consequences attending this Power, as to leave no Doubt concerning the Effects of Acquiescence under it. They have undertaken to give and grant our Money without our Consent, though we have ever exercised an exclusive Right to dispose of our own

Property; Statutes have been passed for extending the Jurisdiction of Courts of Admiralty and Vice-Admiralty beyond their ancient Limits; for depriving us of the accustomed and inestimable Privilege of Trial by Jury in Cases affecting both Life and Property; for suspending the Legislature of one of the Colonies; for interdicting all Commerce to the Capital of another; and for altering fundamentally the Form of Government established by Charter, and secured by Acts of its own Legislature solemnly confirmed by the Crown; for exempting the "Murderers" of Colonists from legal Trial, and in Effect, from Punishment; for erecting in a neighbouring Province, acquired by the joint Arms of Great-Britain and America, a Despotism dangerous to our very Existence; and for quartering Soldiers upon the Colonists in Time of profound Peace. It has also been resolved in Parliament, that Colonists charged with committing certain Offences, shall be transported to England to be tried.

But why should we enumerate our Injuries in detail? By one Statute it is declared, that Parliament can "of right make Laws to bind us in all Cases whatsoever."[4] What is to defend us against so enormous, so unlimited a Power? Not a single Man of those who assume it, is chosen by us; or is subject to our Controul or Influence; but on the Contrary, they are all of them exempt from the Operation of such Laws, and an American Revenue, if not diverted from the ostensible Purposes for which it is raised, would actually lighten their own Burdens in Proportion, as they increase ours. We saw the Misery to which such Despotism would reduce us. We for ten Years incessantly and ineffectually besieged the Throne as Supplicants; we reasoned, we remonstrated with Parliament in the most mild and decent Language.

Administration sensible that we should regard these oppressive Measures as Freemen ought to do, sent over Fleets and Armies to enforce them. The Indignation of the Americans was roused, it is true; but it was the Indignation of a virtuous, loyal, and affectionate People. A Congress of Delegates from the United Colonies was assembled at Philadelphia, on the fifth Day of last September. We resolved again to offer an humble and dutiful Petition to the King, and also addressed our Fellow Subjects of Great-Britain. We have pursued every temperate, every respectful Measure; we have even proceeded to break off our commercial Intercourse with our Fellow Subjects, as the last peaceable Admonition, that our Attachment to no Nation upon Earth should supplant our Attachment to Liberty. This, we flattered ourselves, was the ultimate Step of the Controversy: But

4. This is another reference to the 1766 Declaratory Act. *See* p. 37.

subsequent Events have shewn, how vain was this Hope of finding Moderation in our Enemies.

Several threatening Expressions against the Colonies were inserted in His Majesty's Speech; our Petition, tho' we were told it was a Decent one, and that his Majesty had been pleased to receive it graciously, and to promise laying it before his Parliament, was huddled into both Houses among a Bundle of American Papers, and there neglected.[5] The Lords and Commons in their Address, in the Month of February, said, that "a Rebellion at that Time actually existed within the Province of Massachusetts-Bay; and that those concerned in it, had been countenanced and encouraged by unlawful Combinations and Engagements, entered into by his Majesty's Subjects in several of the other Colonies; and therefore they besought his Majesty, that he would take the most effectual Measures to inforce due Obedience to the Laws and Authority of the Supreme Legislature." Soon after, the commercial Intercourse of whole Colonies, with foreign Countries, and with each other, was cut off by an Act of Parliament; by another, several of them were intirely prohibited from the Fisheries in the Seas near their Coasts, on which they always depended for their Sustenance; and large Re-inforcements of Ships and Troops were immediately sent over to General Gage.

Fruitless were all the entreaties, arguments, and eloquence of an Illustrious Band of the most distinguished Peers, and Commoners, who nobly and strenuously asserted the Justice of our Cause, to stay, or even to mitigate the heedless fury with which these accumulated and unexampled Outrages were hurried on. Equally fruitless was the interference of the City of London, of Bristol, and many other respectable Towns in our Favour. Parliament adopted an insidious Manoeuvre calculated to divide us, to establish a perpetual Auction of Taxations where Colony should bid against Colony, all of them uninformed what Ransom would redeem their Lives; and thus to extort from us, at the Point of the Bayonet, the unknown sums that should be sufficient to gratify, if possible to gratify, ministerial Rapacity, with the miserable indulgence left to us of raising, in our own Mode, the prescribed Tribute. What Terms more rigid and humiliating could have been dictated by remorseless Victors to conquered Enemies? In our circumstances to accept them, would be to deserve them.

Soon after the Intelligence of these proceedings arrived on this Continent, General Gage, who in the course of the last Year had taken Possession of the Town of Boston, in the Province of Massachusetts-Bay, and still occupied it as a

---

5. This is a reference to the Oct. 26, 1774, Petition to King George III. *See* p. 53.

Garrison, on the 19th day of April, sent out from that Place a large detachment of his Army, who made an unprovoked Assault on the Inhabitants of the said Province, at the Town of Lexington, as appears by the Affidavits of a great Number of Persons, some of whom were Officers and Soldiers of that detachment, murdered eight of the Inhabitants, and wounded many others. From thence the Troops proceeded in warlike Array to the Town of Concord, where they set upon another Party of the Inhabitants of the same Province, killing several and wounding more, until compelled to retreat by the country People suddenly assembled to repel this cruel Aggression. Hostilities, thus commenced by the British Troops, have been since prosecuted by them without regard to Faith or Reputation. The Inhabitants of Boston being confined within that Town by the General their Governor, and having, in order to procure their dismission, entered into a Treaty with him, it was stipulated that the said Inhabitants having deposited their Arms with their own Magistrates, should have liberty to depart, taking with them their other Effects. They accordingly delivered up their Arms, but in open violation of Honour, in defiance of the obligation of Treaties, which even savage Nations esteemed sacred, the Governor ordered the Arms deposited as aforesaid, that they might be preserved for their owners, to be seized by a Body of Soldiers; detained the greatest part of the Inhabitants in the Town, and compelled the few who were permitted to retire, to leave their most valuable Effects behind.[6]

By this perfidy Wives are separated from their Husbands, Children from their Parents, the aged and the sick from their Relations and Friends, who wish to attend and comfort them; and those who have been used to live in Plenty and even Elegance, are reduced to deplorable Distress.

The General, further emulating his ministerial Masters, by a Proclamation bearing date on the 12th day of June, after venting the grossest Falsehoods and Calumnies against the good People of these Colonies, proceeds to "declare them all, either by Name or Description, to be Rebels and Traitors, to supersede the course of the Common Law, and instead thereof to publish and order the use and exercise of the Law Martial." His Troops have butchered our Countrymen, have wantonly burnt Charlestown, besides a considerable number of Houses in other Places; our Ships and Vessels are seized; the necessary supplies of Provisions are intercepted, and he is exerting his utmost Power to spread destruction and devastation around him.

6. This disarmament, and many other experiences, inspired the Second Amendment.

We have received certain Intelligence, that General Carleton, the Governor of Canada, is instigating the People of that Province and the Indians to fall upon us; and we have but too much reason to apprehend, that Schemes have been formed to excite domestic Enemies against us.[7] In brief, a part of these Colonies now feel, and all of them are sure of feeling, as far as the Vengeance of Administration can inflict them, the complicated Calamities of Fire, Sword, and Famine. We are reduced to the alternative of chusing an unconditional Submission to the tyranny of irritated Ministers, or resistance by Force. The latter is our choice. We have counted the cost of this contest, and find nothing so dreadful as voluntary Slavery. Honour, Justice, and Humanity, forbid us tamely to surrender that Freedom which we received from our gallant Ancestors, and which our innocent Posterity have a right to receive from us. We cannot endure the infamy and guilt of resigning succeeding Generations to that wretchedness which inevitably awaits them, if we basely entail hereditary Bondage upon them.

Our cause is just. Our union is perfect. Our internal Resources are great, and, if necessary, foreign Assistance is undoubtedly attainable.[8] We gratefully acknowledge, as signal Instances of the Divine Favour towards us, that his Providence would not permit us to be called into this severe Controversy, until we were grown up to our present strength, had been previously exercised in warlike Operation, and possessed of the means of defending ourselves. With hearts fortified with these animating Reflections, we most solemnly, before God and the World, declare, that, exerting the utmost Energy of those Powers, which our beneficent Creator hath graciously bestowed upon us, the Arms we have been compelled by our Enemies to assume, we will, in defiance of every Hazard, with unabating Firmness and Perseverence, employ for the preservation of our Liberties; being with one Mind resolved to die Freemen rather than to live Slaves.

Lest this Declaration should disquiet the Minds of our Friends and Fellow-Subjects in any part of the Empire, we assure them that we mean not to dissolve that Union which has so long and so happily subsisted between us, and which we sincerely wish to see restored. Necessity has not yet driven us into that desperate Measure, or induced us to excite any other Nation to War against them. We have not raised Armies with ambitious Designs of separating from Great-Britain, and

---

7. Instigating Tribes and "domestic Enemies" (slaves) to fight against the colonists continues as a grievance in the Declaration of Independence. *See* p. 96.

8. The Declaration included many not-so-subtle threats. France was interested in potentially helping the colonies in order to destabilize its longtime foe—England.

establishing Independent States. We fight not for Glory or for Conquest. We exhibit to Mankind the remarkable Spectacle of a People attacked by unprovoked Enemies, without any imputation or even suspicion of Offence. They boast of their Privileges and Civilization, and yet proffer no milder Conditions than Servitude or Death.

In our own native Land, in defence of the Freedom that is our Birthright, and which we ever enjoyed till the late Violation of it—for the protection of our Property, acquired solely by the honest Industry of our fore-fathers and ourselves, against Violence actually offered, we have taken up Arms. We shall lay them down when Hostilities shall cease on the part of the Aggressors, and all danger of their being renewed shall be removed, and not before.

With an humble Confidence in the Mercies of the supreme and impartial Judge and Ruler of the Universe, we most devoutly implore his Divine Goodness[9] to protect us happily through this great Conflict, to dispose our Adversaries to reconciliation on reasonable Terms, and thereby to relieve the Empire from the Calamities of civil War.

By order of Congress,
John Hancock,
President.

Attested,
Charles Thomson,
secretary

Philadelphia, July 6th, 1775.

9. This more spiritual closing paragraph appears in Dickinson's draft but not in Jefferson's. Dickinson was deeply religious and Jefferson was at most a deist.

King George III

A Proclamation for Suppressing Rebellion and Sedition

(AUGUST 23, 1775)

Introduction

As the conflict intensified and news of new military conflicts in the colonies reached King George III, he issued A Proclamation for Suppressing Rebellion and Sedition on August 23, 1775. It declared that many of the colonies were in a state of "open and avowed rebellion," which stripped rebellious colonies of rights, treated them as official enemies, and incentivized tribes and slaves to fight against the colonists. It also forced colonists against colonists, as they (and British subjects in England) were required by law to "withstand and suppress such Rebellion" and to disclose the identity of anyone who was sympathetic to the American rebellion.

The Prohibitory Act soon followed (December 1775), which formally severed all trade between Britain and the colonies, removed the colonies from the King's protection, and declared American vessels to be enemy vessels which could be taken and declared prizes of war. John Adams considered this Act

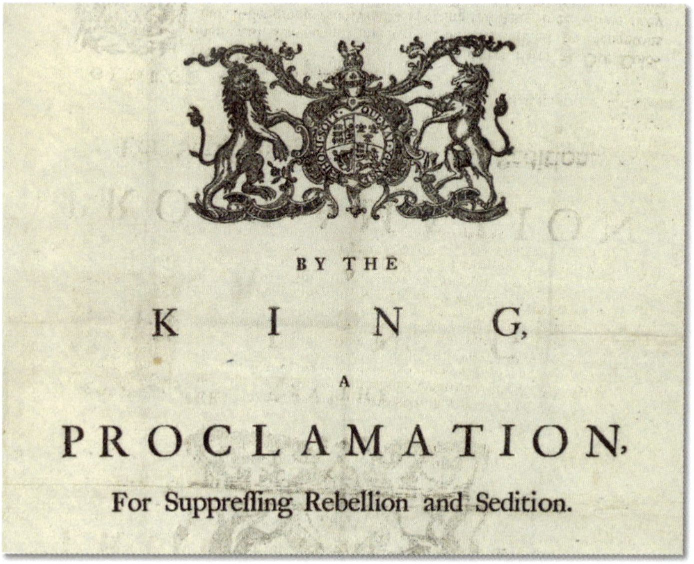

BY THE

K I N G,

A

PROCLAMATION,

For Suppreſſing Rebellion and Sedition.

alone to be a declaration that the colonies were independent. Many colonists considered these actions (along with the large presence of British troops and Hessian mercenaries in the colonies) to be the last straw—they were left with no other options and independence was now a necessity. Natural-law theorists at the time argued that without rights and under a tyrannical attack, colonists were returned to the state of nature, and the first law of nature is self-preservation.

The Second Continental Congress published a rather defiant response on December 6, 1775, and the Declaration of Independence followed the next year.

Excerpt from A Proclamation for Suppressing Rebellion and Sedition

By the
KING,
A
PROCLAMATION,
For suppressing Rebellion and Sedition.

GEORGE R.

Whereas many of our subjects in divers parts of our Colonies and Plantations in North America, misled by dangerous and ill designing men, and forgetting the allegiance which they owe to the power that has protected and supported them; after various disorderly acts committed in disturbance of the publick peace, to the obstruction of lawful commerce, and to the oppression of our loyal subjects carrying on the same; have at length proceeded to open and avowed rebellion, by arraying themselves in a hostile manner, to withstand the execution of the law, and traitorously preparing, ordering and levying war against us:

And whereas, there is reason to apprehend that such rebellion hath been much promoted and encouraged by the traitorous correspondence, counsels and comfort of divers wicked and desperate persons within this Realm: To the end therefore, that none of our subjects may neglect or violate their duty through ignorance thereof, or through any doubt of the protection which the law will afford to their loyalty and zeal, we have thought fit, by and with the advice of our Privy Council, to issue our Royal Proclamation, hereby declaring, that not only all our Officers, civil and military, are obliged to exert their utmost endeavours to suppress such rebellion, and to bring the traitors to justice, but that all our subjects of this Realm, and the dominions thereunto belonging, are bound by law to be aiding and assisting in the suppression of such rebellion, and to disclose and make known all traitorous conspiracies and attempts against us, our crown and dignity; and we do accordingly strictly charge and command all our Officers, as well civil as military, and all others our obedient and loyal subjects, to use their utmost endeavours to withstand and suppress such rebellion, and to disclose and make known all treasons and traitorous conspiracies which they shall know to be against us, our crown and dignity; and for that purpose, that they transmit to one of our principal Secretaries of State, or other proper officer, due and full information of all persons who shall be found carrying on correspondence with, or in any manner or degree aiding or abetting the persons now in open arms and rebellion against our Government, within any of our Colonies and Plantations in North America, in order to bring to condign punishment the authors, perpetrators, and abetters of such traitorous designs.

Given at Our Court at *St. James's*, the Twenty-third Day of *August*, One thousand seven hundred and seventy-five, in the Fifteenth Year of Our Reign.

God save the King.

Declaration of Independence—Redlined

(JULY 4, 1776)

Introduction

Many colonists were quite loyal to Britain after the success of the French and Indian War, and even as their grievances grew over the next decade, blame was often placed on the King's agents or Parliament, not the King. Some leaders actively opposed independence (like John Dickinson), but others like John Adams and his second cousin, Samuel Adams, had been working at the grassroots level to bring the counties and later colonies around to approve independence. The wide circulation of Thomas Paine's *Common Sense* in early 1776 catalyzed this effort; in an easily understood book, Paine persuasively refuted concepts of monarchical and hereditary rule and argued for a new form of government based on popular choice.

Unlike today where citizens can vote out "tyrants," there was no hope of colonists doing so because the King served for life, they had no direct representation in Parliament, and their appeals to the British people were unsuccessful.

(In 1774, British voters chose to return the same members back to Parliament for up to another seven years.) After enduring the Intolerable Acts, a massive invasion of British troops, and for an array of other reasons, some ninety counties and localities had declared or proclaimed independence by June 1776. Many of these local declarations borrowed grievances from, among other places, the 1689 English Declaration of Rights.

As just one example, Chief Justice William Henry Drayton of the South Carolina Supreme Court used the assembling of a grand jury on April 23, 1776, as an opportunity to publicly voice his opinion on independence. South Carolina had declared independence a month earlier and adopted a new constitution. Justice Drayton addressed the grand jury, describing "evil machinations tending to nothing less than absolute tyranny." Under British rule, jury trials had been suspended "in contempt of Magna Charta." He blamed Britain for loosening "the bands of Government," gave a history of the recent monarchs, and then listed specific grievances (but "only some of the most weighty") against King George III:

> Under color of law, the King and Parliament of *Great Britain* have made the most arbitrary attempts to enslave *America*:
>
> - By claiming a right to bind the Colonies "in all cases whatsoever";
> - By laying duties at their mere will and pleasure upon all the Colonies;
> - By suspending the Legislature of *New-York*;
> - By rendering the *American* Charters of no validity, having annulled the most material parts of the Charter of the *Massachusetts-Bay*;
> - By divesting multitudes of the Colonists of their property, without legal accusation or trial;
> - By depriving whole Colonies of the bounty of Providence, on their own proper coasts, in order, to coerce them by famine;
> - By restricting the trade and commerce of *America*;
> - By sending to, and continuing in *America*, in time of peace, an armed, force, without and against the consent of the People;

- By granting impunity to a Soldiery instigated to murder the *Americans*;
- By declaring that the People of *Massachusetts-Bay* are liable, for offences, or pretended offences, done in that Colony, to be sent to, and tried for the same in *England*, or in any Colony where they cannot have the benefit of a jury of the vicinage;
- By establishing in *Quebeck* the *Roman Catholick* Religion, and an arbitrary Government; instead of the *Protestant* Religion and a free Government.

And when colonists petitioned the crown for these grievances, "to their astonishment, their dutiful petition for peace and safety was answered only by an actual commencement of war and military destruction!"

Drayton then compared the conduct of King George III to that of James II. If the conduct of James II justified a revolution (memorialized in the 1689 English Declaration), Drayton's enumerated grievances tried to prove that King George III's conduct was worse. For these and other reasons, King George III was in "breach of the original contract, and violation of fundamental laws." He then gave the legal justifications for, "in [his] opinion," South Carolina's independence from Britain, including citations to the preeminent treatise on English law—Blackstone's Commentaries.[1]

After the powerful colony of Virginia also declared independence and gave instructions to its national delegates to do the same, most of the other colonies followed, but some resisted. Quakers and wealthy leaders who opposed independence controlled Pennsylvania. To address any holdouts, Congress approved a resolution on May 10 stating:

> *Resolved*, That it be recommended to the respective assemblies and conventions of the United Colonies, where no government sufficient to the exigencies of their affairs have been hitherto established, to adopt such government as shall, in the opinion of the representatives of the people, best conduce to the happiness and safety of their constituents in particular, and America in general.

1. Drayton's charge was months before the Declaration of Independence, Virginia Constitution, and Virginia Declaration of Rights, but years after Jefferson's *A Summary View* (1774), which all proclaimed similar grievances.

To John Dickinson, this did not apply to Pennsylvania because the colony *had* a "government sufficient to the exigencies of their affairs." John Adams worked quickly to draft another resolution addressing this concern, stating that no *reasonable* colony could remain loyal to the crown:

> *Whereas* his Britannic Majesty, in conjunction with the lords and commons of Great Britain, has, by a late act of Parliament, excluded the inhabitants of these United Colonies from the protection of his crown; And whereas, no answer, whatever, to the humble petitions of the colonies for redress of grievances and reconciliation with Great Britain, has been or is likely to be given; but, the whole force of that kingdom, aided by foreign mercenaries, is to be exerted for the destruction of the good people of these colonies;
>
> *And whereas*, it appears absolutely irreconcileable to reason and good Conscience, for the people of these colonies now to take the oaths and affirmations necessary for the support of any government under the crown of Great Britain, and it is necessary that the exercise of every kind of authority under the said crown should be totally suppressed, and all the powers of government exerted, under the authority of the people of the colonies, for the preservation of internal peace, virtue, and good order, as well as for the defence of their lives, liberties, and properties, against the hostile invasions and cruel depredations of their enemies; therefore, resolved, &c.

Congress approved this resolution May 15. Adams stated in later letters that he smiled at the passage of this resolution and he considered it to be a declaration of independence, though he knew that additional "formalities" were needed. His plan worked. Within days, citing these resolutions, Pennsylvania essentially overthrew the existing government and arranged a constitutional convention. The new members voted for independence on June 24.

As the consensus formed on national independence, the Continental Congress convened in 1776 with varying intentions and instructions from the states on the issue of independence. Unlike some fictionalized depictions, delegates could not simply vote their conscience—they needed instructions from their home legislatures. Defying those instructions could lead to the delegate being recalled. After delaying long enough for most states to agree, Congress created the Committee of Five to draft a declaration of independence (John Adams, Benjamin Franklin, Thomas Jefferson, Robert Livingston, and Roger Sherman). As you may have seen by now, John Dickinson was the "penman" of the founding and the drafter of several other documents of this book. He likely would have drafted the Declaration of Independence had he not staunchly opposed independence.[2]

Congress was incredibly busy at this time. (Jefferson was on some 34 committees in six months.) Congress and the Committee of Five agreed on much of what they wanted in the Declaration. John Adams arranged the Committee "minutes" (instructions) and the Committee selected Jefferson, from influential Virginia, to assemble a draft. He was finished in a few days.

Jefferson enumerated many of the same grievances in 1774, in his pamphlet *A Summary View of the Rights of British America*. Many of the grievances appear in the same order as they did in *A Summary View*. Jefferson's views on rights and revolution were heavily inspired by the writings of influential Bostonians Samuel Adams and James Otis, Jr. Although he later wrote that he started with no books or parchments, he likely had *A Summary View* in hand or at least in mind, and we know that he referred to the draft of the Virginia Constitution he had recently written (Virginia already had a draft constitution and only incorporated part of Jefferson's in its final 1776 Constitution), and for many other parts he referred to the Virginia Declaration of Rights that George Mason had recently written. Both documents borrowed from the 1689 English Declaration of Rights, but the 1689 Declaration grounded revolution in the king's *abdication of the throne*, whereas Jefferson (and others like Drayton) added *contract theory*—that Britain had violated its contract with the American people. Like many of the prior declarations and petitions in this book, the Declaration also invokes the principle of the consent of the governed.

Members of the Committee of Five (primarily, Adams and Franklin) made approximately forty-seven minor revisions to Jefferson's draft, but the Continental Congress made major revisions. Unfortunately, Congress made its edits when it convened in private as the Committee of the Whole, meaning we do not have the record of the debates around of most of its changes, though some reasons can be gleaned from other sources. By this book's general calculation, the Committee or Congress struck around 39% of Jefferson's draft language and added or substituted around 17% new content. Jefferson opposed many of the changes that Congress made (saying Congress "mutilated" it) and subsequently circulated to friends his own "redlined" version tracking the changes (shown below).

---

2. We can get a sense of how John Dickinson's Declaration of Independence might have read by reviewing his Declaration of the Causes and Necessity of Taking Up Arms. *See* p. 73.

The Continental Congress approved the Declaration around a year after the start of the Revolutionary War (passed on July 2, 1776, dated July 4, 1776, engrossed July 19, 1776), severing the political connections between the American colonies and Great Britain. The Declaration gives reasons for declaring independence including twenty-seven grievances against King George III, infringement on natural rights, and the validity of revolution in such circumstances. Key themes in the Declaration include unalienable rights (today generally spelled "inalienable," meaning rights you cannot give up even if you wanted to consent), usurpation of authority, and the consent of the governed. "Dissolv[ing] the political bands" revokes the "social compact" that the colonists had with Britain, meaning rights revert back to the people who are now free to enter into a new contract.

This book tracks the changes between Jefferson's final draft (he had earlier versions) and the engrossed version.[3]

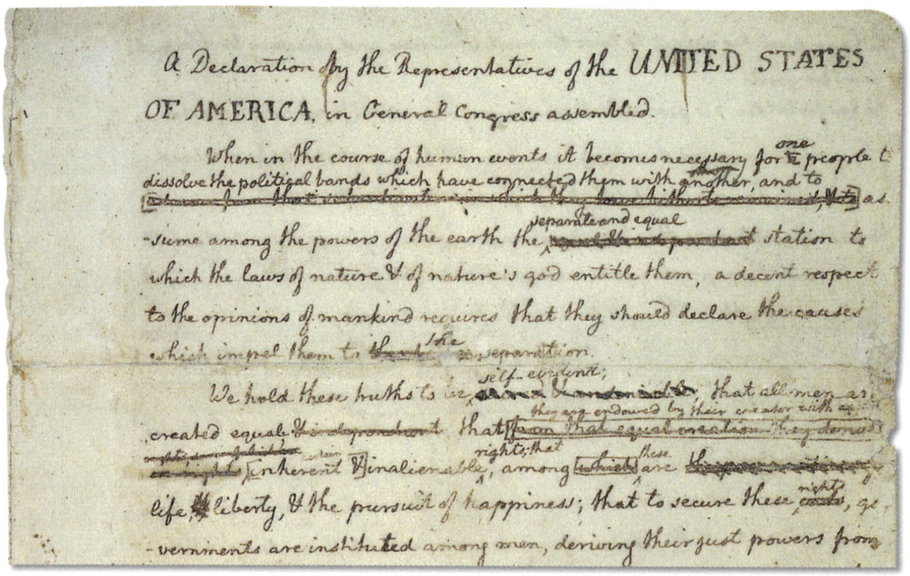
A Declaration by the Representatives of the UNITED STATES OF AMERICA, in General Congress assembled.

When in the course of human events it becomes necessary for one people to dissolve the political bands which have connected them with another, and to assume among the powers of the earth the separate and equal station to which the laws of nature & of nature's god entitle them, a decent respect to the opinions of mankind requires that they should declare the causes which impel them to the separation.

We hold these truths to be self-evident; that all men are created equal; that they are endowed by their creator with inherent & inalienable rights; that among these are life, liberty, & the pursuit of happiness; that to secure these rights, governments are instituted among men, deriving their just powers from

Excerpt from Jefferson's handwritten draft Declaration of Independence

3. Congress made a majority of the changes, but some are from the drafting committee (as indicated in the commentary) and others were last-minute changes that Jefferson made to his own draft. The Engrossed Declaration was based on John Dunlap's printing of Congress's final version. John Dunlap is responsible for most of the spelling changes, and there are stylistic capitalization differences in all versions. (Capitalization at this time was largely stylistic, not substantive.)

IN CONGRESS, JULY 4, 1776.

The unanimous Declaration of the thirteen united States of America,

When in the Course of human events, it becomes necessary for one people to dissolve the political bands which have connected them with another, and to assume among the powers of the earth, the separate and equal station to which the Laws of Nature and of Nature's God entitle them, a decent respect to the opinions of mankind requires that they should declare the causes which impel them to the separation. — We hold these truths to be self-evident, that all men are created equal, that they are endowed by their Creator with certain unalienable Rights, that among these are Life, Liberty and the pursuit of Happiness. — That to secure these rights, Governments are instituted among Men, deriving their just powers from the consent of the governed, — That whenever any Form of Government becomes destructive of these ends, it is the Right of the People to alter or to abolish it, and to institute new Government, laying its foundation on such principles and organizing its powers in such form, as to them shall seem most likely to effect their Safety and Happiness. Prudence, indeed, will dictate that Governments long established should not be changed for light and transient causes; and accordingly all experience hath shewn, that mankind are more disposed to suffer, while evils are sufferable, than to right themselves by abolishing the forms to which they are accustomed. But when a long train of abuses and usurpations, pursuing invariably the same Object evinces a design to reduce them under absolute Despotism, it is their right, it is their duty, to throw off such Government, and to provide new Guards for their future security. — Such has been the patient sufferance of these Colonies; and such is now the necessity which constrains them to alter their former Systems of Government. The history of the present King of Great Britain is a history of repeated injuries and usurpations, all having in direct object the establishment of an absolute Tyranny over these States. To prove this, let Facts be submitted to a candid world. — He has refused his Assent to Laws, the most wholesome and necessary for the public good. — He has forbidden his Governors to pass Laws of immediate and pressing importance, unless suspended in their operation till his Assent should be obtained; and when so suspended, he has utterly neglected to attend to them. — He has refused to pass other Laws for the accommodation of large districts of people, unless those people would relinquish the right of Representation in the Legislature, a right inestimable to them and formidable to tyrants only. — He has called together legislative bodies at places unusual, uncomfortable, and distant from the depository of their public Records, for the sole purpose of fatiguing them into compliance with his measures. — He has dissolved Representative Houses repeatedly, for opposing with manly firmness his invasions on the rights of the people. — He has refused for a long time, after such dissolutions, to cause others to be elected; whereby the Legislative powers, incapable of Annihilation, have returned to the People at large for their exercise; the State remain-

Excerpt from William Stone Engraving of the Declaration of Independence (1823)

In Congress, July 4, 1776

~~*A*~~ The unanimous **Declaration of the** ~~*Representatives of the UNITED STATES OF AMERICA, in General Congress assembled*~~ thirteen united States of America,[4]

[Preamble]

When in the Course of human events, it becomes necessary for ~~*a*~~ one people to ~~*advance from that subordination in*~~ dissolve the political bands which ~~*they*~~ have ~~*hitherto remained, &*~~ connected them with another, and to assume among the powers of the earth, the separate and equal ~~*& independant*~~[5] station to which the

4. Among others, John Locke and Thomas Hobbes informed Jefferson's views on natural rights. This preamble departs from earlier preambles (often beginning with "WHEREAS") and matches the tone of John Dickinson's preamble in the Declaration on Taking Up Arms. *See* p. 73.

5. In what many scholars consider the worst Supreme Court decision of all time, Chief Justice Roger Taney relied on this "separate and equal" language to conclude that "the negro race [i]s a separate class of persons" in *Dred Scott v. Sanford* (1857) (superseded by the Reconstruction Amendments). Abraham Lincoln campaigned on how immoral he thought the *Dred Scott* decision was, winning the presidency in the election of 1860.

BENJAMIN FRANKLIN: Separation is more specific and direct.[[1]]

BENJAMIN FRANKLIN: We cover more people if we consider these to be rational truths that are "self-evident," not ones that might be contingent on a government or particular belief system.[[2]]

THOMAS JEFFERSON: Acceptable. The rights exist without governments.

JOHN DICKINSON: This will destroy my reputation, but silence is guilt. We should not declare independence. We should win the war first—there is no reason to declare independence before winning. We might also offend France and Spain by not waiting until we hear more from them. We do not even have an alternative government. Independence puts the cart before the horse. We are unprepared. This is akin to braving a storm in a skiff made of paper.

JOHN ADAMS: The people want independence, and they have a right to it. The states have approved it. My state is under siege. The British have forced our hands, we have no choice but independence.

Laws of Nature and of Nature's God entitle them, a decent respect to the opinions of mankind requires that they should declare the causes which impel them to the ~~*change*~~ separation.[[1]]

[Rights]

We hold these truths to be ~~*sacred & undeniable;*~~ self-evident,[[2]] that all men are created equal[6] ~~*& independant*~~, that ~~*from*~~ they are endowed by their Creator with certain unalienable Rights, that ~~*equal creation they derive rights inherent & inalienable,*~~ among ~~*which are the preservation of*~~ these are Life, Liberty ~~*&*~~ and the pursuit of Happiness.[7]—That to secure these ~~*ends*~~ rights, Governments are instituted among Men, deriving their just powers from the consent of the governed,—That whenever any Form of Government ~~*shall become*~~ becomes destructive of these ends, it is the Right of the People to alter or to abolish it, and to institute new Government, laying its foundation on such principles and organizing its powers in such form, as to them shall seem most likely to effect their Safety and Happiness. Prudence, indeed, will dictate that Governments long established should not be changed for light and transient causes; and accordingly all experience hath shewn, that mankind are more disposed to suffer, while evils are sufferable, than to right themselves by abolishing the forms to which they are accustomed. But when a long train of abuses[8] and usurpations, ~~*begun at a*~~

Jefferson appears to have made this change himself. The original phrase "equal and independent" is a direct quote from Locke. (Interestingly, Locke included "health" in life, liberty, health, and possessions.) Justice Taney likely could not have relied on the initial language ("equal and independent") for his *Dred Scott* reasoning—Locke opposed the American type of slavery as "vile," inherited status, and labor without consent (though he thought that enslaving enemies could be justified in cases of a just war).

6. According to Kermit Roosevelt and others, "all men created equal" was understood at the time to mean British "insiders" (including colonists) not "outsiders" like slaves. Under this view, the phrase did not take on its modern understanding until at least after the Reconstruction Amendments (when former slaves were included in the American experiment). In this way, Lincoln and the Reconstructionists reimagined the Declaration of Independence in their time just as Coke and Blackstone reimagined Magna Carta in theirs. *See* p. 3 n. 1.

7. Many at the time envisioned "happiness" as the "good life" in the biblical context: sitting "under your own vine and under your own fig tree, and no one will make you afraid." George Washington referenced "vine and fig tree" some fifty times in his writings, often in reference to his home at Mount Vernon. Departing from earlier colonial documents, Jefferson changed "property," to "the pursuit of Happiness," mixing Locke and Epicurus. *See also* 1774 Declaration, p. 39 (stating "property").

8. This line is borrowed from Locke's Second Treatise on Government (1690): the people can accept minor mismanagement and mistakes from leaders "[b]ut if a long train of Abuses, Prevarications, and Artifices, all tending the same way, make the design visible to the People, . . . they should

~~*distinguished period, &*~~ pursuing invariably the same Object~~,~~ evinces a design to ~~*subject*~~ reduce them ~~*to arbitrary power*~~ under absolute Despotism,[[3]] it is their right, it is their duty, to throw off such Government, and to provide new Guards for their future security.—Such has been the patient sufferance of these Colonies; and such is now the necessity which constrains them to ~~*expunge*~~ alter their former Systems of Government. The history of ~~*his*~~ the present ~~*majesty,*~~ King of Great Britain[[4]] is a history of ~~*unremitting*~~ repeated injuries and usurpations, ~~*among which no one fact stands single or solitary to contradict the uniform tenor of the rest,*~~ all ~~*of which have*~~ having in direct object the establishment of an absolute Tyranny over these States. To prove this, let Facts be submitted to a candid world~~*, for the truth of which we pledge a faith yet unsullied by falsehood*~~.

[Grievances] [9]

He has refused his Assent to Laws, the most wholesome and necessary for the public good.

He has forbidden his Governors to pass Laws of immediate and pressing importance, unless suspended in their operation till his Assent should be obtained; and when so suspended, he has utterly neglected ~~*utterly*~~ to attend to them.

He has refused to pass other Laws for the accommodation of large districts of people, unless those people would relinquish the right of Representation in the Legislature, a right inestimable to them~~,~~ and formidable to tyrants ~~*alone:*~~ only.

---

then rouze themselves, and endeavour to put the rule into such hands which may secure to them he ends for which Government was at first erected."

9. For all but a few of these grievances, the Declaration mirrors the Virginia Constitution (drafted by George Mason). For example, the Virginia Constitution lists: "By putting his negative on laws the most wholesome and necessary for the public good; By denying his Governors permission to pass laws of immediate and pressing importance, unless suspended in their operation for his assent, and, when so suspended neglecting to attend to them for many years. By refusing to pass certain other laws, unless the persons to be benefited by them would relinquish the inestimable right of representation in the legislature; By dissolving legislative Assemblies repeatedly and continually, for opposing with manly firmness his invasions of the rights of the people."

Many people who were still loyal to the Crown (and others) criticized the Declaration's charges for being too vague or misleading, particularly the first eight.

BENJAMIN FRANKLIN: Let's change this to "Despotism" to be more specific.[[3]]

JOHN ADAMS: With our independence, he is no longer our majesty. I would go with "King of Great Britain" here.[[4]]

RICHARD HENRY LEE: This document looks like just a copy of Locke's Second Treatise on Government.

JOHN ADAMS: It is also just a compilation of sentiments we've had in Congress for two years now.

THOMAS JEFFERSON: *[In 1825]* It is not our job to invent new ideas or arguments. We are merely to place before mankind, in plain and firm terms, the common sense of the subject of independence. This is intended to be an expression of the American mind, and to give to that expression the proper tone and spirit called for by the occasion.

JOHN ADAMS: *[In 1822]* The document is a bit too personal to King George. I never believed George to be a tyrant in disposition and in nature; I always believed him to be deceived by his courtiers on both sides the Atlantic, and cruel in his official capacity only.

He has called together legislative bodies at places unusual, uncomfortable, and distant from the depository of their public Records, for the sole purpose of fatiguing them into compliance with his measures.[10]

THOMAS JEFFERSON: Local assemblies have been dissolved and courts have been obstructed, leaving people without local government to attend to matters.

He has dissolved Representative Houses repeatedly ~~*& continually*~~, for opposing with manly firmness his invasions on the rights of the people.

JOHN ADAMS: I would add "after such dissolutions" to tie this to the prior grievance.

He has refused for a long ~~*space of*~~ time, after such dissolutions, to cause others to be elected; whereby the Legislative powers, incapable of Annihilation, have returned to the People at large for their exercise; the State remaining in the mean time exposed to all the dangers of invasion from without, and convulsions within.

He has endeavoured to prevent the population of these States; for that purpose obstructing the Laws for Naturalization of Foreigners; refusing to pass others to encourage their migrations hither, and raising the conditions of new Appropriations of Lands.

THOMAS JEFFERSON: Since 1767, the King has taken over payment of judges and other officials, keeping them loyal to him and not us.[[5]]

THE CONGRESS: Technically they are not "our" judges (yet).

He has ~~*suffered*~~ obstructed the Administration of Justice ~~*totally to cease in some of these colonies*~~, by refusing his Assent to Laws for establishing Judiciary powers.

He has made ~~*our*~~ Judges[[5]] ~~*dependant*~~ dependent on his Will alone, for the tenure of their offices, and the amount and payment of their salaries.

He has erected a multitude of New Offices ~~*by a self-assumed power*~~, and sent hither swarms of Officers to harrass our people, and eat out their substance.

THOMAS JEFFERSON: King George II *asked Parliament* if he could have a standing army for a time. King George III should have done the same and obtained the consent of colonial governments to keep standing armies here.

He has kept among us, in times of peace, Standing Armies ~~*& ships of war*~~ without the Consent of our legislatures.[11]

He has affected to render the Military~~, *independant*~~ independent of and superior to the Civil power.

He has combined with others to subject us to a jurisdiction foreign[12] to our constitution~~s~~, and unacknowledged by our laws; giving his Assent to their Acts of pretended ~~*acts of*~~ Legislation:~~;~~

THOMAS JEFFERSON: The British have passed the Quartering Act, requiring our citizens to provide quarters and basic necessities for British troops.

For Quartering large bodies of armed troops among us:

---

10. Many of these added grievances (those that do not borrow from prior documents) directly refer to parts of the Declaratory Act. *See* p. 34.

11. Virginia Constitution: "By keeping among us, in times of peace, standing armies and ships of war." 1689 English Declaration: "By raising and keeping a standing army within this kingdom in time of peace without consent of Parliament, and quartering soldiers contrary to law."

12. "Others" here means Parliament, and "foreign" jurisdiction refers to Britain.

For protecting them, by a mock Trial, from punishment for any Murders which they should commit on the Inhabitants of these States:[13]

For cutting off our Trade with all parts of the world:

For imposing Taxes on us without our Consent:

For depriving us in many cases, of the benefits of Trial by Jury:

For transporting us beyond Seas to be tried for pretended offences:

For abolishing the free System of English Laws in a neighbouring Province,[14] establishing therein an Arbitrary government, and enlarging its Boundaries so as to render it at once an example and fit instrument for introducing the same absolute rule into these Colonies:

For taking away our Charters, & abolishing our most valuable Laws, and[[6]] altering fundamentally the Forms of our Governments:

For suspending our own Legislatures, and declaring themselves invested with power to legislate for us in all cases whatsoever.

He has abdicated Government here,[15] ~~*withdrawing his governors, &*~~ by declaring us out of his ~~*allegiance & protection:*~~ Protection and waging War against us.

He has plundered our seas, ravaged our Coasts, burnt our towns, and destroyed the lives of our people.[16]

He is at this time transporting large Armies of foreign Mercenaries to compleat the works of death, desolation and tyranny, already begun with circumstances of Cruelty & perfidy scarcely paralleled in the most barbarous ages, and totally unworthy the Head of a civilized nation.

BENJAMIN FRANKLIN: Adding "abolishing our most valuable Laws" in this reference to the Intolerable Acts.[[6]]

THE CONGRESS: We can make this draft more concise overall, particularly with the next pages. The bit about slavery needs also to be cut.

13. In 1774, Parliament authorized British soldiers who were accused of murder to be sent to Britain for trial instead of being tried in America with juries of colonists.

14. This is a reference to the Quebec Act that extended the boundaries of Quebec into the Ohio Valley. This prevented the westward expansion of the 13 colonies. The Act was also seen as a bribe to residents in Quebec so they would not protest the abolition of their colonial governments. Finally, it protected and extended Catholicism in Canada, which angered many colonists.

15. Like the 1689 English Declaration, Jefferson still includes abdication as a partial basis for revolution.

16. By this time, the British had destroyed Norfolk, Virginia; Charlestown, Massachusetts; and Falmouth, Massachusetts (now Portland, Maine).

He has constrained our fellow Citizens taken Captive on the high Seas to bear Arms against their Country, to become the executioners of their friends and Brethren, or to fall themselves by their Hands.[17]

He has excited domestic insurrections amongst us, and has endeavoured to bring on the inhabitants of our frontiers, the merciless Indian Savages, whose known rule of warfare, is an undistinguished destruction of all ages, sexes and conditions ~~of existence~~.

~~*he has incited treasonable insurrections in our fellow-subjects, with the allurements of forfeiture & confiscation of our property:*~~[18]

~~*he has waged cruel*~~[[7]] ~~*war against human nature itself, violating it's most sacred rights of life & liberty in the persons of a distant people who never offended him, captivating & carrying them into slavery in another hemisphere, or to incur miserable death in their transportation thither. this piratical warfare, the opprobrium of **infidel** powers, is the warfare of the CHRISTIAN king of Great Britain. determined to keep open a market where MEN should be bought & sold, he has prostituted his negative for suppressing every legislative attempt to prohibit or to restrain this execrable commerce: and that this assemblage of horrors might want no fact of distinguished die, he is now exciting those very people to rise in arms among us, and to purchase that liberty of which he has deprived them, & murdering the people upon whom he also obtruded them; thus paying off former crimes committed against the **liberties** of one people, with crimes which he urges them to commit against the **lives** of another.*~~[19]

THOMAS JEFFERSON: As I said in *A Summary View* in 1774, we must call out the King for perpetuating and benefitting from the evils of slavery, and then offering the slaves freedom and property if they fight for the British *[via* Lord Dunmore's 1775 Proclamation*]*. We would like to prevent the importation of more slaves, but the British won't approve those laws.[[7]]

JOHN ADAMS: I completely agree but there is no way enough others will allow this to remain.

SOUTH CAROLINA AND GEORGIA DELEGATIONS: We are absolutely eliminating any such reference.

---

17. This refers to kidnapping or "impressment" of American men and forcing them to fight for the British.

18. The omitted reference to "treasonable insurrections" refers to the British offering freedom to slaves who agreed to fight on Britain's behalf. It was incorporated into the preceding grievance. Interestingly, Jefferson originally wrote "subjects," but changed it to "citizens" when the draft was submitted to Congress (arguably describing slaves as citizens, contrary to the later *Dred Scott* Supreme Court case).

our fellow-citizens, with

The reference to "treasonable" with "insurrections" further supports this view. According to Blackstone (and English and American law), one must owe allegiance to a country in order to commit treason (and probably insurrection—if committed by foreigners it would be an invasion, not an insurrection). Property would not owe an allegiance to the country—but citizens would. The closing reference to property concerns the King's offer to take land, homes, and personal property from loyal Americans and give it to insurrectionists.

19. Many colonies' willing participation in slavery undermined the blame that Jefferson tried to place exclusively on the King. Virginia Constitution: "By prompting our negroes to rise in arms

In every stage of these Oppressions We have Petitioned for Redress in the most humble terms: Our repeated Petitions have been answered only by repeated injury. A Prince whose character is thus marked by every act which may define a Tyrant, is unfit to be the ruler of a ~~*people who mean to be free. future ages will scarce believe that the hardiness of one man, adventured within the short compass of 12 years only, on so many acts of tyranny without a mask, over a people fostered & fixed in principles of liberty*~~ free people.

Nor have We been wanting in attentions to our Brittish brethren.[[8]] [20] We have warned them from time to time of attempts by their legislature to extend ~~*a*~~ an unwarrantable jurisdiction over ~~*these our states*~~ us. We have reminded them of the circumstances of our emigration and settlement here. ~~*, no one of which could warrant so strange a pretension: that these were effected at the expence of our own blood & treasure, unassisted by the wealth or the strength of Great Britain: that in constituting indeed our several forms of government, we had adopted one common king, thereby laying a foundation for perpetual league & amity with them: but that submission to their parliament was no part of our constitution, nor ever in idea, if history may be credited: and we .*~~ We have appealed to their native justice and magnanimity, ~~*as well as to*~~ and we have conjured them by the ties of our common kindred to disavow these usurpations, which, ~~*were likely to*~~ would inevitably interrupt our connections and correspondence ~~*& connection*~~. They too have been deaf to the voice of justice and of consanguinity. ~~*, & when occasions have been given them, by the regular course of their laws, of removing from their councils the disturbers of our harmony, they have by their free election re-established them in power. at this very time too they are permitting their chief magistrate to send over not only soldiers of our common blood, but Scotch [[9]] & foreign mercenaries to invade & deluge us in blood. these facts have given the last stab to agonizing affection, and manly spirit bids us to renounce for ever these unfeeling brethren.*~~ We must ~~*endeavor to forget*~~, therefore, acquiesce in the necessity, which denounces our ~~*former love for them*~~ Separation, and ~~*to*~~ hold them, as we hold the rest of mankind, Enemies in War, in Peace Friends. ~~*we might have been a free & great people together; but a communication of grandeur & of freedom it seems is below their dignity. be it so, since they will have it: the road to glory & happiness is open to us too; we will climb it in a separate state, and acquiesce in the necessity which pronounces our everlasting Adieu!*~~]

---

against us, those very negroes whom, by an inhuman use of his negative, he hath refused us permission to exclude by law."

20. Here, Jefferson addressed the British people. Congress trimmed this section substantially. Some of the claims were exaggerated, leading to substantial revisions from Congress.

THE CONGRESS:
We still have friends in Britain that we need to keep on our side. Let's tone down these attacks on the British people.[[8]]

JOHN WITHERSPOON:
Please remove references to "Scotch." I, along with James Wilson and others, were born in Scotland.[[9]]

THOMAS JEFFERSON:
Congress is mutilating this document. 😡

BENJAMIN FRANKLIN:
Once, a man was about to open his first shop and sought advice from friends regarding his sign. He proposed "John Thomson, Hatter, makes and sells hats for ready money" with a picture of a hat. One friend thought "hatter" to be redundant. Another that "makes" should be removed because buyers don't care who makes the hats. A third said he thought the words "for ready money," were useless as selling on credit is unusual. The inscription now stood "John Thomson sells hats." "Sells hats" says his next friend? "Nobody will expect you to give them away." His inscription was reduced ultimately to "John Thomson" with the figure of a hat subjoined.

Thus, I have made it a rule, whenever in my power, to avoid becoming the draftsman of papers to be reviewed by a public body.

BENJAMIN FRANKLIN: In signing this, we are signing a death warrant with Britain. This is technically treason. We must all hang together or we will most assuredly all hang separately.

[At least one historian questions whether Franklin said this famous line.]

JOHN ADAMS: Hear hear.

JOHN DICKINSON: I will abstain from voting for this. We should continue to petition the King.

ABIGAIL ADAMS: *[Letter to John Adams, March 31, 1776]*

When you all begin to draft the new laws, be sure to remember the ladies, more than your ancestors.

[Declaration of Independence from Great Britain]

We, therefore, the Representatives of the **united States of America,** in General Congress, Assembled, appealing to the Supreme Judge of the world for the rectitude of our intentions, do, in the Name, and by Authority of the good People of these ~~*states, reject and renounce all allegiance & subjection to the kings of Great Britain & all others who may hereafter claim by, through, or under them; we utterly dissolve & break off all*~~ Colonies, solemnly publish and declare, That these United Colonies are, and of Right ought to be Free and Independent States; that they are Absolved from all Allegiance to the British Crown,[21] and that all political connection ~~*which may have heretofore subsisted*~~ between ~~*us &*~~ them and the ~~*people or parliament*~~ State of Great Britain ~~*; and finally we do assert*~~, is and ~~*declare these a colonies*~~ ought to be ~~*free and independant states,*~~ totally dissolved; and that as **Free and Independent States**, they ~~*shall hereafter*~~ have full Power to levy War, conclude Peace, contract Alliances, establish Commerce, and to do all other Acts and Things which Independent States may of right do. And for the support of this Declaration, with a firm reliance on the protection of divine Providence, we mutually pledge[22] to each other our Lives, our Fortunes and our sacred Honor.

---

21. Congress reworded Jefferson's conclusion and included language from Richard Henry Lee's Resolution that Congress passed on June 7, 1776: "Resolved, That these United Colonies are, and of right ought to be, free and independent States, that they are absolved from all allegiance to the British Crown, and that all political connection between them and the State of Great Britain is, and ought to be, totally dissolved." Lee moved for the resolution based on instructions from the Virginia legislature.

22. This pledge existed in many existing state and local declarations of independence. (Imagine such a pledge today.)

The tone of the Declaration indicates that it was meant to be read aloud before large, public bodies. Compare this with the wordier Declaration on the Causes and Necessity of Taking Up Arms, p. 73.

[Signers, reordered by state][23]

[CONNECTICUT]
Roger Sherman,
Samuel Huntington,
William Williams
Oliver Wolcott

[DELAWARE]
Caesar Rodney,
George Read,
Thomas McKean

[GEORGIA]
Button Gwinnett,
Lyman Hall,
George Walton

[MARYLAND]
Samuel Chase,
William Paca,
Thomas Stone,
Charles Carroll of Carrollton

[MASSACHUSETTS]
John Hancock,
Samuel Adams,
John Adams,
Robert Treat Paine,
Elbridge Gerry

[NEW YORK]
William Floyd,
Philip Livingston,
Francis Lewis,
Lewis Morris

[NEW JERSEY]
Richard Stockton,
John Witherspoon,
Francis Hopkinson,
John Hart,
Abraham Clark

[NEW HAMPSHIRE]
Matthew Thornton,
Josiah Bartlett,
William Whipple

[NORTH CAROLINA]
William Hooper,
Joseph Hewes,
John Penn

[PENNSYLVANIA]
Robert Morris,
Benjamin Rush,
Benjamin Franklin,
John Morton,
George Clymer,
James Smith,
George Taylor,
James Wilson,
George Ross

[RHODE ISLAND]
Stephen Hopkins,
William Ellery

[SOUTH CAROLINA]
Edward Rutledge,
Thomas Heyward, Jr.,
Thomas Lynch, Jr.,
Arthur Middleton

[VIRGINIA]
George Wythe,
Richard Henry Lee,
Thomas Jefferson,
Benjamin Harrison,
Thomas Nelson, Jr.,
Francis Lightfoot Lee,
Carter Braxton

---

23. On July 2, **New York** delegates **did not have permission** to agree to independence and did not sign the Declaration. After the other states approved, New York reconsidered and finally gave delegates permission to join in independence. Congress had the Declaration engrossed in late July, and were then able to add "The unanimous declaration" to the beginning of the Declaration. *See* p. 91. But on July 2, it was not unanimous.

Articles of Confederation—Redlined

(NOVEMBER 15, 1777)

Introduction

The Continental Congress adopted the Articles of Confederation on November 15, 1777. The Articles served as America's first constitution from March 1, 1781, until 1789 when the current Constitution went into effect. The Articles created a "league of friendship" among thirteen sovereign states, with each state retaining a vast majority of all powers. Essentially, a central authority had powers to provide for national defense but had few powers beyond that. The Articles allowed for the taxation of states but provided no enforcement mechanism, resulting in many states refusing to contribute. (The Constitution corrects this by allowing taxation of *individuals*, which can be enforced individually.) The diplomatic standing of the nation also suffered because of the perceived weakness of the national government.

Many members of the Continental Congress hoped that the Articles, a wartime document, would help legitimize the young country in the eyes of the French and Spanish to encourage them to join the American effort. **Richard** Henry Lee of Virginia **moved in Congress** for "a plan of confederation be prepared and transmitted to the respective Colonies for their consideration and approbation."

Under the Articles, each state had one vote. Nine votes were needed to pass a law, but it was often difficult to reach nine votes. Long-distance travel was often arduous and expensive. If only nine states were represented for a given vote, which occurred often due to the difficulties of travel and state infighting, the vote had to be unanimous, compounding the difficulty. The Articles were practically impossible to amend—requiring a unanimous vote of all states. States had their own systems of currency, creating a patchwork of laws and policies rather than having the strength of uniformity. States managed much of their own foreign policy and the Articles made international diplomacy difficult, as the United States might enter into an international agreement only to have an individual state violate it, giving the counterparty cause to breach the agreement, or at least undermining the credibility of the United States.

After only a few years under the Articles, the states were nearing economic catastrophe and the central government was largely powerless to help. Each colony, and the country as a whole, was vulnerable to foreign powers. After failed proposals to **amend the Articles**, the Continental Congress decided to dispense with the Articles.

Among other things, the Constitution takes from the Articles: laws made by the legislature, privileges and immunities, full faith and credit, extradition, speech and debate immunity, and providing for the common defense. Differences include the supremacy of the national government, voting, elections, threshold for amendment and ratification (unanimous in the Articles), and three, co-equal branches in the Constitution (compared to simply a unicameral legislature under the Articles). Additionally, many of the enumerated powers granted to Congress in Article I, § 8 of the Constitution were expressly denied to Congress under the Articles unless nine states voted to grant those powers.

Much of the deliberation over the Articles was in secret, and many of the revisions are only memorialized in general terms in the Journals of the Continental Congress. For example, references to many revisions are in the passive voice and anonymous ("it was moved that"), and voting is reflected generally as "passed in the affirmative."

Benjamin Franklin had an early draft "sketch" of articles of confederation some two years before the actual Articles were adopted and a year before the colonies declared independence. He deserves more credit than he currently receives for first envisioning what the United States would ultimately become.[1]

Articles of Confederation and Perpetual Union proposed by the delegates of the several Colonies of New Hampshire &c in general Congress met at Philadelphia May 10 1775.

Art. I.

The Name of this Confederacy shall henceforth be The United Colonies of North America.

Excerpt from Benjamin Franklin's Sketch of Articles of Confederation (July 21, 1775)

John Dickinson, a delegate from Delaware, is credited with the initial draft that Congress ultimately worked from and approved. Local printers Dunlap & Claypool were commissioned to print 80 copies of the draft for the delegates' consideration.

This book tracks the changes between the Dickinson Draft of the Articles of Confederation and the engrossed version. The organization of the final document differed substantially from Dickinson's original draft. Substantive changes to the text are tracked and identified, but reorganization is not tracked. For exact changes and reorganization, sources of the transcriptions are provided at the end of this book.[2]

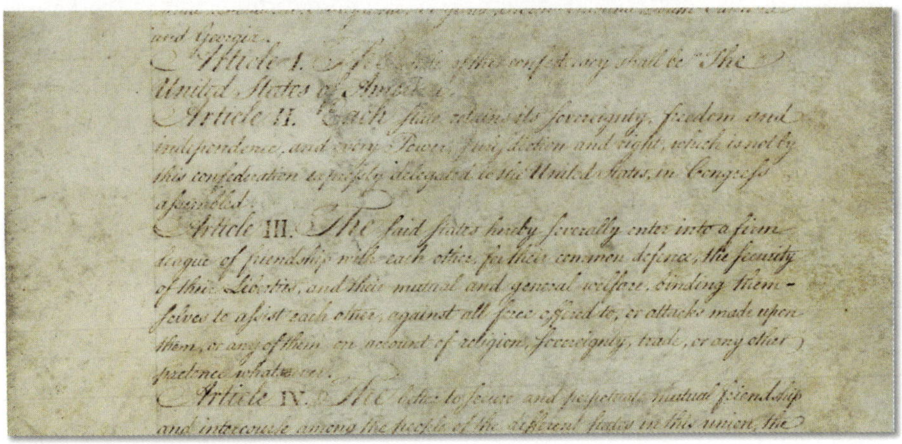

and Georgia.

Article I. The Stile of this confederacy shall be "The United States of America."

Article II. Each state retains its sovereignty, freedom and independence, and every Power, Jurisdiction and right, which is not by this confederation expressly delegated to the United States, in Congress assembled.

Article III. The said states hereby severally enter into a firm league of friendship with each other, for their common defence, the security of their Liberties, and their mutual and general welfare, binding themselves to assist each other, against all force offered to, or attacks made upon them, or any of them, on account of religion, sovereignty, trade, or any other pretence whatever.

Article IV. The better to secure and perpetuate mutual friendship and intercourse among the people of the different states in this union, the

Excerpt from Engrossed Articles of Confederation

1. For more on this, *see* Founders Online, Proposed Articles of Confederation (describing this history of Franklin's "Short Hints" for uniting the northern colonies in 1754, and providing a transcription).

2. Consistent with a theme of this book (the iterative journey of founding documents), in 2023 Chief Justice Roberts relied on the Articles of Confederation to make a structural point about the role of courts in the context of the Elections Clause of the U.S. Constitution (Art. I, § 4) in the landmark case of *Moore v. Harper*, 600 U.S. 1 (2023):

> [M]ultiple state constitutions at the time of the founding regulated federal elections. . . . [T]he Framers did not write the Elections Clause on a blank slate—they instead borrowed from the Articles of Confederation. . . . And around the time the Articles were adopted by the Second Continental Congress, multiple States regulated the "manner" of "appointing delegates," suggesting that the Framers did not understand that language to insulate state legislative action from state constitutional provisions.

Articles of Confederation

To all to whom these Presents shall come, we, the undersigned Delegates of the states affixed to our Names send greeting. Whereas the Delegates of the United States of America in Congress assembled did on the fifteenth day of November in the year of our Lord One Thousand Seven Hundred and Seventy seven, and in the Second Year of the Independence of America agree to certain articles of Confederation and perpetual Union between the states of Newhampshire, Massachusetts-bay, Rhodeisland and Providence Plantations, Connecticut, New York, New Jersey, Pennsylvania, Delaware, Maryland, Virginia, North Carolina, South Carolina, and Georgia in the Words following, viz.

"Articles of Confederation and perpetual Union between the states of Newhampshire, Massachusetts-bay, Rhodeisland and Providence Plantations, Connecticut, New York, New Jersey, Pennsylvania, Delaware, Maryland, Virginia, North Carolina, South Carolina, and Georgia.

JOHN DICKINSON: Although I lost in persuading against independence, I can at least help make sure that that the states have a sound national government.

Article I. [Naming]

~~*THE Name*~~ The Stile of this confederacy shall be "The United States of America."

Article II. [State Sovereignty Retained]

~~*Each Colony shall retain and enjoy as much of*~~ Each state retains [[1]] its ~~*present Laws, Rights and Customs, as it may think fit, and reserves to itself the sole and exclusive Regulation and Government of its internal police, in all matters that shall*~~ sovereignty, freedom and independence, and every Power, Jurisdiction and right, which is not ~~*interfere with the Articles of*~~ by this confederation expressly delegated to the united states, in Congress assembled.[3]

THOMAS BURKE: These revisions guarantee that under the Confederation, supreme authority resides in the states rather than in the central government. The national government should only be for the common defense.[[1]]

JAMES WILSON; RICHARD HENRY LEE: Disagree. We need a stronger central government or these Articles aren't going to work.

[Vote to include language passes 11–1–1.]

3. In an earlier draft, Dickinson added a strong religious-freedom protection, which even applied to the states. (It was also gender-neutral, thought to be the first such use of "his or her" in an American constitution.) The clause was stricken, but a version was added to the U.S. Constitution in the First Amendment. But even that did not apply to the states until after the Fourteenth Amendment (1868).

Article III. [Purpose]

The said ~~*Colonies unite themselves so as never to be divided by any Act whatever, and*~~ states hereby severally enter into a firm league of friendship with each other, for their common defence, the security of their Liberties, and their mutual and general welfare, binding ~~*the said Colonies*~~ themselves to assist ~~*one another*~~ each other, against all force offered to, or attacks made upon them, or any of them, on account of religion, sovereignty, trade, or any other pretence whatever.[4]

Article IV. [Privileges and Immunities; Full Faith and Credit]

The better to secure and perpetuate mutual friendship and intercourse among the people of the different states in this union, the free inhabitants of each of these states, paupers, vagabonds and fugitives from Justice excepted, shall be entitled to all privileges and immunities of free citizens in the several states; and the people of each state shall have free ingress and regress to and from any other state, and shall enjoy therein all the privileges of trade and commerce, subject to the same duties, impositions and restrictions as the inhabitants thereof respectively, provided that such restrictions shall not extend so far as to prevent the removal of property imported into any state, to any other state of which the Owner is an inhabitant; provided also that no imposition, duties or restriction shall be laid by any state, on the property of the united states, or either of them.

~~*The Inhabitants of each Colony shall henceforth always have the same Rights, Liberties, Privileges, Immunities and Advantages, in the other Colonies, which the said Inhabitants now have, in all Cases whatever, except in those provided for by the next following Article.*~~

~~*The Inhabitants of each Colony shall enjoy all the Rights, Liberties, Privileges, Immunities, and Advantages, in Trade, Navigation, and Commerce, in any other Colony, and in going to and from the same from and to any Part of the World, which the Natives of such Colony or any Commercial Society, established by its Authority shall enjoy.*~~

RICHARD HENRY LEE: After many debates in Congress about Mr. Dickinson's draft, our finalizing committee (me, Richard Law, and James Duane) propose rearranging sections from Mr. Dickinson's draft, making some other changes, and adding a version of this paragraph on privileges and immunities.

ELBRIDGE GERRY: Agreed.

[Congress adopts the substance of these changes but uses Gerry's modified wording for most of this paragraph.]

4. Some of the themes in Article III (common defense, security of liberties, and general welfare) are general duties of government that resurface in the revised Preamble to the Constitution. *See* p. 136. But the Constitution's Preamble adds: creating a "more perfect" *Union*, establishing justice (the judicial branch), and ensuring domestic tranquility (instead of domestic turmoil under the Articles).

If any Person guilty of, or charged with, treason, felony, or other high misdemeanor in any state, shall flee from Justice, and be found in any of the united states, he shall upon demand of the Governor or executive power of the state from which he fled, be delivered up, and removed to the state having jurisdiction of his offence.

Full faith and credit shall be given in each of these states to the records, acts and judicial proceedings of the courts and magistrates of every other state.

Article V. [Delegates; Meetings]

For the more convenient management of the general interests of the united states, delegates ~~*should*~~ shall be annually appointed[[2]] in such manner as the legislature of each ~~*Colony*~~ state shall direct, ~~*or such Branches thereof as the Colony shall authorize for that purpose,*~~ to meet in ~~*General*~~ Congress ~~*at the City of Philadelphia, in the Colony of Pennsylvania, until otherwise ordered by Congress the united states assembled; which Meeting shall be*~~ on the first Monday ~~*of*~~ in November, in every year, with a power reserved to ~~*those who appointed the said Delegates, respectively to supercede recall them*~~ each state to recal its delegates, or any of them, at any time within the year, and to send ~~*new Delegates*~~ others in their stead, for the remainder of the Year.

No state shall be represented in Congress by less than two, nor by more than seven Members; and no person shall be capable of being ~~*a*~~ delegate for more than three years, in any term of six years~~.~~ ~~*No Person*~~; nor shall any person, being a delegate, be capable of holding any office under the united states, for which he, or another for his benefit~~,~~ receives any salary, fees~~,~~ or emolument of any kind.

Each ~~*Colony*~~ state shall ~~*support*~~ maintain its own delegates in a meeting of the states, and while they act as members of the committee of the states ~~*herein after mentioned*~~.

In determining questions in the united states, in Congress assembled, each ~~*Colony*~~ state shall have one vote.[[3]]

Freedom of speech and debate[[4]] in Congress shall not be impeached or questioned in any Court, or place out of Congress, and the members of congress shall be protected in their persons from arrests and imprisonments, during the

THOMAS BURKE: I move that we have two houses of Congress.

[Motion fails. Many delegates were more familiar with a unicameral body. There were also fears that a House based on population would overpower smaller states.]

JAMES MADISON: *[In 1783]* This annual appointment and then rotation every three years is undesirable. We need the stability that comes with experience, not a bunch of new people all the time. New members also often do not feel the necessary respect or responsibility for the acts of their predecessors.[[2]]

BENJAMIN FRANKLIN: One vote for each state is highly unfair to larger states.[[3]]

RICHARD HENRY LEE: We need a speech-and-debate clause; our committee proposes this one.[[4]]

JOHN DICKINSON: Shouldn't delegates be required to take an oath to observe and abide by the Articles?

[Not provided for in the Articles but added to the Constitution.]

time of their going to and from, and attendance on congress, except for treason, felony, or breach of the peace.[5]

Article VI. [Powers Denied States]

No ~~*Colony or Colonies*~~ state, without the Consent of the united states, in congress assembled, shall send any embassy to, or receive any embassy from, or enter into any ~~*Treaty, Convention or Conference with the King or Kingdom of Great-Britain, or any foreign Prince or state; nor shall any Colony or Colonies, nor any Servant*~~ conferrence, agreement, alliance, or ~~*Servants*~~ treaty, with any King, prince or state; nor shall any person holding any office of profit or trust under the united states, or any of ~~*any Colony or Colonies*~~ them, accept of any present, emolument, office, or title of any kind whatever, from ~~*the King or Kingdom of Great-Britain*~~ any king, prince, or ~~*any*~~ foreign ~~*Prince or*~~ state; nor shall the united states, in congress assembled, or any ~~*Colony*~~ of them, grant any title of nobility.

No two or more ~~*Colonies*~~ states shall enter into any treaty, confederation, or alliance whatever between them, without the ~~*previous and free Consent and Allowance*~~ consent of the united states, in congress assembled, specifying accurately the purposes for which the same is to be entered into, and how long it shall continue.

~~*Each Colony may assess*~~ No state shall lay any imposts or duties, which may interfere ~~*provided such Imposts or Duties do not interfere*~~ with any stipulations in treaties, entered into by the united states in congress assembled, with any king, prince, or state, in pursuance of any treaties already proposed by congress, to the courts of France and Spain~~*, or any foreign Prince or state*~~.

~~*No standing Army or Body of Forces*~~ No vessels of war shall be kept up ~~*by any Colony or Colonies in Times*~~ in time of peace, by any state, except such number only, as shall be deemed necessary by the united states, in congress assembled, for the defence of such state, or its trade; nor shall any body of

---

5. This privilege is also enshrined in the 1689 English Bill of Rights: "That the freedom of speech and debates or proceedings in Parliament ought not to be impeached or questioned in any court or place out of Parliament." *See* p. 22. The British added this protection in part in response to the *Six Members Case* (1629), which involved the arrest and imprisonment of six members of the English Parliament by King Charles I for their opposition to his demands.

forces be kept up, by any state, in time of peace,[6] except such ~~*a*~~ number only as ~~*may be*~~, in the judgment of the united states, in congress assembled, shall be deemed requisite to garrison the forts necessary for the defence of such ~~*Colony or Colonies:*~~ state; but every ~~*Colony*~~ state shall always keep up a well regulated and disciplined militia, sufficiently armed and accoutred, and shall provide and constantly have ready for use, in public stores, a due number of field pieces and tents, and a proper quantity of arms, ammunition, and ~~*other*~~ camp equipage.[7]

No ~~*Colony or Colonies*~~ state shall engage in any war without the ~~*previous*~~ consent of the united states in congress assembled, unless such ~~*Colony or Colonies*~~ state be actually invaded by enemies, or shall have received certain advice of a resolution being formed by some nation of Indians to invade such ~~*Colony or Colonies*~~ state, and the danger is so imminent~~,~~ as not to admit of a delay~~,~~ till the ~~*other Colonies*~~ united states in congress assembled, can be consulted: nor shall any ~~*Colony or Colonies*~~ state grant commissions to any ships or vessels of war, nor letters of marque or reprisal, except it be after a declaration of war by the united states in congress assembled, and then only against the kingdom or state, and the subjects thereof, against which war has been so declared, and under such regulations as shall be established by the united states in congress assembled, unless such state be infested by pirates, in which case vessels of war may be fitted out for that occasion, and kept so long as the danger shall continue, or until the united states in congress assembled shall determine otherwise.

Article VII. [States Assign Ranks Under Colonel]

When ~~*Troops*~~ land-forces are raised ~~*in*~~ by any ~~*of the Colonies*~~ state, for the common defence, ~~*the Commission Officers proper for the Troops raised in each Colony, except the General Officers*~~ all officers of or under the rank of colonel, shall be appointed by the legislature of each ~~*Colony*~~ state respectively by whom such forces shall be raised, or in such manner as ~~*shall by them be directed.*~~ such

---

6. With all of the concern about standing armies in prior documents, even a grievance in the 1689 English Declaration, it is notable that the Articles (and the Constitution) do not prohibit it (paving the way for a national army but limiting funding of an army to two years. *See* p. 145).

7. Dickinson's earlier draft of the Articles stated the following, which can be compared to the draft and final versions of the Second Amendment (p. 173): "but every Colony shall keep always keep up a well regulated & disciplined Militia sufficiently armed and accoutred, in which every (able bodied) Male White person between the Ages of [blank] and [blank] Years, except (Ministers of the Gospel, and) those who are conscientiously scrupulous of bearing Arms, shall be duely enrolled."

state shall direct, and all vacancies shall be filled up by the state which first made appointment.

Article VIII. [Federal Expenses and Taxes][8]

All charges of war, and all other expenses that shall be incurred for the common defence or general welfare, and allowed by the united states in ~~*General*~~ congress assembled, shall be defrayed out of a common treasury, which shall be supplied by the several ~~*Colonies*~~ states,[[5]] in proportion to ~~*Number of Inhabitants of every Age, Sex and Quality, except Indians not paying Taxes, in each Colony, a true Account of which, distinguishing the white Inhabitants who are not slaves, shall be triennially taken and transmitted to Congress the Assembly of the United States*~~ the value of all land within state, granted to or surveyed for any Person, as such land and buildings and improvements thereon shall be estimated, according to such mode as the united states, in congress assembled, shall, from time to time, direct and appoint. The taxes for paying that proportion shall be laid and levied by the authority and direction of the legislatures of the several ~~*Colonies,*~~ states within the time agreed upon by the united states in congress assembled.

Article IX. [Powers of Congress][9]

The united states, in congress assembled, shall have the sole and exclusive right and power of determining on peace and war, except in the cases mentioned in the ~~*thirteenth Article*~~ Sixth article—of sending and receiving ambassadors—entering into treaties and alliances, provided that no treaty of commerce shall be made, whereby the legislative power of the respective states shall be restrained from imposing such imposts and duties on foreigners, as their own people are subjected to, or from prohibiting the exportation or importation of any species of goods or commodities whatsoever—of establishing rules for deciding, in all cases, what captures on land or water shall be legal, and in what manner prizes taken by land or naval forces in the service of the united states shall be divided or appropriated—of granting letters of marque and reprisal

JAMES MADISON: *[In 1787]* This provision has proven a failure. States simply refuse to comply with payment obligations, and there is no enforcement mechanism. States are also violating US treaty obligations and encroaching on each other.[[5]]

8. This article proved to be a major structural flaw in the Articles. It relied on states to voluntarily contribute funds, and many failed to do so. According to Michael Klarman, the overall compliance rate for requisitions during this period was 37%, and was only 2% by August 1786.

9. Like the Constitution, the article concerning the powers of Congress is the longest and most detailed.

in times of peace—appointing courts for the trial of ~~*all Crimes, Frauds*~~ piracies and felonies committed on the high seas~~*, or on any navigable River, not within the Body of a County or Parish-Establishing Courts;*~~ and establishing courts; for receiving and determining finally appeals in all cases of captures, provided that no member of congress shall be appointed a judge of any of the said courts.

The united states, in congress assembled, shall also be the last resort on appeal, in all disputes and differences now subsisting,[10] or that hereafter may arise between two or more states concerning boundary, jurisdiction, or any other cause whatever; which authority shall always be exercised in the manner following. Whenever the legislative or executive authority, or lawful agent of any state in controversy with another, shall present a petition to congress, stating the matter in question, and praying for a hearing, notice thereof shall be given, by order of congress, to the legislative or executive authority of the other state in controversy, and a day assigned for the appearance of the parties by their lawful agents, who shall then be directed to appoint, by joint consent, commissioners or judges to constitute a court for hearing and determining the matter in question: but if they cannot agree, congress shall name three persons out of each of the united states, and from the list of such persons each party shall alternately strike out one, the petitioners beginning, until the number shall be reduced to thirteen; and from that number not less than seven, nor more than nine names, as congress shall direct, shall, in the presence of congress, be drawn out by lot, and the persons whose names shall be so drawn, or any five of them, shall be commissioners or judges, to hear and finally determine the controversy, so always as a major part of the judges, who shall hear the cause, shall agree in the determination: and if either party shall neglect to attend at the day appointed, without showing reasons which congress shall judge sufficient, or being present, shall refuse to strike, the congress shall proceed to nominate three persons out of each state, and the secretary of congress shall strike in behalf of such party absent or refusing; and the judgment and sentence of the court, to be appointed in the manner before prescribed, shall be final and conclusive; and if any of the parties shall refuse to submit to the authority of such court, or to appear or defend their claim or cause, the court shall nevertheless proceed to pronounce sentence, or judgment, which shall in like manner be final and decisive; the judgment or sentence and other proceedings being in either case transmitted to congress, and lodged among the acts of congress,

10. Without a judicial branch, Congress created ad hoc courts to handle disputes.

for the security of the parties concerned: provided that every commissioner, before he sits in judgment, shall take an oath to be administered by one of the judges of the supreme or superior court of the state where the cause shall be tried, "well and truly to hear and determine the matter in question, according to the best of his judgment, without favour, affection, or hope of reward: "provided, also, that no state shall be deprived of territory for the benefit of the united states.

All controversies concerning the private right of soil claimed under different grants of two or more states, whose jurisdictions as they may respect such lands, and the states which passed such grants are adjusted, the said grants or either of them being at the same time claimed to have originated antecedent to such settlement of jurisdiction, shall, on the petition of either party to the congress of the united states, be finally determined, as near as may be, in the same manner as is before prescribed for deciding disputes respecting territorial jurisdiction between different states.

The united states, in congress assembled, shall also have the sole and exclusive right and power of regulating the alloy and value of coin struck by their own authority, or by that of the respective states—[11] fixing the standard of weights and measures throughout the united states—regulating the trade and managing all affairs[12] with the Indians, not members of any of the states; provided that the legislative right of any state, within its own limits, be not

11. The colonies (now states) were still printing paper money to raise revenue and as a workaround to English prohibitions on coining money, and each state's different currency substantially complicated commerce and the war effort. States secured their currency in various ways, including with tobacco, crops, government promises, and land (including land that the states did not own, in the case of Georgia and the Creek Indians). To fund the Revolutionary War, the Continental Congress printed "continental currency" of its own, but devalued it so much (and it was also heavily counterfeited by the British) that it lost almost all of its value by the end of the war, leading to the phrase "not worth a continental." The Constitution tries to resolve this in Article I, § 8 (p. 144). After decentralization of banking by the Andrew Jackson administration, there were some 5,000 state-charted banks before the Civil War. The value of this currency varied wildly (with banks regulating the value, going in and out of business, etc.). The most widely circulated magazines at the time were currency circulators, as people tried to keep up with the changing values of various currency. Abraham Lincoln resolved much of this in the National Banking Act (1863), which standardized "greenbacks" as a national currency.

12. Notice that Art. I, § 8, of the Constitution references "commerce" but does not expressly reference Congressional power over "all affairs with Indians," as the Articles do. *See* p. 111. Some argue that the Constitution therefore gives Congress less authority when dealing with Tribes, while others respond that, structurally, that cannot be correct because the goal of the Constitution was a stronger (not weaker) central government.

infringed or violated—~~*Limiting the Bounds of those Colonies, which by Charter or Proclamation, or under any Pretence, are said to extend to the South Sea, and ascertaining those Bounds of any other Colony that appear to be indeterminate-Assigning Territories for new Colonies, either in Lands to he thus separated from Colonies and heretofore purchased or obtained by the Crown of Great-Britain from the Indians, or hereafter to be purchased or obtained from them-Disposing of all such Lands for the general Benefit of all the United Colonies-Ascertaining Boundaries to such new Colonies, within which Forms of Government are to be established on the Principles of Liberty*~~—establishing and regulating post-offices from one state to another, throughout all the united states, and exacting such postage on the papers passing through the same, as may be requisite to defray the expenses of the said office—appointing all officers of the land forces in the service of the united states, excepting regimental officers—appointing all the officers of the naval forces, and commissioning all officers whatever in the service of the united states; making rules for the government and regulation of the said land and naval forces, and directing their operations.

JAMES MADISON: *[In 1787]* The Articles needed a commerce clause. Under these Articles, states were incentivized to undermine each other, which has proven unsustainable. The 1787 Constitution improves on this by allowing at least some centralized management of commerce.

~~*Appointing a Council of state, and such Committees and civil Officers as may be necessary for managing the general Affairs of the united states, under their Direction while assembled, and in their Recess, of the Council of state-Appointing one of their number to preside, and a suitable Person for Secretary-And adjourning to any Time within the Year. The Council of state shall consist of one Delegate from each Colony, to be named annually by the Delegates of each Colony, and where they cannot agree, by the united states assembled.*~~

The united states, in congress assembled, shall have authority to appoint a committee, to sit in the recess of congress,[13] to be denominated, "A Committee of the states," and to consist of one delegate from each state; and to appoint such other committees and civil officers as may be necessary for managing the general affairs of the united states under their direction—to appoint one of their number to preside; provided that no person be allowed to serve in the office of president more than one year in any term of three years; to ascertain the necessary sums of money to be raised for the service of the united states, and

13. A Committee of States conducted business when Congress was not in session. There was no executive to manage affairs when Congress was in recess; each year, Congress selected an individual to serve as the President of Congress to preside over proceedings. Fearful of a tyrant or monarch, the role of "President" under the Articles was largely ceremonial and administrative.

to appropriate and apply the same for defraying the public expenses; to borrow money or emit bills on the credit of the united states, transmitting every half year to the respective states an account of the sums of money so borrowed or emitted,—to build and equip a navy—to agree upon the number of land forces, and to make requisitions from each ~~*Colony*~~ state for its quota, in proportion to the number of white inhabitants[[6]] in such ~~*Colony*~~ state, which requisition shall be binding; and thereupon the legislature of each ~~*Colony*~~ state shall appoint the regimental officers, raise the men, and clothe, arm, and equip them, in a soldier-like manner, at the expense of the united states; and the officers and men so clothed, armed, and equipped, shall march to the place appointed, and within the time agreed on by the united states, in congress assembled; but if the united states, in congress assembled, shall, on consideration of circumstances, judge proper that any ~~*Colony or Colonies*~~ state should not raise men, or should raise a smaller number than its quota, and that any other ~~*Colony or Colonies*~~ state should raise a greater number of men than the quota thereof, such extra number shall be raised, officered, clothed, armed, and equipped in the same manner as the quota of such ~~*Colony or Colonies*~~ state, unless the legislature of such ~~*Colony or Colonies*~~ state shall judge that such extra number cannot be safely spared out of the same, in which case they shall raise, officer, clothe, arm, and equip, as many of such extra number as they judge can be safely spared. And the officers and men so clothed, armed, and equipped, shall march to the place appointed, and within the time agreed on by the united states in congress assembled.

~~*But the united states assembled shall never impose or levy any Taxes or Duties, except in managing the Post-Office, nor interfere in the internal Police of any Colony, any further than such Police may be affected by the Articles of this Confederation.*~~ The united states, in congress assembled, shall never engage ~~*the United Colonies*~~ in a war, nor grant letters of marque and reprisal in time of peace, nor enter into any treaties or alliances, nor coin money, nor regulate the value thereof~~,~~ nor ~~*agree upon nor fix*~~ ascertain the sums and expenses necessary for the defence and welfare of the united ~~*Colonies*~~ states, or any of them, nor emit bills, nor borrow money on the credit of the united ~~*Colonies*~~ states, nor ~~*raise Naval Forces*~~ appropriate money, nor agree upon the number of ~~*Land*~~ vessels of war to be built or purchased, or the number of land or sea forces to be raised, nor appoint a commander in chief of the army or navy, unless ~~*the Delegates of*~~ nine ~~*Colonies freely*~~ states assent to the same, nor shall a question on any other point, except for adjourning from day to day, be determined, unless by the votes of a majority of the united states in congress assembled ~~*unless the*~~

NJ AND PA DELEGATIONS:
The Declaration of Independence that we just passed says, "all men are created equal." We think that the reference to "white inhabitants" here should be changed to all inhabitants.

[Motions fail 6 to 3, 1 divided.][[6]]

~~*Delegates of seven Colonies vote in the affirmative*~~. The congress of the united states shall have power to adjourn to any time within the year, and to any place within the united states, so that no period of adjournment be for a longer duration than the space of six Months, and shall publish the Journal of their proceedings monthly, except such parts thereof relating to treaties, alliances, or military operations, as in their judgment require secrecy; and the yeas and nays of the delegates of each state, on any question, shall be entered on the Journal, when it is desired by any delegate; and the delegates of a state, or any of them, at his or their request, shall be furnished with a transcript of the said Journal, except such parts as are above excepted, to lay before the legislatures of the several states.

~~*The Business and Duty of This Council shall have Power to receive and open all Letters directed to the united states, and to return proper Answers; but not to make any Engagements that shall be binding on the united states-To correspond with the Legislature of each Colony, and all Persons acting under the Authority of the united states, or of the said Legislatures-To apply to such Legislatures, or to the Officers in the several Colonies who are entrusted with the executive Powers of Government, for occasional Aid whenever and wherever necessary-To give Counsel to the Commanding Officers, and to direct military Operations by Sea and Land, not changing any Objects or Expeditions determined on by the united states assembled, unless an Alteration of Circumstances which shall come to the Knowledge of the Council after the Recess of the states, shall malice such Change absolutely necessary-To attend to the Defence and Preservation of Forts and strong Posts, and to prevent the Enemy from acquiring new Holds—To procure Intelligence of the Condition and Designs of the Enemy-To expedite the Execution of such Measures as may be resolved on by the united states assembled, in Pursuance of the Powers hereby given to them-To draw upon the Treasurers for such Sums as may be appropriated by the united states assembled, and for the Payment of such Contracts as the said Council may make in Pursuance of the Powers hereby given to them—To superintend and controul or suspend all Officers civil and military, acting under the Authority of the united states-In Case of the Death or Removal of any Officer within the Appointment of the united states assembled, to employ a Person to fulfill the Duties of such Office until the Assembly of the states meet-To publish and disperse authentic Accounts of military Operations-To summon an Assembly of the states at an earlier Day than that appointed for their next Meeting, if any great and unexpected Emergency*~~

~~should render it necessary for the Safety or Welfare of the United Colonies or any of them-To prepare Matters for the Consideration of the united states, and to lay before them at their next Meeting all Letters and Advices received by the Council, with a Report of their Proceedings-To appoint a proper Person for their Clerk, who shall take an Oath of Secrecy and Fidelity, before he enters on the Exercise of his Office—Seven Members shall have Power to act-In Case of the Death of any Member, the Council shall immediately apply to his surviving Colleagues to appoint some one of themselves to be a Member thereof till the Meeting of the states, and if only one survives, they shall give him immediate Notice, that he may take his Seat as a Councilor till such Meeting.~~

~~When the Boundaries of any Colony shall be ascertained by Agreement, or in the Manner herein after directed, all the other Colonies shall guarantee to such Colony the full and peaceable Possession of, and the free and entire Jurisdiction in and over the Territory included within such Boundaries.~~

~~The Assembly of the united states to publish the Journal of their Proceedings monthly, except such Parts thereof relating to Treaties, Alliances, or military Operations, as in their Judgment require Secrecy-The Yeas and Nays of the Delegates of each Colony on any Question to he entered on the Journal, where it is desired by any Delegate; and the Delegates of a Colony, or any of them, at his or their Request, to be furnished with a Transcript of the said Journal, except such Parts as are above excepted, to lay before the Legislatures of the several Colonies.~~

Article X. [Recess Powers]

The committee of the states, or any nine of them, shall be authorized to execute, in the recess of congress, such of the powers of congress as the united states, in congress assembled, by the consent of nine states, shall, from time to time, think expedient to vest them with; provided that no power be delegated to the said committee, for the exercise of which, by the articles of confederation, the voice of nine states, in the congress of the united states assembled, is requisite.

Article XI. [Admission of New States]

Canada[14] acceding to this confederation, and ~~*entirely*~~ joining in the measures of the united ~~*Colonies*~~ states, shall be admitted into, and entitled to all the advantages of this union: but no other colony shall be admitted into the same, unless such admission be agreed to by ~~*the Delegates of*~~ nine ~~*Colonies*~~ states.[15]

Article XII. [Assumption of Debt and Credit]

All bills of credit emitted, monies borrowed, and debts contracted by or under the authority of congress, before the assembling of the united states, in pursuance of the present confederation, shall be deemed and considered as a charge against the united states, for payment and satisfaction whereof the said united states and the public faith are hereby solemnly pledged.

JOHN DICKINSON: I wonder if we shouldn't add an article prohibiting the importation of slaves.

[Unlike the Constitution and Articles of Association, the Articles of Confederation are largely silent on slavery, leaving the issue to the states. There are brief references to "free inhabitants" and "property imported into any state" in Article IV, and a reference to "white inhabitants" in Article IX. Many slave states passed laws allowing slavery, concerned that courts would outlaw slavery after the English case Somerset v. Stewart *(1772) effectively ended slavery in England on the basis that there was no positive English law allowing slavery in England.]*

Article XIII. [Supremacy; Perpetual Existence; Amendments]

Every ~~*Colony*~~ State shall abide by the determinations of the united states, in congress assembled, ~~*concerning the Services performed and Losses or Expences incurred by every Colony for the common Defence or general Welfare, and no Colony or Colonies shall in any Case whatever endeavor by Force to procure Redress of any Injury or Injustice supposed to be done by the United States to such Colony or Colonies in not granting such Satisfactions, Indemnifications, Compensations, Retributions, Exemptions, or Benefits of any Kind, as such Colony or Colonies may think just or reasonable*~~ on all questions which by this confederation are submitted to them.

~~*These Articles shall be proposed to the Legislatures of all the United Colonies, to be by them considered, and if approved by them, they are advised to authorize their Delegates to ratify the same in the Assembly of the United States, which being done, the foregoing*~~

---

14. Many colonists hoped that Canada would join the call for independence and join the Union (a particular obsession for Jefferson).

15. Note that Article XI appears to admit Canada automatically if it consents, and requires nine existing states to agree to the admission of other new states. This was either a substantial oversight (What happens when there are 20, 30, or more states? Is the agreement of only nine states—a minority—enough to admit new states?) or there was perhaps a view that most new land would be considered a *territory* and not a state. The Constitution fixes this by requiring a majority vote in Congress instead of a specific number of states. *See* p. 157.

And the Articles of this confederation shall be inviolably *be* observed by every ~~Colony~~ state, and the union ~~*is to*~~ shall be perpetual~~:~~;[16] nor shall any alteration *be* at any time hereafter be made in ~~*these Articles or*~~ any of them, unless such alteration be agreed to in ~~*an Assembly*~~ a congress of the united states, and be afterwards confirmed by the legislatures of every ~~Colony~~ state.

And Whereas it hath pleased the Great Governor of the World to incline the hearts of the legislatures we respectively represent in congress, to approve of, and to authorize us to ratify the said articles of confederation and perpetual union, **Know Ye,** that we, the undersigned delegates, by virtue of the power and authority to us given for that purpose, do, by these presents, in the name and in behalf of our respective constituents, fully and entirely ratify and confirm each and every of the said articles of confederation and perpetual union, and all and singular the matters and things therein contained. And we do further solemnly plight and engage the faith of our respective constituents, that they shall abide by the determinations of the united states in congress assembled, on all questions, which by the said confederation are submitted to them. And that the articles thereof shall be inviolably observed by the states we respectively represent, and that the union shall be perpetual. In Witness whereof, we have hereunto set our hands, in Congress. Done at Philadelphia, in the state of Pennsylvania, the ninth Day of July, in the Year of our Lord one Thousand seven Hundred and Seventy eight, and in the third year of the Independence of America.

~~*Resolved, That eighty copies, and no more, of the confederation, as brought in by the committee, be immediately printed, and deposited with the secretary, who shall deliver one copy to each member:*~~

~~*That a committee of be appointed to superintend the press, who shall talk care that the foregoing resolution [unfinished]*~~

~~*That the printer be under oath to deliver all the copies, which he shall print, together with the copy sheet, to the secretary, and not to disclose either directly or indirectly, the contents of the said confederation:*~~

---

16. Notice that the Articles were supposed to be "perpetual," and could not be amended without unanimous agreement. But the new Constitution was initially approved *without* unanimous agreement (only requiring nine states to ratify, *see* p. 160). Thus, so far by the ratification of the 1787 Constitution we have (1) treason by declaring independence from Britain, and (2) a Constitution that might technically be unconstitutional. Many policy arguments have been made to justify the Constitution's legitimacy, including arguments based on necessity, popular sovereignty (citizens voted to ratify the Constitution, but not the Articles), and subsequent ratification/acquiescence by all states.

[Signed:][17]

CONNECTICUT
Roger Sherman,
Samuel Huntington,
Oliver Wolcott,
Titus Hosmer,
Andrew Adams

DELAWARE
Thomas McKean,
John Dickinson,
Nicholas Van Dyke

GEORGIA
John Walton,
Edward Telfair,
Edward Langworthy

MARYLAND
John Hanson,
Daniel Carroll

MASSACHUSETTS BAY
John Hancock,
Samuel Adams,
Elbridge Gerry,
Francis Dana,
James Lovell,
Samuel Holten

NEW HAMPSHIRE
Josiah Bartlett,
John Wentworth Jr.

NEW JERSEY
John Witherspoon,
Nathaniel Scudder

NEW YORK
James Duane,
Francis Lewis,
William Duer,
Gouverneur Morris

NORTH CAROLINA
John Penn,
Cornelius Harnett,
John Williams

PENNSYLVANIA
Robert Morris,
Daniel Roberdeau,
Jonathan Bayard Smith,
William Clingan,
Joseph Reed

RHODE ISLAND AND PROVIDENCE PLANTATIONS
William Ellery,
Henry Marchant,
John Collins

SOUTH CAROLINA
Henry Laurens,
William Henry Drayton,
John Mathews,
Richard Hutson,
Thomas Heyward Jr.

VIRGINIA
Richard Henry Lee,
John Banister,
Thomas Adams,
John Harvie,
Francis Lightfoot Lee

---

17. After approving the Articles, Congress ordered 300 copies to be printed and disseminated to the states. Congress then moved to other business, including creating a committee to "collect and digest the late useful discoveries for making molasses and spirits from the juice of corn stalks, and report a plan for communicating the said discoveries to the inhabitants of the several states."

Northwest Ordinance

(JULY 13, 1787)

Introduction

As described in the chapter on the Declaration of Rights and Grievances of 1765, the King had prohibited westward expansion of the colonies, including in the 1763 Royal Proclamation, which forbade any settlement west of the Appalachian Mountains. England ceded some western lands to the United States after the Revolutionary War, and the Confederated Congress[1] passed the Northwest Ordinance on July 13, 1787, to manage the land.

The Ordinance established the first U.S. territory outside of the thirteen colonies. The Northwest Territory was south of the Great Lakes and north of the Mississippi and Ohio rivers, consisting of what would become Ohio, Indiana, Illinois, Michigan, Wisconsin, and part of Minnesota. Importantly, Congress passed the Northwest Ordinance while the Constitutional Convention was convening (May 25 to September 17, 1787).[2] It was not clear at all that under the Articles of Con-

1. Congress is referred to as the Confederated Congress at this time because it was operating under the Articles of Confederation. After ratification of the Constitution, Congress passed the Northwest Ordinance Act of 1789 to bring the Ordinance into harmony with the new Constitution.

2. Delegates to the Convention had copies of the Ordinance and referenced it during the proceedings. Some even left the Convention so that Congress would have a quorum to vote on the Northwest Ordinance.

federation the Confederated Congress had the power to manage the Northwest Territory in the way it did. The Constitution fixes this in the Territories Clause, Article I, § 3. *See* p. 157.

Under the Ordinance, Congress directly administered the territory (an early foray into federalism) and laid the groundwork for the admission of new states. It assured that territories would not be forced to remain territories forever. Initially, the territory would be overseen by a governor, a secretary, and three judges (who had life tenure) appointed by Congress. Once the territory reached a population of 5,000 free male inhabitants, it could elect a territorial legislature. When the population reached 60,000, the territory could draft a state constitution and apply for statehood, on an equal footing with the original states.

After experiencing mistreatment by a foreign power as colonists, the Confederate Congress vowed in the Northwest Ordinance to do better than that for its territories. In addition to the "equal footing" provision described above, the Ordinance included a bill of rights guaranteeing freedom of religion, the right to a trial by jury, a prohibition against takings without just compensation, and other civil liberties. It prohibited excessive fines and cruel or unusual punishment, and included a protection for the writ of habeas corpus. It encouraged the establishment of schools and stressed the importance of education for good governance and the happiness of mankind. The Ordinance stated that the utmost good faith would always be observed towards Native Americans, and their lands and property would not be taken without their consent, although this principle was often violated in practice.

The Ordinance prohibited slavery and involuntary servitude in the Northwest Territory, except as punishment for crimes.[3] This set the stage for many disputes about slavery in America, and the Ohio River became a de facto barrier between free and slave states. Some have argued that the Northwest Ordinance kept slavery out of Northern states, states that might have otherwise ultimately been slave states. Without the Ordinance's prohibition of slavery, and with the balance of free and slave states tipped even more in favor of slave states, 19th-century America might have looked very different.

Notice that the first clause of Article Six of the Northwest Ordinance is virtually identical to the Thirteenth Amendment and the rest of Article Six is the

---

3. In 1784, Thomas Jefferson drafted an ordinance similar to the Northwest Ordinance, but before its passing Congress struck the antislavery provision from Jefferson's draft.

Fugitive Slave Clause that would appear in the Constitution. It is notable that the latter made it into the original Constitution, but not the former.

> NORTHWEST ORDINANCE: There shall be neither slavery nor involuntary servitude in the said territory, otherwise than in the punishment of crimes whereof the party shall have been duly convicted.
>
> THIRTEENTH AMENDMENT: Neither slavery nor involuntary servitude, except as a punishment for crime whereof the party shall have been duly convicted, shall exist within the United States, or any place subject to their jurisdiction.
>
> NORTHWEST ORDINANCE: Provided, always, That any person escaping into the same, from whom labor or service is lawfully claimed in any one of the original States, such fugitive may be lawfully reclaimed and conveyed to the person claiming his or her labor or service as aforesaid.
>
> ARTICLE IV, SECTION 2, CLAUSE 3: No Person held to Service or Labour in one State, under the Laws thereof, escaping into another, shall, in Consequence of any Law or Regulation therein, be discharged from such Service or Labour, but shall be delivered up on Claim of the Party to whom such Service or Labour may be due.

By putting these important documents next to each other, we see that the Articles of Association prohibited the importation of slaves, the Articles of Confederation are silent on the issue, the Northwest Ordinance bans all slavery in the Northwest Territory, and the Constitution *prevents* Congress from banning of the importation of slavery for twenty years after ratification.

Ultimately, the Ordinance established a blueprint for the orderly expansion and governance of new territories, which influenced the constitutional framework for handling the admission of new states. It significantly influenced the drafting of the Constitution in other important ways like underscoring the authority of the federal government, protecting civil liberties, and trying to address the contentious issue of slavery. According to some scholars, the Ordinance expressed the sentiment that slavery would be contained to existing states, and that westward expansion of America would entail freedom, not slavery.[4]

---

4. To the extent that this sentiment existed in 1787, it was short-lived, and slavery expanded into new states through subsequent acts and compromises. Several theories have been suggested to explain why the Southern states voted (unanimously) in favor of the Northwest Ordinance. They could have seen the compromise as worthwhile in that it tacitly guaranteed slavery south of the Ohio and

An Ordinance for the Government of the Territory of the United States Northwest of the River Ohio

Section 1. Be it ordained by the United States in Congress assembled, That the said territory, for the purposes of temporary government, be one district, subject, however, to be divided into two districts, as future circumstances may, in the opinion of Congress, make it expedient.

Sec 2. Be it ordained by the authority aforesaid, That the estates, both of resident and nonresident proprietors in the said territory, dying intestate, shall descent to, and be distributed among their children, and the descendants of a deceased child, in equal parts; the descendants of a deceased child or grandchild to take the share of their deceased parent in equal parts among them: And where there shall be no children or descendants, then in equal parts to the next of kin in equal degree; and among collaterals, the children of a deceased brother or sister of the intestate shall have, in equal parts among them, their deceased parents' share; and there shall in no case be a distinction between kindred of the whole and half blood; saving, in all cases, to the widow of the intestate her third part of the real estate for life, and one third part of the personal estate; and this law relative to descents and dower, shall remain in full force until altered by the legislature of the district. And until the governor and judges shall adopt laws as hereinafter mentioned, estates in the said territory may be devised or bequeathed by wills in writing, signed and sealed by him or her in whom the estate may be (being of full age), and attested by three witnesses; and real estates may be conveyed by lease and release, or bargain and sale, signed, sealed and delivered by the person being of full age, in whom the estate may be, and attested by two witnesses, provided such wills be duly proved, and such conveyances be acknowledged, or the execution thereof duly proved, and be recorded within one year after proper magistrates, courts, and registers shall be appointed for that purpose; and personal property may be transferred by delivery; saving, however to the French and Canadian inhabitants, and other settlers of the Kaskaskies, St. Vincents and the neighboring villages who have heretofore pro-

---

Mississippi rivers. It also might have been seen as protectionist—as there would be no risk of slave labor in the North competing with slave labor in the South. There might have been handshake agreements for concessions in the forthcoming Constitution, like the Three-Fifths Clause.

fessed themselves citizens of Virginia, their laws and customs now in force among them, relative to the descent and conveyance, of property.

Sec. 3. Be it ordained by the authority aforesaid, That there shall be appointed from time to time by Congress, a governor, whose commission shall continue in force for the term of three years, unless sooner revoked by Congress; he shall reside in the district, and have a freehold estate therein in 1,000 acres of land, while in the exercise of his office.

Sec. 4. There shall be appointed from time to time by Congress, a secretary, whose commission shall continue in force for four years unless sooner revoked; he shall reside in the district, and have a freehold estate therein in 500 acres of land, while in the exercise of his office. It shall be his duty to keep and preserve the acts and laws passed by the legislature, and the public records of the district, and the proceedings of the governor in his executive department, and transmit authentic copies of such acts and proceedings, every six months, to the Secretary of Congress: There shall also be appointed a court to consist of three judges, any two of whom to form a court, who shall have a common law jurisdiction, and reside in the district, and have each therein a freehold estate in 500 acres of land while in the exercise of their offices; and their commissions shall continue in force during good behavior.

Sec. 5. The governor and judges, or a majority of them, shall adopt and publish in the district such laws of the original States, criminal and civil, as may be necessary and best suited to the circumstances of the district, and report them to Congress from time to time: which laws shall be in force in the district until the organization of the General Assembly therein, unless disapproved of by Congress; but afterwards the Legislature shall have authority to alter them as they shall think fit.

Sec. 6. The governor, for the time being, shall be commander in chief of the militia, appoint and commission all officers in the same below the rank of general officers; all general officers shall be appointed and commissioned by Congress.

Sec. 7. Previous to the organization of the general assembly, the governor shall appoint such magistrates and other civil officers in each county or township, as he shall find necessary for the preservation of the peace and good order in the same: After the general assembly shall be organized, the powers and duties of the magistrates and other civil officers shall be regulated and defined by the said assembly; but all magistrates and other civil officers not herein otherwise directed, shall during the continuance of this temporary government, be appointed by the governor.

Sec. 8. For the prevention of crimes and injuries, the laws to be adopted or made shall have force in all parts of the district, and for the execution of process, criminal and civil, the governor shall make proper divisions thereof; and he shall proceed from time to time as circumstances may require, to lay out the parts of the district in which the Indian titles shall have been extinguished, into counties and townships, subject, however, to such alterations as may thereafter be made by the legislature.

Sec. 9. So soon as there shall be five thousand free male inhabitants of full age in the district, upon giving proof thereof to the governor, they shall receive authority, with time and place, to elect a representative from their counties or townships to represent them in the general assembly: Provided, That, for every five hundred free male inhabitants, there shall be one representative, and so on progressively with the number of free male inhabitants shall the right of representation increase, until the number of representatives shall amount to twenty five; after which, the number and proportion of representatives shall be regulated by the legislature: Provided, That no person be eligible or qualified to act as a representative unless he shall have been a citizen of one of the United States three years, and be a resident in the district, or unless he shall have resided in the district three years; and, in either case, shall likewise hold in his own right, in fee simple, two hundred acres of land within the same; Provided, also, That a freehold in fifty acres of land in the district, having been a citizen of one of the states, and being resident in the district, or the like freehold and two years residence in the district, shall be necessary to qualify a man as an elector of a representative.[5]

Sec. 10. The representatives thus elected, shall serve for the term of two years; and, in case of the death of a representative, or removal from office, the governor shall issue a writ to the county or township for which he was a member, to elect another in his stead, to serve for the residue of the term.

Sec. 11. The general assembly or legislature shall consist of the governor, legislative council, and a house of representatives. The Legislative Council shall consist of five members, to continue in office five years, unless sooner removed by Congress; any three of whom to be a quorum: and the members of the Council shall be nominated and appointed in the following manner, to wit: As soon as representatives shall be elected, the Governor shall appoint a time and place

5. Compare this requirement for representatives to own land to the debate at the Constitutional Convention, p. 141.

for them to meet together; and, when met, they shall nominate ten persons, residents in the district, and each possessed of a freehold in five hundred acres of land, and return their names to Congress; five of whom Congress shall appoint and commission to serve as aforesaid; and, whenever a vacancy shall happen in the council, by death or removal from office, the house of representatives shall nominate two persons, qualified as aforesaid, for each vacancy, and return their names to Congress; one of whom congress shall appoint and commission for the residue of the term. And every five years, four months at least before the expiration of the time of service of the members of council, the said house shall nominate ten persons, qualified as aforesaid, and return their names to Congress; five of whom Congress shall appoint and commission to serve as members of the council five years, unless sooner removed. And the governor, legislative council, and house of representatives, shall have authority to make laws in all cases, for the good government of the district, not repugnant to the principles and articles in this ordinance established and declared. And all bills, having passed by a majority in the house, and by a majority in the council, shall be referred to the governor for his assent; but no bill, or legislative act whatever, shall be of any force without his assent. The governor shall have power to convene, prorogue, and dissolve the general assembly, when, in his opinion, it shall be expedient.

Sec. 12. The governor, judges, legislative council, secretary, and such other officers as Congress shall appoint in the district, shall take an oath or affirmation of fidelity and of office; the governor before the president of congress, and all other officers before the Governor. As soon as a legislature shall be formed in the district, the council and house assembled in one room, shall have authority, by joint ballot, to elect a delegate to Congress, who shall have a seat in Congress, with a right of debating but not voting during this temporary government.

Sec. 13. And, for extending the fundamental principles of civil and religious liberty, which form the basis whereon these republics, their laws and constitutions are erected; to fix and establish those principles as the basis of all laws, constitutions, and governments, which forever hereafter shall be formed in the said territory: to provide also for the establishment of States, and permanent government therein, and for their admission to a share in the federal councils on an equal footing with the original States, at as early periods as may be consistent with the general interest:

Sec. 14. It is hereby ordained and declared by the authority aforesaid, That the following articles shall be considered as articles of compact between the original States and the people and States in the said territory and forever remain unalterable, unless by common consent, to wit:[6]

Art. 1. No person, demeaning himself in a peaceable and orderly manner, shall ever be molested on account of his mode of worship or religious sentiments, in the said territory.

Art. 2. The inhabitants of the said territory shall always be entitled to the benefits of the writ of habeas corpus, and of the trial by jury; of a proportionate representation of the people in the legislature; and of judicial proceedings according to the course of the common law. All persons shall be bailable, unless for capital offenses, where the proof shall be evident or the presumption great. All fines shall be moderate; and no cruel or unusual punishments shall be inflicted. No man shall be deprived of his liberty or property, but by the judgment of his peers or the law of the land; and, should the public exigencies make it necessary, for the common preservation, to take any person's property, or to demand his particular services, full compensation shall be made for the same. And, in the just preservation of rights and property, it is understood and declared, that no law ought ever to be made, or have force in the said territory, that shall, in any manner whatever, interfere with or affect private contracts or engagements, bona fide, and without fraud, previously formed.[7]

Art. 3. Religion, morality, and knowledge, being necessary to good government and the happiness of mankind, schools and the means of education shall forever be encouraged. The utmost good faith shall always be observed towards the Indians; their lands and property shall never be taken from them without their consent; and, in their property, rights, and liberty, they shall never be invaded or disturbed, unless in just and lawful wars authorized by Congress; but laws founded in justice and humanity, shall from time to time be made for preventing wrongs being done to them, and for preserving peace and friendship with them.

Art. 4. The said territory, and the States which may be formed therein, shall forever remain a part of this Confederacy of the United States of America, subject to the Articles of Confederation, and to such alterations therein as shall be

---

6. Virtually all of these articles end up as protections in either the original Constitution or the Bill of Rights.

7. This provision prohibiting interference with private contracts was included in the Constitution—even after the delegates rejected it and used alternative language. *See* p. 147.

constitutionally made; and to all the acts and ordinances of the United States in Congress assembled, conformable thereto. The inhabitants and settlers in the said territory shall be subject to pay a part of the federal debts contracted or to be contracted, and a proportional part of the expenses of government, to be apportioned on them by Congress according to the same common rule and measure by which apportionments thereof shall be made on the other States; and the taxes for paying their proportion shall be laid and levied by the authority and direction of the legislatures of the district or districts, or new States, as in the original States, within the time agreed upon by the United States in Congress assembled. The legislatures of those districts or new States, shall never interfere with the primary disposal of the soil by the United States in Congress assembled, nor with any regulations Congress may find necessary for securing the title in such soil to the bona fide purchasers. No tax shall be imposed on lands the property of the United States; and, in no case, shall nonresident proprietors be taxed higher than residents. The navigable waters leading into the Mississippi and St. Lawrence, and the carrying places between the same, shall be common highways and forever free, as well to the inhabitants of the said territory as to the citizens of the United States, and those of any other States that may be admitted into the confederacy, without any tax, impost, or duty therefor.

Art. 5. There shall be formed in the said territory, not less than three nor more than five States; and the boundaries of the States, as soon as Virginia shall alter her act of cession, and consent to the same, shall become fixed and established as follows, to wit: The western State in the said territory, shall be bounded by the Mississippi, the Ohio, and Wabash Rivers; a direct line drawn from the Wabash and Post Vincents, due North, to the territorial line between the United States and Canada; and, by the said territorial line, to the Lake of the Woods and Mississippi. The middle State shall be bounded by the said direct line, the Wabash from Post Vincents to the Ohio, by the Ohio, by a direct line, drawn due north from the mouth of the Great Miami, to the said territorial line, and by the said territorial line. The eastern State shall be bounded by the last mentioned direct line, the Ohio, Pennsylvania, and the said territorial line: Provided, however, and it is further understood and declared, that the boundaries of these three States shall be subject so far to be altered, that, if Congress shall hereafter find it expedient, they shall have authority to form one or two States in that part of the said territory which lies north of an east and west line drawn through the southerly bend or extreme of Lake Michigan. And, whenever any of the said States shall have sixty thousand free inhabitants therein, such State shall be admitted, by its delegates, into the Congress of the United States, on an equal footing with the original States in all respects whatever, and shall be at liberty to form a permanent constitution and State government: Provided, the constitution and government so to be formed, shall be republican, and in conformity to the principles contained in these articles; and, so far as it can be consistent with the general interest of the confederacy, such admission shall be allowed at an earlier period, and when there may be a less number of free inhabitants in the State than sixty thousand.

Art. 6. There shall be neither slavery nor involuntary servitude in the said territory, otherwise than in the punishment of crimes whereof the party shall have been duly convicted: Provided, always, That any person escaping into the same, from whom labor or service is lawfully claimed in any one of the original States, such fugitive may be lawfully reclaimed and conveyed to the person claiming his or her labor or service as aforesaid.

Be it ordained by the authority aforesaid, That the resolutions of the 23rd of April, 1784, relative to the subject of this ordinance, be, and the same are hereby repealed and declared null and void.

Done by the United States, in Congress assembled, the 13th day of July, in the year of our Lord 1787, and of their sovereignty and independence the twelfth.

Constitution of the United States—Redlined

(SEPTEMBER 17, 1787)

Introduction

The Constitution of the United States is generally considered to be the most influential legal document ever created. It is an agreement of "We the People" to enshrine our core principles, establish and operate a government, grant and restrict government powers, manage relationships between the states, and protect certain rights and interests. The Declaration severed ties between Britain and the colonists, who were then returned to the state of nature and free to enter into new contracts for government. Because, at least as Thomas Hobbes posited, life in the state of nature is "solitary, poor, nasty, brutish, and short," and people are inclined to band together to give up some of their freedoms for the protection of rights and interests, colonists turned to creating state governments for this purpose. The Articles then tried to arrange some affairs between states, but not people. In the 1787 Constitution, the *states* gave up some of their power to a national government. The great reimagining of the federal government as a protector of individual liberties (even protecting against state intrusion) was not widely recognized until after the Reconstruction Amendments (what historian Eric Foner described as the "Second Founding").

As this book shows, the Framers did not create the 1787 Constitution from scratch. They looked to enlightenment thinkers, earlier American documents, the British system of government, and the state constitutions. Toward the end of the eighteenth century, America had prevailed in the Revolutionary War, but it was clear that the Articles of Confederation were failing the young country. The states were nearing economic disaster, and without a sufficient central government, disputes over territory, treaties, taxation, and trade threatened the termination of the American experiment. Congress could not compel the states to contribute money to the national treasury, could not control commerce between the states or with foreign nations, and could not even assemble a quorum to conduct business much of the time. Congress convened a Constitutional Convention (May 25 to September 17, 1787) to study solutions to the problem. The Convention first considered amending the Articles of Confederation but ultimately (and controversially) decided to create an entirely new constitution.

The Convention appointed members to the Committee of Detail (Oliver Ellsworth, Nathaniel Gorham, Edmund Randolph, John Rutledge, and James Wilson) to summarize principles that were largely agreed upon at the Convention. On August 6, 1787, the Committee of Detail produced a draft to the Convention. The Convention deliberated over the draft and made several changes. This book tracks the changes between the "proof copy" of that draft (delivered to the Convention on August 5–6) and the final, engrossed (written) version of the Constitution.

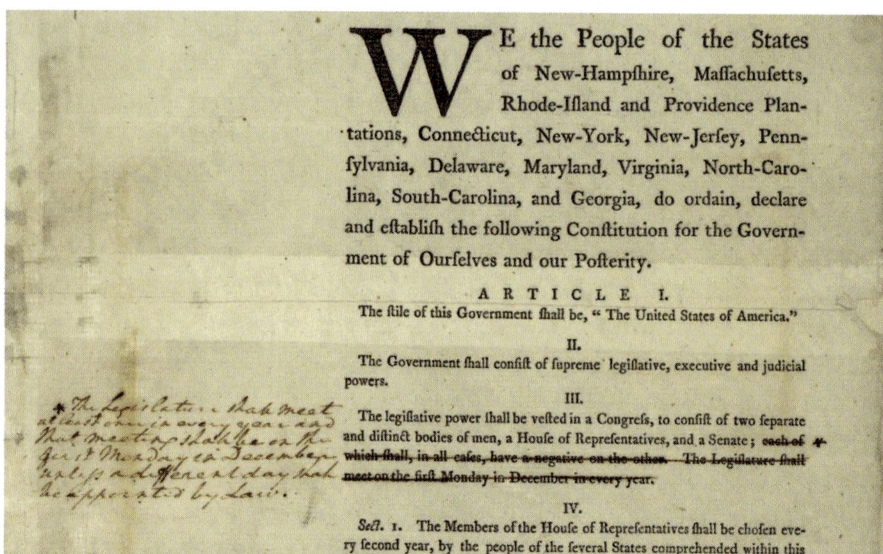

WE the People of the States of New-Hampſhire, Maſſachuſetts, Rhode-Iſland and Providence Plantations, Connecticut, New-York, New-Jerſey, Pennſylvania, Delaware, Maryland, Virginia, North-Carolina, South-Carolina, and Georgia, do ordain, declare and eſtabliſh the following Conſtitution for the Government of Ourſelves and our Poſterity.

ARTICLE I.

The ſtile of this Government ſhall be, "The United States of America."

II.

The Government ſhall conſiſt of ſupreme legiſlative, executive and judicial powers.

III.

The legiſlative power ſhall be veſted in a Congreſs, to conſiſt of two ſeparate and diſtinct bodies of men, a Houſe of Repreſentatives, and a Senate; ~~each of which ſhall, in all caſes, have a negative on the other. The Legiſlature ſhall meet on the firſt Monday in December in every year.~~ *

* The Legislature shall meet at least once in every year, and that meeting shall be on the first Monday in December, unless a different day shall be appointed by Law.

IV.

Sect. 1. The Members of the Houſe of Repreſentatives ſhall be choſen every ſecond year, by the people of the ſeveral States comprehended within this

Excerpt from George Washington's annotated Committee of Detail draft

Throughout the Convention, local printers Dunlap & Claypoole had been printing drafts for use by the delegates, including the August 6 Committee of Detail draft. After all agreements had been reached and revisions made, the provisions were sent to the Committee of Style (William Samuel Johnson, Alexander Hamilton, Gouverneur Morris, James Madison, and Rufus King) to combine everything and ensure uniformity. The Committee of Style worked with Dunlap & Claypoole to print near-final versions of the Constitution in mid-September, which went back to the Convention for final revisions.

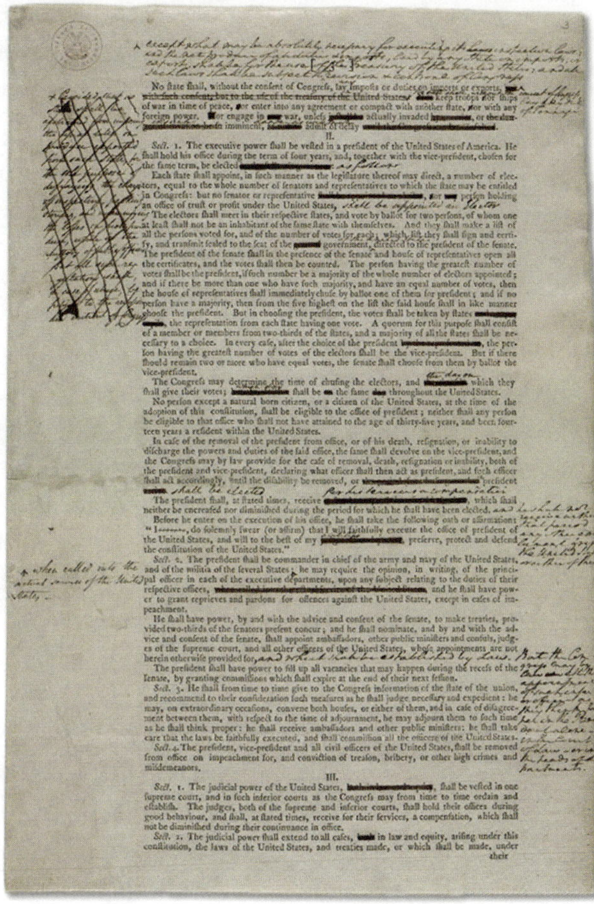

Excerpt from George Washington's annotated copy of Committee of Style draft

On September 15, the Convention had made all of its major agreements on a final constitution and instructed scribe Jacob Shallus to complete an engrossed copy. The Convention also had Dunlap & Claypoole print 500 copies of the final Constitution for distribution to the delegates of the Convention.

Shallus presented the beautiful, engrossed Constitution to the Convention on September 17, and after a last-minute change to representation in the House (from a maximum of 40,000 to 30,000, *see* p. 138), the Convention approved and signed the Constitution that same day. State ratification conventions followed.

America has been inconsistent regarding which document is the "official" version of the Constitution. Is it the engrossed and signed version that Americans are familiar with and is prominently displayed at the National Archives? Is it the version that appears in the statute books? (The statute books have varied on which version they use.) Some other version? Surprisingly, this has been an unsettled question for generations, and variations between versions crept in due to stylistic differences between printers, spelling and punctuation preferences, or typesetting errors. These were, of course, copied and typeset by hand, so mistakes and variations are inevitable. For legally binding documents (particularly, the United States Constitution), it goes without saying that it is crucial to identify the actual document that is binding.

Let us take inventory. As discussed above, by September 15, 1787, the Convention had made all of its major agreements on a final constitution and instructed Jacob Shallus to complete an engrossed copy (the "Engrossed Version."). It also hired Dunlap & Claypoole to print 500 copies of the final Constitution for use among the delegates (the "Convention Version"). It does not appear that the new Convention Versions were circulated to the delegates before their final deliberation and vote on September 17. Therefore, in voting to approve the Constitution the delegates likely either reviewed the single Engrossed Version or (more likely) their existing September 12 Committee of Style version (marked up as necessary). On September 18, the final 500 printed copies of Dunlap & Claypoole's Convention Version were completed and distributed to the remaining delegates.[1] But by this point, the delegates had already voted on and approved the Constitution. The Convention Version differs in spelling and punctuation from the Engrossed Version.

Recall that the Convention was a creature of Congress, and the full Congress was still needed to send any new Constitution to the states for ratification. Congress was convening in New York at the time, and the "Report of the Convention" (consisting of the Engrossed Constitution, ratification resolution, and letter from George Washington) reached New York on September 20. On September 28, Congress voted unanimously to send the Constitution to the states and authorized the printing of yet another 100 copies to be sent to the states (the "Congress Version"). Subsequent comparisons (including mine) reveal that the Congress Version was based on Convention Version, as its variations—some of which are unique—track much closer to the Convention Version than the Engrossed Version.

The states reprinted the Congress Version for distribution to their citizens for potential ratification. (Those also had variants.) Only one original Congress Version is known to exist; it was found in a Resolve Book of the Office of Foreign Affairs covering the term of John Jay (as Secretary of Foreign Affairs) from May 7, 1784, to January 15, 1790. The Congress Version was reprinted in a 1961 Senate Report and the original is now available at the National Archives:

---

1. Only thirteen copies of the Convention Version are known to exist, and a copy sold in 2021 for $43.2 million.

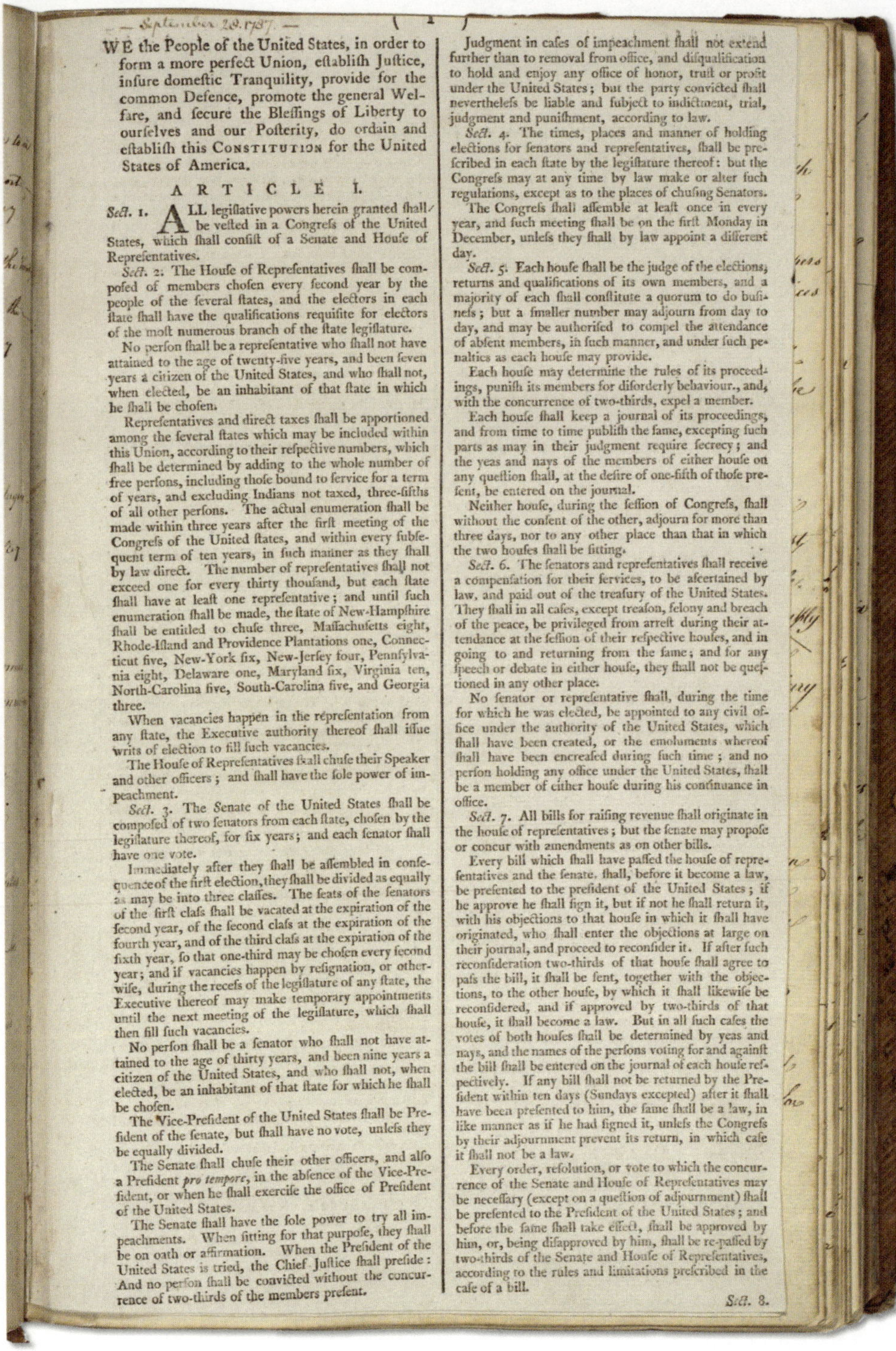

— September 28. 1787. — (1)

WE the People of the United States, in order to form a more perfect Union, eſtabliſh Juſtice, inſure domeſtic Tranquility, provide for the common Defence, promote the general Welfare, and ſecure the Bleſſings of Liberty to ourſelves and our Poſterity, do ordain and eſtabliſh this CONSTITUTION for the United States of America.

ARTICLE I.

Sect. 1. ALL legiſlative powers herein granted ſhall be veſted in a Congreſs of the United States, which ſhall conſiſt of a Senate and Houſe of Repreſentatives.

Sect. 2. The Houſe of Repreſentatives ſhall be compoſed of members choſen every ſecond year by the people of the ſeveral ſtates, and the electors in each ſtate ſhall have the qualifications requiſite for electors of the moſt numerous branch of the ſtate legiſlature.

No perſon ſhall be a repreſentative who ſhall not have attained to the age of twenty-five years, and been ſeven years a citizen of the United States, and who ſhall not, when elected, be an inhabitant of that ſtate in which he ſhall be choſen.

Repreſentatives and direct taxes ſhall be apportioned among the ſeveral ſtates which may be included within this Union, according to their reſpective numbers, which ſhall be determined by adding to the whole number of free perſons, including thoſe bound to ſervice for a term of years, and excluding Indians not taxed, three-fifths of all other perſons. The actual enumeration ſhall be made within three years after the firſt meeting of the Congreſs of the United ſtates, and within every ſubſequent term of ten years, in ſuch manner as they ſhall by law direct. The number of repreſentatives ſhall not exceed one for every thirty thouſand, but each ſtate ſhall have at leaſt one repreſentative; and until ſuch enumeration ſhall be made, the ſtate of New-Hampſhire ſhall be entitled to chuſe three, Maſſachuſetts eight, Rhode-Iſland and Providence Plantations one, Connecticut five, New-York ſix, New-Jerſey four, Pennſylvania eight, Delaware one, Maryland ſix, Virginia ten, North-Carolina five, South-Carolina five, and Georgia three.

When vacancies happen in the repreſentation from any ſtate, the Executive authority thereof ſhall iſſue writs of election to fill ſuch vacancies.

The Houſe of Repreſentatives ſhall chuſe their Speaker and other officers; and ſhall have the ſole power of impeachment.

Sect. 3. The Senate of the United States ſhall be compoſed of two ſenators from each ſtate, choſen by the legiſlature thereof, for ſix years; and each ſenator ſhall have one vote.

Immediately after they ſhall be aſſembled in conſequence of the firſt election, they ſhall be divided as equally as may be into three claſſes. The ſeats of the ſenators of the firſt claſs ſhall be vacated at the expiration of the ſecond year, of the ſecond claſs at the expiration of the fourth year, and of the third claſs at the expiration of the ſixth year, ſo that one-third may be choſen every ſecond year; and if vacancies happen by reſignation, or otherwiſe, during the receſs of the legiſlature of any ſtate, the Executive thereof may make temporary appointments until the next meeting of the legiſlature, which ſhall then fill ſuch vacancies.

No perſon ſhall be a ſenator who ſhall not have attained to the age of thirty years, and been nine years a citizen of the United States, and who ſhall not, when elected, be an inhabitant of that ſtate for which he ſhall be choſen.

The Vice-Preſident of the United States ſhall be Preſident of the ſenate, but ſhall have no vote, unleſs they be equally divided.

The Senate ſhall chuſe their other officers, and alſo a Preſident *pro tempore*, in the abſence of the Vice-Preſident, or when he ſhall exerciſe the office of Preſident of the United States.

The Senate ſhall have the ſole power to try all impeachments. When ſitting for that purpoſe, they ſhall be on oath or affirmation. When the Preſident of the United States is tried, the Chief Juſtice ſhall preſide: And no perſon ſhall be convicted without the concurrence of two-thirds of the members preſent.

Judgment in caſes of impeachment ſhall not extend further than to removal from office, and diſqualification to hold and enjoy any office of honor, truſt or profit under the United States; but the party convicted ſhall nevertheleſs be liable and ſubject to indictment, trial, judgment and puniſhment, according to law.

Sect. 4. The times, places and manner of holding elections for ſenators and repreſentatives, ſhall be preſcribed in each ſtate by the legiſlature thereof: but the Congreſs may at any time by law make or alter ſuch regulations, except as to the places of chuſing Senators.

The Congreſs ſhall aſſemble at leaſt once in every year, and ſuch meeting ſhall be on the firſt Monday in December, unleſs they ſhall by law appoint a different day.

Sect. 5. Each houſe ſhall be the judge of the elections, returns and qualifications of its own members, and a majority of each ſhall conſtitute a quorum to do buſineſs; but a ſmaller number may adjourn from day to day, and may be authoriſed to compel the attendance of abſent members, in ſuch manner, and under ſuch penalties as each houſe may provide.

Each houſe may determine the rules of its proceedings, puniſh its members for diſorderly behaviour, and, with the concurrence of two-thirds, expel a member.

Each houſe ſhall keep a journal of its proceedings, and from time to time publiſh the ſame, excepting ſuch parts as may in their judgment require ſecrecy; and the yeas and nays of the members of either houſe on any queſtion ſhall, at the deſire of one-fifth of thoſe preſent, be entered on the journal.

Neither houſe, during the ſeſſion of Congreſs, ſhall without the conſent of the other, adjourn for more than three days, nor to any other place than that in which the two houſes ſhall be ſitting.

Sect. 6. The ſenators and repreſentatives ſhall receive a compenſation for their ſervices, to be aſcertained by law, and paid out of the treaſury of the United States. They ſhall in all caſes, except treaſon, felony and breach of the peace, be privileged from arreſt during their attendance at the ſeſſion of their reſpective houſes, and in going to and returning from the ſame; and for any ſpeech or debate in either houſe, they ſhall not be queſtioned in any other place.

No ſenator or repreſentative ſhall, during the time for which he was elected, be appointed to any civil office under the authority of the United States, which ſhall have been created, or the emoluments whereof ſhall have been encreaſed during ſuch time; and no perſon holding any office under the United States, ſhall be a member of either houſe during his continuance in office.

Sect. 7. All bills for raiſing revenue ſhall originate in the houſe of repreſentatives; but the ſenate may propoſe or concur with amendments as on other bills.

Every bill which ſhall have paſſed the houſe of repreſentatives and the ſenate, ſhall, before it become a law, be preſented to the preſident of the United States; if he approve he ſhall ſign it, but if not he ſhall return it, with his objections to that houſe in which it ſhall have originated, who ſhall enter the objections at large on their journal, and proceed to reconſider it. If after ſuch reconſideration two-thirds of that houſe ſhall agree to paſs the bill, it ſhall be ſent, together with the objections, to the other houſe, by which it ſhall likewiſe be reconſidered, and if approved by two-thirds of that houſe, it ſhall become a law. But in all ſuch caſes the votes of both houſes ſhall be determined by yeas and nays, and the names of the perſons voting for and againſt the bill ſhall be entered on the journal of each houſe reſpectively. If any bill ſhall not be returned by the Preſident within ten days (Sundays excepted) after it ſhall have been preſented to him, the ſame ſhall be a law, in like manner as if he had ſigned it, unleſs the Congreſs by their adjournment prevent its return, in which caſe it ſhall not be a law.

Every order, reſolution, or vote to which the concurrence of the Senate and Houſe of Repreſentatives may be neceſſary (except on a queſtion of adjournment) ſhall be preſented to the Preſident of the United States; and before the ſame ſhall take effect, ſhall be approved by him, or, being diſapproved by him, ſhall be re-paſſed by two-thirds of the Senate and Houſe of Repreſentatives, according to the rules and limitations preſcribed in the caſe of a bill.

Sect. 8.

Excerpt from Resolve Book of the Office of Foreign Affairs

Over the years, Congress has relied on different documents as the "official" version. The Engrossed Version quickly went into storage once Congress could rely on printed copies, and various printed versions were relied upon (and reprinted, sometimes with variations) as official versions. The Engrossed Version gained popularity after it was displayed during centennial celebrations, and efforts were undertaken to perfectly transcribe the Engrossed Version and then rely on it as the "official" version. But because the Congress Version was the version that was sent to the states for ratification, most scholars today believe that the Congress Version (September 28, 1787) is the archetype or "correct" version of the Constitution. Accordingly, that version is included as the "clean" version at the end of this book. Other than the addition of space for the reader's notes, that text appears as it does in the September 28, 1787, Congress Version.

We the People of the United States, in Order to form a more perfect Union, establish Justice, insure domestic Tranquility, provide for the common defence, promote the general Welfare, and secure the Blessings of Liberty to ourselves and our Posterity, do ordain and establish this Constitution for the United States of America.

Article. I.

Section. 1. All legislative Powers herein granted shall be vested in a Congress of the United States, which shall consist of a Senate and House of Representatives.

Section. 2. The House of Representatives shall be composed of Members chosen every second Year by the People of the several States, and the Electors in each State shall have the Qualifications requisite for Electors of the most numerous Branch of the State Legislature.

No Person shall be a Representative who shall not have attained to the Age of twenty five Years, and been seven Years a Citizen of the United States, and who shall not, when elected, be an Inhabitant of that State in which he shall be chosen.

Representatives and direct Taxes shall be apportioned among the several States which may be included within this Union, according to their respective Numbers, which shall be determined by adding to the whole Number of free Persons, including those bound to Service for a Term of Years, and excluding Indians not taxed, three fifths of all other Persons. The actual Enumeration shall be made within three Years after the first Meeting of the Congress of the United States, and within every subsequent Term of ten Years, in such Manner as they shall by Law direct. The Number of Representatives shall not exceed one for every thirty Thousand, but each State shall have at Least one Representative; and until such enumeration shall be made, the State of New Hampshire shall be entitled to chuse three, Massachusetts eight, Rhode-Island and Providence Plantations one, Connecticut five, New-York six, New Jersey four, Pennsylvania eight, Delaware one, Maryland six, Virginia ten, North Carolina five, South Carolina five, and Georgia three.

When vacancies happen in the Representation from any State, the Executive Authority thereof shall issue Writs of Election to fill such Vacancies.

The House of Representatives shall chuse their Speaker and other Officers; and shall have the sole Power of Impeachment.

Section. 3. The Senate of the United States shall be composed of two Senators from each State, chosen by the Legislature thereof, for six Years; and each Senator shall have one Vote.

Immediately after they shall be assembled in Consequence of the first Election, they shall be divided as equally as may be into three Classes. The Seats of the Senators of the first Class shall be vacated at the Expiration of the second Year, of the second Class at the Expiration of the fourth Year, and of the third Class at the Expiration of the sixth Year, so that one third may be chosen every second Year; and if Vacancies happen by Resignation, or otherwise, during the Recess of the Legislature of any State, the Executive thereof may make temporary Appointments until the next Meeting of the Legislature, which shall then fill such Vacancies.

No Person shall be a Senator who shall not have attained to the Age of thirty Years, and been nine Years a Citizen of the United States, and who shall not, when elected, be an Inhabitant of that State for which he shall be chosen.

The Vice President of the United States shall be President of the Senate, but shall have no Vote, unless they be equally divided.

The Senate shall chuse their other Officers, and also a President pro tempore, in the Absence of the Vice President, or when he shall exercise the Office of President of the United States.

The Senate shall have the sole Power to try all Impeachments. When sitting for that Purpose, they shall be on Oath or Affirmation. When the President of the United States is tried, the Chief Justice shall preside: And no Person shall be convicted without the Concurrence of two thirds of the Members present.

Judgment in Cases of Impeachment shall not extend further than to removal from Office, and disqualification to hold and enjoy any Office of honor, Trust or Profit under the United States: but the Party convicted shall nevertheless be liable and subject to Indictment, Trial, Judgment and Punishment, according to Law.

Section. 4. The Times, Places and Manner of holding Elections for Senators and Representatives, shall be prescribed in each State by the Legislature thereof; but the Congress may at any time by Law make or alter such Regulations, except as to the Places of chusing Senators.

The Congress shall assemble at least once in every Year, and such Meeting shall be on the first Monday in December, unless they shall by Law appoint a different Day.

Section. 5. Each House shall be the Judge of the Elections, Returns and Qualifications of its own Members, and a Majority of each shall constitute a Quorum to do Business; but a smaller Number may adjourn from day to day, and may be authorized to compel the Attendance of absent Members, in such Manner, and under such Penalties as each House may provide.

Each House may determine the Rules of its Proceedings, punish its Members for disorderly Behaviour, and, with the Concurrence of two thirds, expel a Member.

Excerpt from Engrossed Constitution of the United States of America

In the margin commentary that follows, some of the views that are expressed are from after the Convention. (For example, from Thomas Jefferson, who was in France during the Convention.) Such commentary is identified with explanatory brackets. Additionally, Gouverneur Morris served in the Convention and on the Committee of Style, and he has interesting commentary from both of those roles (also indicated in brackets).

This book also includes the "forgotten" letter from George Washington to the President of Congress, transmitting the Constitution. The letter was intended to transmit the proposed Constitution from the Convention to the public, where it would undergo scrutiny and potential ratification by the states. It was a sales pitch to the public, similar to the forthcoming Federalist Papers. Washington's letter emphasized the necessity of a stronger central government and highlighted the inadequacies of the Articles of Confederation, particularly in areas such as making war, peace, treaties, levying money, and regulating commerce. The letter eloquently addressed the challenge of balancing state sovereignty with national unity, acknowledged the spirit of compromise that characterized the Constitutional Convention, and expressed hope that the new Constitution would promote a future of "lasting welfare" for the young country.

The Constitution of the United States of America

GOUVERNEUR MORRIS: *[Committee of Style revision]* Allow me to reword this Preamble to focus more on national unity.

PIERCE BUTLER: *[In 1788]* We had all of the great ancient and modern constitutions before us when drafting this Constitution. We looked at England's primarily, and improved on its weak points. We especially limited the executive's powers so that he is not a king.

Preamble

We the People[2] of the United States, ~~*states of New-Hampshire, Massachusetts, Rhode-Island and Providence Plantations, Connecticut, New-York, New-Jersey, Pennsylvania, Delaware, Maryland, Virginia, North-Carolina, South-Carolina, and Georgia,*~~ in Order to form a more perfect Union, establish Justice, insure domestic Tranquility, provide for the common defence, promote the general Welfare, and secure the Blessings of Liberty to ourselves and our Posterity, do ordain~~, *declare,*~~ and establish ~~*the following*~~ this Constitution for the United States of America ~~*government of ourselves and our posterity*~~.[3]

Article. I.
[*Legislative Branch*]

~~*The style of the Government shall be, "The United States of America."*~~

~~*The Government shall consist of supreme Legislative, Executive, and Judicial powers.*~~

GOUVERNEUR MORRIS: *[Committee of Style revision]* I have added "herein granted" to clarify that Congress's power is limited to what the Constitution provides, and I've changed "the" power to "all . . . powers." [[1]]

Section. 1. [Vesting Clause]

~~*The*~~ All legislative Powers herein granted[[1]][4] shall be vested in a Congress of the United States, which shall consist of a Senate and House of Representatives.

---

2. Among others, the Framers were inspired by John Locke and Jean-Jacques Rousseau's ideas of popular sovereignty and society as a contract between the people. ("We the People . . . do ordain.")

3. The Committee of Style was tasked with finalizing the document. The Committee reworded the Preamble and added six new objects. The revisions were substantial. (For example, the People of a unified nation vs. people of individual states.) Also compare this Preamble with the Preamble in the Articles of Confederation, which reveals this to be a much more nationalist document. *See* p. 104.

Several Supreme Court cases (*see, e.g.*, *Nixon v. United States* (1993); *Powell v. McCormack* (1969)) apply a presumption that the Committee of Style only made stylistic changes. Changes to the Preamble introduce interesting questions about that presumption. Soon after ratification, Supreme Court justices cited these added words to explain the object and structure of the Constitution. *See* *Chisholm v. Georgia* (1793). Today the Preamble is largely considered hortatory.

4. Desiring a strong executive and judiciary, Gouverneur Morris did not add this qualifier ("herein granted") to the vesting clauses of Articles II or III. Some scholars argue that Morris snuck

~~*to consist of two separate and distinct bodies of men, a House of Representatives and a Senate; each of which shall in all cases have a negative on the other.*~~

Section. 2. [House of Representatives][[2]]

The ~~*members of the*~~ House of Representatives shall be composed of Members chosen every second Year~~,~~ by the People of the several States, ~~*comprehended within this Union. The qualifications of the electors shall be the same from time to time, as those of the electors in the several States, of the most numerous branch of their own Legislatures*~~ and the Electors in each State shall have the Qualifications requisite for Electors of the most numerous Branch of the State Legislature.

No Person shall be a Representative who shall not have attained to the Age of twenty five Years, and been seven Years a Citizen of the United States, and who shall not, when elected, be an Inhabitant of that State in which he shall be chosen. ~~*Every member of the House of Representatives shall be of the age of twenty-five years at least; shall have been a citizen in the United States for at least three years before his election; and shall be, at the time of his election, a resident of the State in which he shall be chosen.*~~

Representatives and direct Taxes shall be apportioned among the several States which may be included within this Union, according to their respective Numbers, which shall be determined by adding to the whole Number of free Persons, including those bound to Service for a Term of Years, and excluding Indians not taxed, three fifths[[3]] of all other Persons.[5]

~~*The proportions of direct taxation shall be regulated by the whole number of white and other free citizens and inhabitants of every age, sex and condition, including those bound to servitude for a term of years, and three-fifths of all other persons not comprehended in the foregoing description, (except Indians not paying taxes); which number shall, within six years after the first*~~

WILLIAM PATERSON: States should be equally represented in Congress.[[2]]

EDMUND RANDOLPH: We should have a bicameral legislature with representation based on population or wealth.

ROGER SHERMAN AND OLIVER ELLSWORTH: Let's enter into a grand compromise: a bicameral legislature with an upper house of equal representation from each state, and a lower house with proportional representation based on a state's population.

JOHN DICKINSON: I've been proposing that for months.

[Passed 5 to 4 to 1.]

CHARLES COTESWORTH PINCKNEY: South Carolina and her slaves contribute massively to the American economy. We should be able to count our slaves in full, not some fraction of them.[[3]]

GOUVERNEUR MORRIS: No. You can't say that they are non-voting property but then count them as full citizens for apportionment purposes.

JAMES WILSON AND ROBERT SHERMAN: We propose a compromise: count three-fifths of the slave populations.

[Passed 6 to 2 to 2.]

in many such changes that his fellow delegates missed or did not consider significant.

5. The Thirteenth Amendment abolished slavery, and the Fourteenth Amendment (among other things) modified the Three-Fifths Clause. Although we can never know for sure, some have argued that Jefferson would have lost the close election of 1800 without the Three-Fifths Clause (increasing Southern voting power with the benefit of counting three fifths of the slave population). A majority of states in 1787 (8 of 13) were slave states, to some extent explaining the many slavery concessions in the Constitution.

GEORGE MASON: The people lack sufficient representation in the House.

NATHANIAL GORHAM: Perhaps, to lessen objection to the document, this could be 30,000 so that representatives have smaller districts and are more accountable to the people. Then we might be unanimous in approving the draft constitution.[[4]]

GEORGE WASHINGTON: *[The only time rising to speak in Convention]* I agree.

~~*meeting of the Legislature, and within the term of every ten years afterwards, be taken in such a manner as the said Legislature shall direct.*~~[6]

The actual Enumeration[7] shall be made within three Years after the first Meeting of the Congress of the United States, and within every subsequent Term of ten Years, in such Manner as they shall by Law direct. The Number of Representatives shall not exceed one for every thirty Thousand,[8] [[4]] but each State shall have at Least one Representative; and until such enumeration shall be made, the State of New Hampshire shall be entitled to chuse three, Massachusetts eight, Rhode-Island and Providence Plantations one, Connecticut five, New-York six, New Jersey four, Pennsylvania eight, Delaware one, Maryland six, Virginia ten, North Carolina five, South Carolina five, and Georgia three.

~~*As the proportions of numbers in different States will alter from time to time; as some of the States may hereafter be divided: as others may be enlarged by addition of territory; as two or more States may be united; as new States will be erected within the limits of the United States, the legislature shall, in each of these cases, regulate the number of Representatives by the number of inhabitants, according*~~

---

6. **Fourteenth Amendment § 2** [Equal Protection, Apportionment]: Representatives shall be apportioned among the several States according to their respective numbers, counting the whole number of persons in each State, excluding Indians not taxed. But when the right to vote at any election for the choice of electors for President and Vice-President of the United States, Representatives in Congress, the Executive and Judicial officers of a State, or the members of the Legislature thereof, is denied to any of the male inhabitants of such State, being twenty-one years of age, and citizens of the United States, or in any way abridged, except for participation in rebellion, or other crime, the basis of representation therein shall be reduced in the proportion which the number of such male citizens shall bear to the whole number of male citizens twenty-one years of age in such State.

Twenty-Sixth Amendment [Reduction in Voting Age]: The right of citizens of the United States, who are eighteen years of age or older, to vote shall not be denied or abridged by the United States or by any State on account of age.

7. Justice Stevens and Justice Thomas debated the Committee of Style's addition of "actual Enumeration" in *Utah v. Evans* (2002).

Justice Stevens: The Committee of Style lacked authority to change substance; adding "actual enumeration" merely distinguishes the census from the process of apportionment for the first Congress.

Justice Thomas: The ratified *text* is binding. The addition of "actual enumeration" explicitly rules out estimation.

8. This last-minute change from forty to thirty is clearly visible in the engrossed Constitution (which scribe Jacob Shallus notes, *see* p. 160): 

~~*to the provisions hereinafter made, at the rate of one for every forty thousand. The House of Representatives shall, at its first formation, and until the number of citizens and inhabitants shall be taken in the manner hereinafter described, consist of sixty-five members, of whom three shall be chosen in New-Hampshire, eight in Massachusetts, one in Rhode-Island and Providence Plantations, five in Connecticut, six in New-York, four in New-Jersey, eight in Pennsylvania, one in Delaware, six in Maryland, ten in Virginia, five in North-Carolina, five in South-Carolina, and three in Georgia.*~~

When vacancies happen in the Representation from any State, the Executive Authority thereof shall issue Writs of Election to fill such Vacancies. ~~*Vacancies in the House of Representatives shall be supplied by writs of election from the Executive authority of the state in the representation from which they shall happen.*~~

The House of Representatives shall ~~*have the sole power of impeachment. It shall choose its speaker and other officers*~~ chuse their Speaker and other Officers; and shall have the sole Power of Impeachment.

Section. 3. [Senate]

~~*The Senate of the United States shall have power to make treaties,*~~[[5]] ~~*and to appoint ambassadors, and Judges of the Supreme Court.*~~

The Senate of the United States shall be ~~*chosen by the Legislatures of the several States. Each Legislature shall choose two members*~~ composed of two Senators from each State, chosen by the Legislature thereof [[6]] [9] for six Years; and each Senator shall have one Vote.

~~*The Senators shall be chosen for six years; but*~~ Immediately after they shall be assembled in Consequence of the first Election, they shall be divided~~*, by lot,*~~ as ~~*nearly*~~ equally as may be into three Classes~~*, numbered one, two, and three*~~. The Seats of the ~~*members*~~ Senators of the first Class shall be vacated at the Expiration of the second Year~~;~~, of the second Class at the Expiration of the fourth Year~~;~~, and of the third Class at the Expiration of the sixth Year~~;~~, so that ~~*a*~~ one third ~~*part of the members*~~ may be chosen every second Year; ~~*Vacancies may be supplied by the*~~

9. **Seventeenth Amendment** [Popular Election of Senators]: The Senate of the United States shall be composed of two Senators from each State, elected by the people thereof, for six years; and each Senator shall have one vote. The electors in each State shall have the qualifications requisite for electors of the most numerous branch of the State legislatures. . . .

JAMES MADISON:
The President should be an agent in treaties. Also, we should consider that there are different types of treaties, so we might separate treaty power by type of treaty. [[5]]

CHARLES COTESWORTH PINCKNEY:
Having Congress approve treaties failed us under the Articles. We had to get nine states to approve a treaty, and if only nine states were present, the approval had to be unanimous (which was rare). Let's move this to the Executive, upon advice and consent of the Senate.

JAMES WILSON:
We should have popular election of senators, not "chosen by the Legislature" of the states.[[6]]

JAMES MADISON:
No, the version as drafted protects states' power and links the states and the federal government.

[Wilson's motion failed, but the Seventeenth Amendment adopts his view.]

GEORGE MASON: What's this new position: a vice-president? That's unnecessary, and an encroachment on the Senate/ separation of powers. We can't have someone from the executive branch leading the Senate. [[7]]

ELBRIDGE GERRY: Agreed.

[Vote to include anyway passes 8 to 2.]

~~*Executive until the next meeting of the Legislature.*~~ and if Vacancies happen by Resignation, or otherwise, during the Recess of the Legislature of any State, the Executive thereof may make temporary Appointments until the next Meeting of the Legislature, which shall then fill such Vacancies.[10]

~~*Every member of the Senate shall be of the age of thirty years at least; shall have been a citizen in the United States for at least four years efore his election; and shall be, at the time of his election, a resident of the State for which he shall be chosen.*~~

No Person shall be a Senator who shall not have attained to the Age of thirty Years, and been nine Years a Citizen of the United States,[11] and who shall not, when elected, be an Inhabitant of that State for which he shall be chosen.

The Vice President [[7]] of the United States shall be President of the Senate, but shall have no Vote, unless they be equally divided.

~~*The Senate shall choose its own President and other officers.*~~ The Senate shall chuse their other Officers, and also a President pro tempore, in the Absence of the Vice President, or when he shall exercise the Office of President of the United States.

The Senate shall have the sole Power to try all Impeachments.[12] When sitting for that Purpose, they shall be on Oath or Affirmation. When the President of the United States is tried, the Chief Justice shall preside: And no Person shall be convicted without the Concurrence of two thirds of the Members present.

Judgment~~,~~ in Cases of Impeachment~~,~~ shall not extend further than to removal from Office, and disqualification to hold and enjoy any Office of honor, Trust or Profit~~,~~ under the United States~~.~~: ~~*But*~~ but the Party convicted shall nev-

---

10. **Seventeenth Amendment** [Popular Election of Senators]: . . . When vacancies happen in the representation of any State in the Senate, the executive authority of such State shall issue writs of election to fill such vacancies: Provided, That the legislature of any State may empower the executive thereof to make temporary appointments until the people fill the vacancies by election as the legislature may direct.

11. The nine-year-citizenship requirement was at issue in 1870 in the case of Mississippi Senator Hiram Revels, the first Black member of Congress. His opponents argued that because *Dred Scott v. Sanford* (1857) held that people of African descent were ineligible for citizenship, Revels lacked the constitutionally required nine years as a citizen to hold a seat in the Senate. The Senate voted along party lines (48 to 8) that Revels was qualified. Before secession, Jefferson Davis, who later became the president of the Confederacy, held the other Senate seat from Mississippi.

12. An earlier Pickney draft contemplated the Supreme Court trying all cases of impeachment. *See* Art. 3, § 2. The vote to have the Senate try impeachments instead passed 9 to 2.

ertheless be liable and subject to Indictment, Trial, Judgment and Punishment, according to Law.[13]

Section. 4. [Congressional Elections]

The Times, Places and Manner of holding ~~*the*~~ Elections for ~~*the members of each House*~~ Senators and Representatives, shall be prescribed ~~*by the Legislature of each State*~~ in each State by the Legislature thereof; but ~~*their provisions concerning them may at any time, be altered by the Legislature of the United States*~~ the Congress may at any time by Law make or alter such Regulations, except as to the Places of chusing Senators.

~~*The Legislature of the United States shall have authority to establish such uniform qualifications of the members of each House, with regard to property,*~~[[8]] ~~*as to the said Legislature shall seem expedient.*~~

The ~~*Legislature*~~ Congress shall ~~*meet*~~ assemble at least once in every Year, and such Meeting shall be on the first Monday in December[14] ~~*in every year*~~, unless they shall by Law appoint a different Day.

Section. 5. [Congressional Proceedings][15]

Each House shall be the Judge of the Elections, Returns~~,~~ and Qualifications~~,~~ of its Members. ~~*In each house*~~, and a Majority of ~~*the members*~~ each shall constitute a Quorum to do Business; but a smaller Number may adjourn from day to day, and may be authorized to compel the Attendance of absent Members, in such Manner, and under such Penalties as each House may provide.

Each House may determine the Rules of its Proceedings~~;~~, ~~*may*~~ punish its Members for disorderly Behaviour~~;~~, and ~~*may*~~, with the Concurrence of two thirds, expel a Member.

13. In the Committee of Detail draft, the final paragraph (judgment in impeachment cases) appears in an article covering the judicial branch, not the legislative branch, consistent with the initial idea of having the Supreme Court try impeachment cases.

14. **Twentieth Amendment § 2** [Meetings of Congress]: The Congress shall assemble at least once in every year, and such meeting shall begin at noon on the 3d day of January, unless they shall by law appoint a different day.

15. In the Committee of Detail's draft, Congress was the subject of seven separate articles. The Committee of Style restructured these into three articles for the three branches.

CHARLES COTESWORTH PINCKNEY:
We should have a property requirement for members of each branch. I am open to ideas, but perhaps a minimum of $100,000 for President, $50,000 for judges, and in like proportion for Congressmen. Leaders need to have a vested interest in this country.[[8]]

BENJAMIN FRANKLIN:
Absolutely not. I know honest poor people, and some of the greatest rogues I was ever acquainted with were the richest rogues. A property requirement will also discourage some of the world's greatest minds from wanting to move to America.

JAMES MADISON:
A property requirement is antithetical to everything we are trying to achieve.

HUGH WILLIAMSON:
Agreed. Comprising a legislature of only a certain type of men—lawyers, for example—will lead to them ensuring that only people like them ever serve.

GOUVERNEUR MORRIS:
I move to strike "with regard to property."

[This vote on August 10, 1787, failed 4 to 7, but the requirement was deleted later in the Convention.]

OLIVER ELLSWORTH: I am now convinced that requiring states to pay salaries makes the federal government too dependent on the states. I move to strike that and replace it with "out of the Treasury of the United States." *[Completely reversing his earlier position.]* [[9]]

GOUVERNEUR MORRIS: Agreed. And it puts a disproportionate burden on smaller states and states that are further away, having to pay for travel expenses.

JOHN LANGDON: Concur.

PIERCE BUTLER: I disagree. Payment by the states reminds members that they are dependent on their state's support.

JAMES MADISON: I am for the national government paying but putting caps on either extreme.

ELBRIDGE GERRY: If the states pay, they can prevent the functioning of the federal government by not paying members of Congress.

JOHN DICKINSON: Agreed. If the part can destroy the whole, we might as well have never met in this *[sweaty and smelly]* room.

[Passes 9 to 2.]

~~*The House of Representatives, and the Senate when it shall be acting in a legislative capacity,*~~ Each House shall keep a Journal of ~~*their*~~ its Proceedings~~;~~, and ~~*shall,*~~ from time to time publish the~~*m*~~ same~~;~~, excepting such Parts as may in their Judgment require Secrecy; and the Yeas and Nays of the Members of ~~*each*~~ either House~~,~~ on any question~~,~~ shall, at the Desire of one fifth ~~*part*~~ of ~~*the members*~~ those Present, be entered on the Journal.

Neither House, during the Session of Congress, shall, without the Consent of the other, adjourn for more than three days, nor to any other Place than that ~~*at*~~ in which the two Houses ~~*are*~~ shall be sitting. ~~*But this regulation shall not extend to the Senate when it shall exercise the powers mentioned in the—Article.*~~

Section. 6. [Congressional Pay, Privileges, Immunities, Incompatibility]

The ~~*members of each House*~~ Senators and Representatives shall receive a Compensation for their Services, to be ascertained by Law, and paid out of the Treasury of the United States[[9]] ~~*by the State in which they shall be chosen*~~. ~~*;and the members of each House*~~ They shall in all Cases, except Treason, Felony~~,~~ and Breach of the Peace, be privileged from Arrest during their Attendance at ~~*Congress*~~ the Session of their respective Houses, and in going to and returning from ~~*it*~~ the same; and for any Speech or Debate in either House, they shall not be questioned in any other Place.[16] ~~*Freedom of speech and debate in the Legislature shall not be impeached or questioned in any court or place out of the Legislature.*~~

~~*The members of each House shall be ineligible to, and incapable of holding, any office under the authority of the United States, during the time for which they shall respectively be elected: and the members of the Senate shall be ineligible to, and incapable of holding, any such office for one year afterwards.*~~

No Senator or Representative shall, during the Time for which he was elected, be appointed to any civil Office under the Authority of the United States, which shall have been created, or the Emoluments whereof shall have been encreased during such time; and no Person holding any Office under the United States, shall be a Member of either House during his Continuance in Office.[17]

16. Speech or Debate Immunity carried over from the Articles of Confederation, after colonists observed abuses in England, including the *Six Members Case*. *See* p. 22.

17. **Twenty-Seventh Amendment** [Congressional Compensation]: No law, varying the compensation for the services of the Senators and Representatives, shall take effect, until an election of

Section. 7. [Legislation]

~~*The enacting style of the laws of the United States shall be, "Be it enacted, and it is hereby enacted, by the House of Representatives, and by the Senate of the United States, in Congress assembled."*~~

~~*Each House shall possess the right of originating bills, except in the cases beforementioned.*~~

All Bills for raising Revenue[[10]] ~~*or appropriating money, and for fixing the salaries of the officers of government,*~~ shall originate in the House of Representatives ~~*and shall not be altered or amended by the Senate*~~; but the Senate may propose or concur with Amendments as on other Bills.

Every Bill~~,~~ which shall have passed the House of Representatives and the Senate, shall, before it become~~*s*~~ a Law, be presented to the President of the United States ~~*for his revision*~~; If~~*, upon such revision,*~~ he approve ~~*of it,*~~ he shall sign~~*ify his approbation by signing*~~ it, but if~~*, upon such revision, it shall appear to him improper for being passed into a law,*~~ not he shall return it, ~~*together*~~ with his Objections ~~*against it,*~~ to that House in which it shall have originated~~;~~, who shall enter the Objections at large on their Journal, and proceed to reconsider ~~*the bill*~~ it. ~~*But if*~~ If after such Reconsideration~~,~~ two-thirds of that House shall~~*, notwithstanding the objections of the President,*~~ agree to pass ~~*it*~~ the Bill, it shall be sent, together with ~~*his*~~ the Objections, ~~*be sent*~~ to the other House, by which it shall likewise be re-considered, and if approved by two-thirds of that House ~~*the other house also*~~, it shall become a Law. But in all such Cases the Votes of both Houses shall be determined by yeas and Nays~~;~~, and the Names of the Persons voting for ~~*or*~~ and against the Bill~~,~~ shall be entered on the Journal of each House respectively. If any Bill shall not be returned by the President within ten ~~*seven*~~ Days (Sundays excepted) after it shall have been presented to him, ~~*it*~~ the Same shall be a Law, in like Manner as if he had signed it, unless the ~~*Legislature*~~ Congress by their Adjournment~~,~~ prevent its Return~~;~~, in which Case it shall not be a Law.[18]

Every Order, Resolution, or Vote to which the Concurrence of the Senate and House of Representatives may be necessary (except on a question of Ad-

---

Representatives shall have intervened.

18. The "Presentment Clause" of Section 7 (presenting laws to the President) is another example of checks and balances—requiring the President to sign legislation. However, it also allows Congress to override a veto if the President refuses to sign, addressing the prior grievance of an executive who can unilaterally withhold consent to law. *See, e.g.*, p. 93.

CALEB STRONG: Having the People's House originate revenue-raising bills brings taxation closer to representation.[[10]]

GEORGE MASON: Completely agree, we need to take this power away from the Senate, who can already sell the whole country by means of treaties!

GOUVERNEUR MORRIS: No, that is unnecessary and inconvenient.

JAMES MADISON: I've seen many drafts go back and forth between 2/3 and 3/4 here, causing confusion. There is also much debate, but it should be 2/3, when we compare the danger of weakness at 2/3 vs. the unworkability of 3/4.[[11]]

ROGER SHERMAN: Did someone change the comma after "Excises" to a semicolon? We didn't approve that; instead of limiting Congress's ability to tax to (1) debts, (2) defense and, (3) welfare, it is arguably a completely separate and unlimited grant of power to Congress.[[12]]

GOUVERNEUR MORRIS: Must have been a typo by our Committee of Style or the printer. Let's change it back.

JAMES MADISON: *[In subsequent letters]* This must have been a scrivener's or printer's error; it does not change the substance.

[According to some scholars, this was no typo, and Sherman caught Morris trying to sneak in a substantive change. (Not shown here because there was no semicolon in the Committee of Detail draft or the engrossed version, it only appeared in the Committee of Style draft.)]

journment) shall be presented to the President of the United States; and before the Same shall take Effect, shall be approved by him, or being disapproved by him, shall be repassed by two thirds [[11]] of the Senate and House of Representatives, according to the Rules and Limitations prescribed in the Case of a Bill.

Section. 8. [Enumerated Powers]

The ~~*Legislature of the United States*~~ Congress shall have ~~*the*~~ Power To lay and collect Taxes, Duties, Imposts and Excises,[[12]] to pay the Debts and provide for the common Defence and general Welfare of the United States; but all Duties, Imposts and Excises shall be uniform throughout the United States;

To regulate Commerce with foreign Nations, and among the several States, and with the Indian Tribes;[19]

To establish an uniform Rule of Naturalization, and uniform Laws on the subject of Bankruptcies throughout the United States;

To coin Money~~;~~, regulate the Value thereof, and of foreign Coin~~;~~, and fix the Standard of Weights and Measures;

To provide for the Punishment of counterfeiting the Securities and current Coin of the United States;

To establish Post-Offices and post Roads;[[13]]

To promote the Progress of Science and useful Arts, by securing for limited Times to Authors and Inventors the exclusive Right to their respective Writings and Discoveries;[20]

To constitute Tribunals inferior to the supreme Court;

19. This broad Commerce Clause is one of the most important clauses in the Constitution. Its aim is to streamline commerce, and to prevent state infighting and competition in commerce and trade that proved unworkable under the Articles.

20. The Intellectual Property Clause encourages American innovation and addresses the patchwork of state laws on copyrights and patents that plagued the Articles. It is also a response to British laws that stifled innovation and manufacturing in the colonies. Many colonists contended that English wanted to merely use the colonies to extract resources for Britain, and that Britain did not want the colonies innovating and threatening British superiority.

~~*To declare the law and punishment of*~~ To define and punish Piracies and Felonies committed on the high Seas, ~~*and the punishment of counterfeiting the coin of the United States,*~~ and Offences against the Law of Nations;

To ~~*make*~~[[14]] declare War,[21] grant Letters of Marque and Reprisal, and make Rules concerning Captures on Land and Water;

To raise and support Armies, but no Appropriation of Money to that Use shall be for a longer Term than two Years;[[15]]

~~*To build and equip fleets;*~~ To provide and maintain a Navy;

To make Rules for the Government and Regulation of the land and naval Forces;[22]

To ~~*call*~~ provide for calling forth[[16]] the ~~*aid of the*~~ Militia, ~~*in order*~~ to execute the Laws of the Union, ~~*enforce treaties,*~~ suppress Insurrections, and repel Invasions;

~~*To subdue a rebellion in any State, on the application of its Legislature;*~~

~~*To appoint a Treasurer by ballot;*~~ [[17]]

To provide for organizing, arming, and disciplining, the Militia, and for governing such Part of them as may be employed in the Service of the United States, reserving to the States respectively, the Appointment of the Officers, and the Authority of training the Militia according to the discipline prescribed by Congress;

To exercise exclusive Legislation in all Cases whatsoever, over such District (not exceeding ten Miles square) as may, by Cession of particular States, and the Acceptance of Congress, become the Seat of the Government of the United States, and to exercise like Authority over all Places purchased by the Consent of the Legislature of the State in which the Same shall be, for the Erection of Forts, Magazines, Arsenals, dock-Yards, and other needful Buildings;—And

21. Under Articles I and II, Congress declares and funds wars and the President commands them day to day. "Letters of marque and reprisal" authorize or encourage private shipowners to attack and capture enemy vessels without being deemed pirates.

22. Under Section 8, Congress can make separate rules (and rights) for the military, which led to the Uniform Code of Military Justice.

THOMAS JEFFERSON: *[In subsequent letter to James Madison]* I am a bit concerned about the addition of "post roads." It could be a boundless patronage to the executive, jobbing to members of Congress and their friends, and a bottomless abyss of public money. Perhaps states should handle this.[[13]]

JAMES MADISON; ELBRIDGE GERRY: Move to change "make" to "declare" war, the latter limiting Congress's power over day-to-day affairs of war. The President should also have the limited ability to repel sudden attacks without Congress because Congress only meets once per year.[[14]]

ELBRIDGE GERRY: This provision tries to limit dreaded standing armies. It would limit army appropriations to one year, not two.[[15]]

ROGER SHERMAN: It is a *maximum* of two years, nothing prevents the Congress from only approving one, and we might need the flexibility of two at some point.

GOUVERNEUR MORRIS: *[In Convention]* I move to revise this to "provide for calling forth." It gives Congress more flexibility and Congress can delegate this authority if desired.[[16]]

~~*And, to*~~ To make all Laws ~~*that*~~ which shall be necessary and proper[[18]] for carrying into Execution the foregoing Powers, and all other Powers vested by this Constitution in the Government of the United States, or in any Department or Officer thereof.[23]

Section. 9. [Powers Denied Congress]

~~*No tax or duty shall be laid . . . on the migration or importation of such persons as the several States shall think proper to admit; nor shall such migration or importation be prohibited.*~~

The Migration or Importation of such Persons as any of the States now existing shall think proper to admit, shall not be prohibited by the Congress prior to the Year one thousand eight hundred and eight, but a Tax or duty may be imposed on such Importation,[[19]] not exceeding ten dollars for each Person.[24]

The Privilege of the Writ of Habeas Corpus[25][[20]] shall not be suspended, unless when in Cases of Rebellion or Invasion the public Safety may require it.

No Bill of Attainder[26] or ex post factoLaw shall be passed.

No Capitation, or other direct, Tax shall be laid, unless in Proportion to the Census or enumeration herein before directed to be taken.[27]

---

23. The "Necessary and Proper Clause" or "Elastic Clause" gives Congress broad, flexible powers to make "necessary and proper" laws to carry out its powers. The Supreme Court took an expansive view of the clause in ***McCulloch v. Maryland*** (1819).

24. **Thirteenth Amendment** [Prohibition on Slavery and Involuntary Servitude]: Neither slavery nor involuntary servitude, except as a punishment for crime whereof the party shall have been duly convicted, shall exist within the United States, or any place subject to their jurisdiction.

25. A writ of habeas corpus (rooted in Magna Carta, *see* p. 10) allows a prisoner or detainee to challenge their confinement.

26. A bill of attainder is congressional legislation that declares someone guilty of a crime, usually without a trial. They were used in England to circumvent due process and habeas rights.

27. **Amendment Sixteen** [Income Tax]: The Congress shall have power to lay and collect taxes on incomes, from whatever source derived, without apportionment among the several States, and without regard to any census or enumeration.

JOHN RUTLEDGE: The treasurer should be appointed by the executive. Move to strike this.[[17]]

ROGER SHERMAN: I oppose. The two houses appropriate money, they should appoint the officer to keep it.

CHARLES COTESWORTH PINCKNEY: We have the legislature appoint treasurers in S.C. and we get . . . not the brightest people.

[Motion fails at first but later passes 8 to 3.]

ELBRIDGE GERRY: This "necessary and proper" clause is far too broad.[[18]]

GEORGE MASON: Completely agree. Under the clause, the Congress may grant monopolies in trade and commerce, constitute new crimes, inflict unusual and severe punishments, and extend their powers as far as they shall think proper; so that the State legislatures have no security for the powers now presumed to remain to them, or the people for their rights.

CHARLES COTESWORTH PINCKNEY; CHARLES PINCKNEY: We will never vote for something that allows a tax on slaves—that is too burdensome on Southern economies. In all ages one half of mankind have been slaves.[[19]]

~~*No navigation act*~~[28] [[21]] ~~*shall be passed without the assent of two-thirds of the members present in each House.*~~

No Tax or Duty shall be laid on Articles exported from any State.

No Preference shall be given by any Regulation of Commerce or Revenue to the Ports of one State over those of another: nor shall Vessels bound to, or from, one State, be obliged to enter, clear, or pay Duties in another.

No Money shall be drawn from the ~~*public*~~ Treasury, but in ~~*pursuance*~~ Consequence of Appropriations made by Law[29] ~~*that shall originate in the House of Representatives.*~~; and a regular Statement and Account of the Receipts and Expenditures of all public Money shall be published from time to time.

~~*The United States shall not grant any title of nobility.*~~ No Title of Nobility [[22]] shall be granted by the United States: And no Person holding any Office of Profit or Trust under them, shall, without the Consent of the Congress, accept of any present, Emolument, Office, or Title, of any kind whatever, from any King, Prince, or foreign State.

Section. 10. [Powers Denied States]

No State shall~~*, without the consent of the Legislature of the United States,*~~ enter into any Treaty, Alliance, or Confederation; ~~*nor*~~ grant Letters of Marque and Reprisal; coin Money;[30] emit Bills of Credit; make any Thing but gold and silver Coin a Tender in Payment of Debts; pass any Bill of Attainder, ex post facto Law, or Law impairing the Obligation of Contracts,[[23]] ~~*n*~~or grant any Title of Nobility.

No State shall, without the Consent of the ~~*Legislature of the United States*~~ Congress, ~~*emit bills of credit, or make any thing but specie a tender in payment of debts; nor*~~ lay any Imposts or Duties on Imports~~;~~ or Exports, except what may be

JOHN DICKINSON: I think it's inadmissible to even allow importation of slaves. This practice needs to end.

JAMES MADISON: The Constitution should not admit the idea of property in men.

GEORGE MASON: I propose that we do almost the opposite: we outlaw this diabolical and disgraceful trade after 1800.

[Proposal fails.]

CHARLES PINCKNEY: We need to add protections for habeas corpus, allowing a separate branch (the Judiciary) to check the legality of the Executive's detentions.[[20]]

GOUVERNEUR MORRIS: *[In Convention]* The Northern states want to ban the importation of slaves as we did in the Articles of Association. The Southern states do not, but they are also afraid that the navigation acts discussed in this draft will disproportionately benefit Northern states. I think there is some room here for negotiation.[[21]]

[This issue was committed to the Committee of Eleven and a major compromise was reached that benefitted both sides: strike the paragraph prohibiting navigation acts, but add a prohibition on banning the importation of slaves until 1808, as seen in the redlines in Art. I, § 9.]

---

28. Great Britain heavily regulated trade through Navigation Acts (enforced in proceedings without juries).

29. This important provision prevents the government from spending any money without a law passed by Congress (with a particular focus on the President, after observing this under various kings).

30. Article I, Section 8 gives the federal government authority to coin money, and Section 10 prohibits states from coining money. Varying state currencies led to economic instability under the Articles. Notably, the credit and specie items were moved from the paragraph requiring the consent of Congress (second paragraph) to an absolute bar (first paragraph), along with other reorganization and additions.

absolutely necessary for executing it's inspection Laws: and the net Produce of all Duties and Imposts, laid by any State on Imports or Exports, shall be for the Use of the Treasury of the United States; and all such Laws shall be subject to the Revision and Controul of the Congress.

No State shall, without the Consent of ~~*Legislature of the United States*~~ Congress, lay any Duty of Tonnage, keep Troops, or Ships of War in time of Peace~~;~~, ~~*nor*~~ enter into any Agreement or Compact with another State, or with *any* a foreign Power~~;~~, or engage in *any* War, unless ~~*it shall be*~~ actually invaded ~~*by enemies*~~, or ~~*the danger of invasion be so imminent as not to admit of a delay until the Legislature of the United States can be consulted*~~ in such imminent Danger as will not admit of delay.

Article. II.[[24]]

[*Executive Branch*]

Section. 1. [Vesting Clause, President's Role, Election, Qualifications, Succession, Pay, Oath][[25]]

The executive Power ~~*of the United States*~~ shall be vested in a ~~*single person. His style shall be, "The*~~ President of the United States of America~~*" and his title shall be, "His Excellency." He shall be elected by ballot by the Legislature*~~. He shall hold his Office during the Term of ~~*seven*~~ four Years~~;~~[[26]] ~~*but shall not be elected a second time*~~, and, together with the Vice President, chosen for the same Term, be elected, as follows

Each State shall appoint, in such Manner as the Legislature thereof may direct, a Number of Electors, equal to the whole Number of Senators and Representatives to which the State may be entitled in the Congress: but no Senator or Representative, or Person holding an Office of Trust or Profit under the United States, shall be appointed an Elector.[[27]]

The Electors[31] shall meet in their respective States, and vote by Ballot for two Persons, of whom one at least shall not be an Inhabitant of the

31. The original election procedure only worked because George Washington was the obvious choice during the drafting. Washington is often compared to Cincinnatus because, like the Roman leader, he demonstrated civic virtue by relinquishing power voluntarily after serving his country

CHARLES COTESWORTH PINCKNEY: We need this clause on titles of nobility to avoid (1) a monarchy and (2) foreign interference. [[22]]

GOUVERNEUR MORRIS: *[Committee of Style revision]* Even though a similar provision has been voted down, I'm adding "or Law impairing the Obligation of Contracts" here and hoping no one objects. And I won't qualify "contracts" with "public" or "private" because this Contracts Clause should apply to both. [[23]]

JAMES MADISON: I propose a revision to Section 10, adding: "No State shall violate the equal rights of conscience, or the freedom of the press, or the trial by jury in criminal cases."

[Proposal fails. See also, p. 171]

EDMUND RANDOLPH: We need three presidents from three parts of the country. A single executive will be the foetus of a monarchy.[[24]]

ALEXANDER HAMILTON: *[In Federalist No. 70]* History shows that plural executive systems fail. A plurality is unworkable, unmanageable, will introduce confusion and weakness, and will result in disputes between them.[[25]]

same State with themselves. And they shall make a List of all the Persons voted for, and of the Number of Votes for each; which List they shall sign and certify, and transmit sealed to the Seat of the Government of the United States, directed to the President of the Senate. The President of the Senate shall, in the Presence of the Senate and House of Representatives, open all the Certificates, and the Votes shall then be counted. The Person having the greatest Number of Votes shall be the President, if such Number be a Majority of the whole Number of Electors appointed; and if there be more than one who have such Majority, and have an equal Number of Votes, then the House of Representatives shall immediately chuse by Ballot one of them for President; and if no Person have a Majority, then from the five highest on the List the said House shall in like Manner chuse the President. But in chusing the President, the Votes shall be taken by States, the Representation from each State having one Vote; A quorum for this Purpose shall consist of a Member or Members from two thirds of the States, and a Majority of all the States shall be necessary to a Choice. In every Case, after the Choice of the President, the Person having the greatest Number of Votes of the Electors shall be the Vice President. But if there should remain two or more who have equal Votes, the Senate shall chuse from them by Ballot the Vice President.[32]

The Congress may determine the Time of chusing the Electors, and the Day on which they shall give their Votes; which Day shall be the same throughout the United States.

No Person except a natural born Citizen, or a Citizen of the United States, at the time of the Adoption of this Constitution, shall be eligible to the Office of President; neither shall any Person be eligible to that Office who shall not

---

for two terms as President. The election of 1796 led to political rivals (Adams and Jefferson) being forced to serve together (often actively against each other) as President and Vice President. The election of 1800 prompted the Twelfth Amendment. Jefferson and Burr received the same number of votes and each claimed victory. That election went to the House, and eventually Hamilton convinced the Federalists to vote for Jefferson as the lesser of two evils who was more likely to act in the best interests of the Nation.

32. **Twelfth Amendment** [Election of President]; **Twentieth Amendment** § 3: *See* pp. 193, 210.

JAMES MADISON:
I agree with Mr. Hamilton.

PIERCE BUTLER:
[In 1788] The President's powers would probably not be so great if we all hadn't had the great General Washington in mind when drafting.[[26]]

GOUVERNEUR MORRIS:
Should his term be "during good behaviour" (i.e., indefinitely) instead of seven years? Then the President is beholden to the Legislature.

JAMES MADISON:
No, the branches are not separate if the Executive is dependent upon the Legislature.

GUNNING BEDFORD, JR.:
Agreed. And impeachment won't solve it, that only reaches misfeasance, not incapacity.

ALEXANDER HAMILTON:
Agreed. And what if a monster is elected? Seven years is too long, it should be four.

[Change to "four" passes 10 to 1.]

GOUVERNEUR MORRIS:
We should have popular election of electors for the Executive.[[27]]

[Proposal fails, 5 to 6.]

JAMES WILSON:
I agree, but because that failed, I propose a type of electoral college.

JAMES MADISON: The President of the Senate should not be the successor to the President. The Senate could simply retard the appointment of a President in that case.[[28]]

GOUVERNEUR MORRIS: Perhaps this should be the Chief Justice, not the President of the Senate?

[Later in the Convention, the role of Vice President was introduced.]

NATHANIAL GORHAM: I oppose a Vice President being next in line without the consultation of the Senate.

GEORGE MASON: The President should not be able to pardon treason. One might instigate crime and then use this power to insulate himself from discovery of his own guilt.[[29]]

EDMUND RANDOLPH: Yes. The prerogative of pardon in these cases is too great a trust. The President may himself be guilty. The Traytors may be his own instruments.

GOUVERNEUR MORRIS: So you would leave the pardon power for treason with the legislature? That's worse.

have attained to the Age of thirty five Years, and been fourteen Years a Resident within the United States.[33]

> In Case of ~~*his*~~ the Removal~~, *as aforesaid,*~~ of the President from Office, or of his Death, Resignation, or ~~*disability*~~ Inability to discharge the Powers and Duties of ~~*his*~~ the said Office, the Same shall devolve on the ~~*President of the Senate*~~[[28]] Vice President, and the Congress may by Law provide for the Case of Removal, Death, Resignation or Inability, both of the President and Vice President, declaring what Officer shall then act as President, and such Officer shall act accordingly, until ~~*another President of the United States be chosen, or until the disability of the President be removed*~~ the Disability be removed, or a President shall be elected.[34]

~~*He*~~ The President shall, at stated Times, receive for his Services, a Compensation, which shall neither be ~~i~~encreased nor diminished during ~~*his continuance in office*~~ the Period for which he shall have been elected, and he shall not receive within that Period any other Emolument from the United States, or any of them.

Before he ~~*shall*~~ enter on the ~~*duties of his department*~~ Execution of his Office, he shall take the following Oath or Affirmation:—"I do solemnly swear~~,~~ (or affirm) that I will faithfully execute the Office of President of the United States ~~*of America*~~, and will to the best of my Ability, preserve, protect and defend the Constitution of the United States."

---

33. **Twenty-Second Amendment §1** [Presidential Term Limits]: No person shall be elected to the office of the President more than twice, and no person who has held the office of President, or acted as President, for more than two years of a term to which some other person was elected President shall be elected to the office of the President more than once. . . .

34. **Twenty-Fifth Amendment** [Presidential Vacancy]: *See* p. 217.

Before the Twenty-Fifth Amendment, it was not clear whether the Vice President permanently or temporarily served the president. Today, federal law provides that the next in line after the Vice President is the Speaker of the House. Some scholars have questioned the wisdom of that statute, as the Speaker is often from a different party or ideology than the President and Vice President.

Section. 2. [President's Powers]

~~*He*~~ The President shall be Commander in Chief of the Army and Navy of the United States, and of the Militia of the several States, when called into the actual Service of the United States; he may require the Opinion, in writing, of the principal Officer in each of the executive Departments, upon any Subject relating to the Duties of their respective Offices, and he shall have Power to grant Reprieves and Pardons~~,~~[[29]] for Offences against the United States, except in Cases of Impeachment ~~*but his pardon shall not be pleadable in bar of an impeachment*~~.

He shall have Power, by and with the Advice and Consent of the Senate, to make Treaties,[[30]] provided two thirds of the Senators present concur; and he shall nominate, and by and with the Advice and Consent of the Senate, shall appoint Ambassadors, other public Ministers and Consuls, Judges of the supreme Court, and all other Officers of the United States, whose Appointments are not herein otherwise provided for, and which shall be established by Law: but the Congress may by Law vest the Appointment of such inferior Officers, as they think proper, in the President alone, in the Courts of Law, or in the Heads of Departments.[35]

The President shall have Power to fill up all Vacancies that may happen during the Recess of the Senate, by granting Commissions which shall expire at the End of their next Session.

Section. 3. [President's Duties]

He shall~~,~~ from time to time~~,~~ give ~~*information to the Legislature,*~~ to the Congress Information of the State of the Union~~.~~,[36] ~~*He may*~~ and recommend to their Consideration such Measures as he shall judge necessary~~,~~ and expedient; ~~*He may convene them on extraordinary occasions.*~~ he may, on extraordinary Occasions, convene both Houses, or either of them, and in ~~*In*~~ Case of Disagreement between ~~*the Houses*~~ them, with ~~*regard*~~ Respect to the Time of Adjournment, he

RUFUS KING:
I agree with Morris; involving the legislature violates separation of powers. And legislatures are too possessed by passions. In Massachusetts, one assembly would have hung all insurgents while the next would pardon them all.

JAMES WILSON:
Pardon is necessary even for cases of treason, and is best placed in the hands of the President.

[Proposal to except treason fails 8 to 2 to 1.]

JAMES WILSON:
We should add House of Representatives to this, approving treaties. Because treaties have the force of law, they should be passed like laws.[[30]]

ROGER SHERMAN:
That is unnecessary. Also, sometimes these need to be negotiated in secret, and the Senate can maintain that secrecy better than the whole legislature.

JOHN ADAMS:
[In February 1825, after his son won the presidency] No man who ever held the office of President would congratulate a friend on obtaining it.

---

35. The 1689 English Declaration of Rights established an earlier limitation on executive power: the king cannot unilaterally make or suspend laws, and "levying money for or to the use of the Crown by pretence of prerogative, without grant of Parliament, for longer time, or in other manner than the same is or shall be granted, is illegal." *See* p. 21.

36. Although it is common today to give oral addresses to Congress as the "State of the Union," Thomas Jefferson submitted written reports, possibly based on a lisp and stutter.

may adjourn them to such Time as he ~~*thinks*~~ shall think proper~~.~~; He shall receive Ambassadors and other public Ministers~~*, and may correspond with the supreme executives of the several States.*~~; he shall take Care that the Laws ~~*of the United States*~~ be ~~*duly and*~~ faithfully executed~~.~~, ~~*He*~~ and shall Commission all the Officers of the United States~~*, and shall appoint officers in all cases not otherwise provided for by this Constitution.*~~]

GEORGE MASON: The impeachment provisions are inconsistent between this and Art. I, § 3. We should add here "and disqualified from holding or enjoying any office of honor, trust or profit under the United States."[[31]]

[Ultimately not added.]

ALEXANDER HAMILTON: *[In Federalist 78]* An independent judiciary is essential. It will always be the least dangerous to the political rights of the Constitution. It has no influence over the sword or the purse.[[32]]

GOUVERNEUR MORRIS: I tend to agree, though I do want a strong judiciary to check the other branches.

Section. 4. *[Impeachment]*[[31]]

~~*He*~~ The President, Vice President and all civil Officers of the United States, shall be removed from ~~*his*~~ Office on Impeachment ~~*by the House of Representatives, and conviction, in the Supreme Court, of treason, bribery or corruption.*~~ for, and Conviction of, Treason, Bribery, or other high Crimes and Misdemeanors.[37]

Article. III.[[32]]
[*Judicial Branch*]

Section. 1. [Vesting Clause/Judicial Power]

The judicial Power of the United States, shall be vested in one supreme Court, and in such inferior Courts as ~~*shall, when necessary, from time to time, be constituted by the Legislature of the United States*~~ the Congress may from time to time ordain and establish. The Judges, both of the supreme ~~*Court,*~~ and ~~*of the*~~ inferior Courts, shall hold their Offices during good Behaviour~~.~~, ~~*They*~~ and shall, at stated Times, receive for their Services, a Compensation, which shall not be diminished during their Continuance in Office.

---

37. The Convention added the phrase "against the United States" to the end of this section, limiting impeachments to crimes against the United States and arguably to those related to performance of duties in office. The Committee of Style removed that phrase. This issue was raised in the impeachment proceedings of Presidents Clinton and Trump (whether the alleged conduct must be "against the United States"). The language "against the United States" does not appear here because it was not in the Committee of Detail draft or in the final version of the Constitution.

Like the addition of "actual enumeration" in Art. I, § 2, these seemingly unauthorized changes by the Committee of Style raise interesting questions about which version should be enforced—the final text, the version that the Convention approved, or something else?

Section. 2. [Justiciability, Supreme Court Jurisdiction, Jury Trials][38]

The judicial Power ~~*jurisdiction of the Supreme Court*~~[[33]] shall extend to all Cases, in Law and Equity, arising under this Constitution, the Laws ~~*passed by the Legislature*~~ of the United States, and Treaties made, or which shall be made, under their Authority;—to all Cases affecting Ambassadors, other public Ministers and Consuls; ~~*to the trial of impeachments of officers of the United States;*~~—to all Cases of admiralty and maritime Jurisdiction;—to Controversies to which the United States shall be a Party;—to Controversies between two or more States; ~~*(except such as shall regard territory or jurisdiction);*~~—between a State and Citizens of another State,—between Citizens of different States,—between Citizens of the same State claiming Lands under Grants of different States, and between a State, or the Citizens thereof, and foreign States, Citizens or Subjects.[39]

In ~~*cases of impeachment,*~~ all Cases affecting Ambassadors, other public Ministers and Consuls, and those in which a State shall be Party, ~~*this jurisdiction shall be original*~~ the supreme Court shall have original Jurisdiction. In all the other Cases before mentioned, ~~*it shall be appellate,*~~ the supreme Court shall have appellate Jurisdiction, both as to Law and Fact, with such Exceptions, and under such Regulations~~,~~ as the ~~*Legislature*~~ Congress shall make.

~~*The Legislature may assign any part of the jurisdiction above mentioned (except the trial of the President of the United States) in the manner and under the limitations which it shall think proper, to such inferior courts as it shall constitute from time to time.*~~[[34]]

38. Notably, the text of Article III does not expressly provide that federal courts possess the power of judicial review (the ability to declare acts of the President or Congress unconstitutional). Many Framers commented that courts have this power, and the Supreme Court formally acknowledged judicial review in *Marbury v. Madison* (1803).

George Washington separately asked Patrick Henry and Alexander Hamilton (in a roundabout way) if either would serve as Chief Justice and both declined. At the time, the pay was insufficient, the position lacked prestige (according to John Jay), and Justices disliked "riding circuit" and hearing cases for months at a time away from home.

39. **Eleventh Amendment** [Suits Against States]: The Judicial power of the United States shall not be construed to extend to any suit in law or equity, commenced or prosecuted against one of the United States by Citizens of another State, or by Citizens or Subjects of any Foreign State.

JAMES MADISON; JAMES WILSON:
We should have the Supreme Court review and revise all laws after they pass in Congress. This saves time, preventing unconstitutional laws.[[33]]

CHARLES COTESWORTH PINCKNEY:
No, that mixes the branches too much. And it gives proposed laws the previous tincture of lawfulness.

[Proposal fails 8 to 3.]

JOHN DICKINSON:
I'm not sure the judiciary should have the power to declare laws unconstitutional. (Though I'm at a loss as to a good substitute.)

GEORGE MASON:
I am concerned that a judiciary might interpret the law in a way that would be unfavorable to the interests of the states and individual rights—particularly without a bill of rights.

JOHN DICKINSON:
We need lower federal courts, but let the legislature institute them.[[34]]

JAMES MADISON; JAMES WILSON:
Yes. Our motion is to give Congress the power to create lower courts, but it is not obligated to do so: "such inferior Courts as the United States the Congress may from time to time ordain and establish."

[Passed 8 to 2 to 1.]

ELBRIDGE GERRY: We need juries to protect against corrupt judges, prosecutors, and police. Juries serve as a critical democratic check against abuses by the government. [[35]]

GEORGE MASON: We should add "or encreased" in § 1 regarding judges' compensation to prevent the legislature from influencing their decisions with the allure of more money.

[Proposal fails.]

JOHN RUTLEDGE: Throwing out ideas here, but maybe we should have decisions of state judges appealable to the national legislature.[[36]]

JAMES MADISON: Another idea: we can have the Senate appoint federal judges.

ALEXANDER HAMILTON: I prefer having the President nominate and the Senate confirm.

The Trial of all ~~*criminal offences*~~ Crimes, except in Cases of Impeachment, shall be ~~*in the State where they shall be committed; and shall be by jury.*~~ by Jury; [[35]] and such Trial shall be held in the State where the said Crimes shall have been committed; but when not committed within any State, the Trial shall be at such Place or Places as the Congress may by Law have directed.[40]

~~*In all disputes*~~ [[36]] ~~*and controversies now subsisting, or that may hereafter subsist, between two or more States, respecting jurisdiction or territory, the Senate shall possess the following powers:—Whenever the Legislature or the Executive authority, or lawful agent of any State, in controversy with another, shall, by memorial to the Senate, state the matter in question, and apply for a hearing, notice of such memorial and application shall be given, by order of the Senate, to the Legislature, or the Executive authority, of the other State in controversy. The Senate shall also assign a day for the appearance of the parties, by their agents, before that House. The agents shall be directed to appoint, by joint consent, commissioners or judges to constitute a court for hearing and determining the matter in question. But if the agents cannot agree, the Senate shall name three persons out of each of the several States; and from the list of such persons, each party shall alternately strike out one, until the number shall be reduced to thirteen; and from that number, not less than seven, nor more than nine, names, as the Senate shall direct, shall, in their presence, be drawn out by lot; and the persons whose names shall be so drawn, or any five of them, shall be commissioners or judges to hear and finally determine the controversy; provided a majority of the judges who shall hear the cause agree in the determination. If either party shall neglect to attend at the day assigned, without showing sufficient reasons for not attending, or being present shall refuse to strike, the Senate shall proceed to nominate three persons out of each State, and the Clerk of the Senate shall strike in behalf of the party absent or refusing. If any of the parties shall refuse to submit to the authority of such court, or shall not appear to prosecute or defend their claim or cause, the court shall nevertheless proceed to pronounce judgment. The judgment shall be final and conclusive. The proceedings shall be transmitted to the President of the Senate, and shall be lodged among the public records for the security of the parties concerned. Every commissioner shall, before he sit in judgment, take an oath to be administered by one of the Judges of the Supreme or Superior Court of the State where the cause shall be tried, "well and truly to hear and determine the*~~

40. This clause constitutionalizes jury-trial rights and the location of trials, which are grievances and rights described in earlier documents in this book.

~~*matter in question, according to the best of his judgment, without favor, affection, or hope of reward."*~~[41]

~~*All controversies concerning lands claimed under different grants of two or more States, whose jurisdictions, as they respect such lands, shall have been decided or adjusted subsequently to such grants, or any of them, shall, on application to the Senate, be finally determined, as near as may be, in the same manner as is before prescribed for deciding controversies between different States.*~~

Section. 3. [Treason]

Treason against the United States, shall consist only in levying War against ~~*the United States, or any of*~~ them~~;~~, ~~*and*~~ or [[37]] in adhering to ~~*the enemies of the United States, or any of them*~~ their Enemies, giving them Aid and Comfort. No Person shall be convicted of Treason~~,~~ unless on the Testimony of two Witnesses to the same overt Act,[[38]] or on Confession in open Court.[42] [[39]]

The ~~*Legislature of the United States*~~ Congress shall have Power to declare the Punishment of Treason~~.~~, but no ~~*No*~~ Attainder of Treason shall work Corruption of Blood, ~~*n*~~or Forfeiture~~,~~ except during the Life of the Person attainted.

JAMES MADISON: We should change this "and" to an "or" so that there is no confusion that both are required.[[37]]

BENJAMIN FRANKLIN: There were many political abuses of the treason charge in England, and treason was far too easy to prove. I like the addition of "to the same overt act." Prosecutions for treason were generally virulent; and perjury too easily made use of against innocence.[[38]]

[Passed 8 to 3.]

LUTHER MARTIN: A traitor could also confess. We should add "or on confession of open court."[[39]]

[Passed 7 to 3.]

---

41. By striking the parenthetical "except such as shall regard territory or jurisdiction" earlier in Article III, § 2 (*see* p. 153), the Framers took from the Senate the power to decide jurisdiction and territorial disputes between states and gave the power to the Supreme Court. The Constitution therefore no longer needed this long provision, carried over from the Articles of Confederation. *See* p. 111.

Note that Article II, § 2 and Article III, § 1 both refer to "Judges" of the Supreme Court and not "Justices." (Although Article I, § 3 refers to the Chief Justice, a term taken from English tradition.) Congress started using the term "justices" in the Federal Judiciary Act (1789) ("That the supreme court of the United States shall consist of a chief justice and five associate justices. . . .").

42. This section was borrowed largely from English law but narrows the definition of treason to prevent abuse. In England, "treason" was interpreted broadly and carried harsh penalties that included death. The final sentence clarifies that the treason conviction does not extend beyond the life of the person convicted (meaning their families can, among other things, still inherit property).

In the English and American tradition, treason can only be committed by someone who actually has an allegiance to the country. (For example, a foreign terrorist plotting against America doesn't commit "treason.") Curiously, the Framers neglected to include this important limitation in the Treason Clause. This was quickly fixed in a treason statute enacted in 1790, which added "owing allegiance to the United States of America."

Article. IV.[43]

[*State Relationships*]

Section. 1. [Full Faith and Credit]

Full Faith and Credit shall be given in each State to the public Acts ~~*of the Legislatures*~~, ~~*and to the*~~ Records, and judicial Proceedings ~~*of the courts and magistrates,*~~ of every other State. And the Congress may by general Laws prescribe the Manner in which such Acts, Records and Proceedings shall be proved, and the Effect thereof.

Section. 2. [Interstate Comity: Privileges and Immunities, Extradition, Slavery]

The Citizens of each State shall be entitled to all Privileges and Immunities of Citizens in the several States.[44]

~~*Any*~~ A Person charged in any State with Treason, Felony, or other Crime ~~*high misdemeanor in any State*~~, who shall flee from Justice, and ~~*shall*~~ be found in ~~*any other*~~ another State, shall~~,~~ on Demand of the executive ~~*power*~~ Authority of the State from which he fled, be delivered up, ~~*and*~~ to be removed to the State having Jurisdiction of the ~~*offence*~~ Crime.

No Person held to Service or Labour in one State, under the Laws thereof, escaping into another, shall, in Consequence of any Law or Regulation therein, be discharged from such Service or Labour, but shall be

43. This important Article tries to avoid conflicts between states. It requires state courts to respect the laws and valid judgments of courts in other states. As just one example, without this Article individuals or businesses could simply litigate issues in various states until they get a favorable outcome. Then disputes would arise over which outcome is binding. Under Article IV, as long as the original court had jurisdiction, its decision is typically binding. This Article also allows the enforcement of one state's judgements in another state, ensuring that wrongdoers cannot avoid liability by simply moving to another state.

44. Notably, the Articles of Confederation excluded from privileges and immunities "paupers, vagabonds and fugitives" (poor, homeless, and fugitives) and slaves. *See* p. 105.

delivered up [[40]] on Claim of the Party to whom such Service or Labour may be due. [45]

Section. 3. [Addition of New States] [46] [[41]]

New States ~~*lawfully constituted or established within the limits of the United States*~~ may be admitted~~,~~ by the ~~*Legislature*~~ Congress~~,~~ into this ~~*government*~~ Union; but no new State shall be formed or erected within the Jurisdiction of any other State; nor any State be formed by the Junction of two or more States, or Parts of States, without the Consent of the Legislatures of the States concerned as well as of the Congress. ~~*to such admission the consent of two-thirds of the members present in each House shall be necessary. If a new State shall arise within the limits of any of the present States, the consent of the Legislatures of such States shall be also necessary to its admission. If the admission be consented to, the new States shall be admitted on the same terms with the original States. But the Legislature may make conditions with the new States concerning the public debt which shall be then subsisting.*~~

The Congress shall have Power to dispose of and make all needful Rules and Regulations respecting the Territory or other Property belonging to the United States; and nothing in this Constitution shall be so construed as to Prejudice any Claims of the United States, or of any particular State.

PIERCE BUTLER; CHARLES PINCKNEY: We should require fugitive slaves and servants to be delivered up like criminals. [[40]]

JAMES WILSON: That would oblige the Executive of the State to do it, at the public expence. Quite an infringement on States' rights.

ROGER SHERMAN: There is no more propriety in the public seizing and surrendering a slave or servant than a horse.

[Compromise to include passed 11 to 0.]

GOUVERNEUR MORRIS: *[Committee of Style revision]* I will revise this section to make it a little harder for newly acquired territories to become states and ensure that Congress controls the rules of admission. I am concerned that new states will (1) be slave states, (2) overpower the original thirteen states, and (3) have bad or disgruntled leaders who fled from existing states. [[41]]

---

45. **Thirteenth Amendment** [Prohibition on Slavery and Involuntary Servitude]: Neither slavery nor involuntary servitude, except as a punishment for crime whereof the party shall have been duly convicted, shall exist within the United States, or any place subject to their jurisdiction.

The Committee of Detail's draft did not include a Fugitive Slave Clause; the clause was added at the Convention. The Convention's version included the word "justly" to describe the slave service or labor, which would have arguably resulted in the Constitution contemplating "just" slavery. The Committee of Style removed "justly" when it reworded this clause in the final version. (Several Committee members opposed slavery.)

The Constitution takes great pains to avoid using the word "slaves" (although the term was used regularly in Convention). This was the work of Northern states who wanted to avoid expressly mentioning slavery in such an important document. It was also likely for diplomatic reasons, and to give abolitionists at least an argument in the future (however weak) that the Constitution was not really talking about slavery. Compare this to the Confederate Constitution (pp. 229, 235, 244, and 245), which replaces many such euphemisms with "slaves" or "slavery."

46. This section anticipates westward expansion—not just thirteen states. There was no debate or opposition to the last-minute addition of the last paragraph. Morris later conceded that if the delegates truly understood what he was trying to do (effectively governing new territories as provinces rather than states), "strong opposition would have been made."

ELIZABETH WILLING POWEL: *[After the Convention]* So, what sort of government is this? [[42]]

BENJAMIN FRANKLIN: It's a republic, if you can keep it.

JAMES MADISON: *[In Federalist 39]* A republic derives all of its powers directly or indirectly from the great body of the people. It is *essential* that our republic is derived from the great body of the society, not from an inconsiderable proportion, or some favored class.

JAMES MADISON: Perhaps the greatest flaw of the Articles of Confederation was that amendments had to be unanimously approved states. Article V strikes the perfect balance.[[43]]

THOMAS JEFFERSON: *[In 1789 and 1816]* Each generation should have an opportunity to revisit the Constitution to repair it as they see fit. That is roughly every 19 or 20 years. The earth belongs to the living.

JAMES MADISON: *[In 1790]* I disagree. If the dead improve the earth, the living owe it to the dead to honor those improvements.

JAMES WILSON: Shall it be "two-thirds" of the several states? [[44]]

[Vote fails and Wilson amends to three-fourths.]

JOHN RUTLEDGE: South Carolina can never agree to let provisions relating to slaves be promptly amended after ratification by free states. We should add: "provided that no amendments, which may be made prior

Section. 4. [Republican Form of Government] [[42]]

The United States shall guarantee to ~~*each*~~ every State in this Union a Republican Form of Government~~;~~, and shall protect each ~~*State*~~ of them against ~~*foreign*~~ Invasions~~,~~; and~~,~~ on Application of ~~*its*~~ the Legislature, or of the Executive (when the Legislature cannot be convened), against domestic Violence.[47]

Article. V. [[43]]
[*Amending the Constitution*]

~~*On the application of the Legislatures of two-thirds of the States in the Union, for an amendment of this Constitution, the Legislature of the United States shall call a convention for that purpose.*~~

The Congress, whenever two thirds of both Houses shall deem it necessary, shall propose Amendments to this Constitution, or, on the Application of the Legislatures of two thirds of the several States, shall call a Convention for proposing Amendments, which, in either Case, shall be valid to all Intents and Purposes, as Part of this Constitution, when ratified by the Legislatures of three fourths of the several States, or by Conventions in three fourths [[44]] thereof, as the one or the other Mode of Ratification may be proposed by the Congress; Provided that no Amendment which may be made prior to the Year One thousand eight hundred and eight shall in any Manner affect the first and fourth Clauses in the Ninth Section of the first Article; and that no State, without its Consent, shall be deprived of it's equal Suffrage in the Senate. [[45]]

47. This section enjoyed renewed significance during Reconstruction, where reconstructionists tried to ensure a Republican form of government even for former slaves. Those efforts were undermined after the assassination of Abraham Lincoln, during the presidency of Andrew Johnson and thereafter.

Article. VI.
[*Debts Validated; Supreme Law; No Religious Tests; Oath*]

All Debts contracted and Engagements entered into, before the Adoption of this Constitution, shall be as valid against the United States under this Constitution, as under the Confederation.[48]

~~*The acts of the Legislature*~~ This Constitution, and the Laws of the United States which shall be made in Pursuance thereof ~~*of this Constitution*,~~; and all Treaties made, or which shall be made, under the Authority of the United States, shall be the supreme Law [[46]] of ~~*the several States, and of their citizens and inhabitants*~~ the Land~~,~~; and the Judges in ~~*the several*~~ every State*s* shall be bound thereby ~~*in their decisions*~~, any Thing in the Constitution*s* or Laws of ~~*the several*~~ any State*s* to the Contrary notwithstanding.

The ~~*members of the Legislatures*~~ Senators and Representatives before mentioned, and the Members of the several State Legislatures, and all executive and judicial Officers ~~*of the United States*~~, both of the United States~~,~~ and of the several States, shall be bound by Oath or Affirmation, to support this Constitution; but no religious Test shall[[47]] ever be required as a Qualification to any Office or public Trust under the United States.

48. Debt validation avoids the perception that the Constitution was a declaration of bankruptcy that voided all debts and contracts.

to the year 1808, shall in any manner affect the fourth and fifth sections of the seventh article." [[45]]

[Passed 9 to 1 to 1]

[As discussed on p. 147, this was based on a compromise to strike the provision governing navigation acts. Congress can pass navigation acts by a simple majority, but can't prohibit the importation of slaves for twenty years.]

GOUVERNEUR MORRIS:
[Committee of Style revision] This should be reworded to be crystal clear that federal law is supreme, and that Supreme Court precedents are binding on all states.[[46]]

GEORGE MASON:
Treaties being the supreme law gives the President and Senate effectively an exclusive power of legislation, improperly excluding the House. See my comments on pp. 138, 143, and 150.

CHARLES PINCKNEY:
We need a line here that prohibits religious tests. There were many abuses in England when religion was entangled with national government.[[47]]

JAMES MADISON:
This should be 7, requiring a concurrence of a majority of the States and the people. [[48]]

ROGER SHERMAN:
This should be 13, all of the States.

[Motion fails.]

ROGER SHERMAN:
OK, 10.

[Motion fails 4 to 7.]

GEORGE MASON:
The people are accustomed to 9 under the Articles of Confederation.

[Motion passes 8 to 3.]

RUFUS KING:
Let's make this binding only between the states "so ratifying," to address non-ratifying states.

[Motion passes 9 to 1.]

GOUVERNEUR MORRIS:
I move to strike "of the Conventions." We can let the states decide how to ratify.

RUFUS KING:
Conventions are the only way to avoid the complexities of the state legislatures, and to avoid those currently in power who are enemies of the Constitution.

NATHANIAL GORHAM:
I say we urge the expediency of conventions.

[Motion fails. This is addressed in the Resolutions that accompany the Constitution. See p. 165.]

Article. VII.
[*Ratification*]

The Ratification of the Conventions[49] of ~~*[blank]*~~ nine[[48]] States, shall be sufficient for ~~*organizing*~~ the Establishment of this Constitution between the States so ratifying the Same.

[Errata][50]

The Word, "the", being interlined between the seventh and eighth Lines of the first Page, The Word "Thirty" being partly written on an Erazure in the fifteenth Line of the first Page, The Words "is tried" being interlined between the thirty second and thirty third Lines of the first Page and the Word "the" being interlined between the forty third and forty fourth Lines of the second Page.

49. Some feared that state legislatures would reject ratification if it was left up to them (the Constitution reduced state power). Art. VII largely bypasses state legislatures and prefers ratification directly by a vote of the people. *See also* Ratification Resolution, p. 165 (recommending a vote of the people for ratification).

50. Scribe Jacob Shallus documented his last-minute changes and corrections here.

Done in Convention by the Unanimous Consent of the States present the Seventeenth Day of September in the Year of our Lord one thousand seven hundred and Eighty seven and of the Independance of the United States of America the Twelfth. In witness whereof We have hereunto subscribed our Names,[[49]]

EDMUND RANDOLPH:
Gentlemen, I will not be signing this document. It gives too much power to the federal government. Nine states will not ratify this anyway and it will all have been in vain.[[49]]

GEORGE MASON:
Agree. This does not adequately protect individual rights. I'm going to campaign against this.

ELBRIDGE GERRY:
Agree with both of these,
I am also not signing.

BENJAMIN FRANKLIN:
I do not agree with everything in here, but now being an old man, I have experienced many instances of changing my mind, even on important subjects, that I once thought right but later found to be otherwise. Sirs, would you join with me in a little doubt of your own infallibility, and sign this so that we can show the people and the world that we are unanimous? What if we add:

"Done in Convention by the unanimous consent of the states present, the 17th of September, &c. In witness whereof, we have hereunto subscribed our names."

If we add that language, your signature serves as authentication, despite your objections, simply saying that the states *present* were unanimous? So you would be signing that form, not the Constitution.

ALEXANDER HAMILTON: Gentlemen, please appreciate Dr. Franklin's wisdom. Refusing to sign might do infinite mischief by kindling the latent sparks that lurk under an enthusiasm. I'm not even sure that this document will last a generation, but we must start somewhere.

GOUVERNEUR MORRIS: I agree that it is not perfect but it is the best that we can do at this time. Shall we have a national government or not?

EDMUND RANDOLPH: Regrettably, I am still a no.

GEORGE MASON: Same.

ELBRIDGE GERRY: Same. I fear that a civil war is brewing and this Constitution does not prevent it; in fact it could have the contrary effect.

CHARLES COTESWORTH PINCKNEY: We are not likely to gain many converts by the ambiguity of Dr. Franklin's proposed form of signing. Let's get on with signing.

JAMES MADISON: Ratification is what matters. The Constitution is nothing more than a dead letter until life and validity are breathed into it by the voice of the people, speaking through the several State Conventions.

PRESIDT. AND DEPUTY FROM VIRGINIA
Go. Washington

DELAWARE
Geo: Read,
Gunning Bedford jun,
John Dickinson,
Richard Bassett,
Jaco: Broom

MARYLAND
James McHenry,
Dan of St. Thos. Jenifer,
Danl. Carrol

VIRGINIA
John Blair,
James Madison Jr.

NORTH CAROLINA
Wm. Blount,
Richd. Dobbs Spaight,
Hu Williamson

SOUTH CAROLINA
J. Rutledge,
Charles Cotesworth Pinckney,
Charles Pinckney,
Pierce Butler

GEORGIA
William Few,
Abr Baldwin

Attest
William Jackson, Secretary

NEW HAMPSHIRE
John Langdon,
Nicholas Gilman

MASSACHUSETTS
Nathaniel Gorham,
Rufus King

CONNECTICUT
Wm: Saml. Johnson,
Roger Sherman

NEW YORK
Alexander Hamilton

NEW JERSEY
Wil: Livingston,
David Brearley,
Wm. Paterson,
Jona: Dayton

PENSYLVANIA
B Franklin,
Thomas Mifflin,
Robt. Morris,
Geo. Clymer,
Thos. FitzSimons,
Jared Ingersoll,
James Wilson,
Gouv Morris

Letter of George Washington to the President of Congress[51]

In Convention, September 17, 1787

SIR,

WE have now the honor to submit to the consideration of the United States in Congress assembled, the Constitution which has appeared to us the most adviseable.

The friends of our country have long seen and desired, that the power of making war, peace and treaties, that of levying money and regulating commerce, and the correspondent executive and judicial authorities should be fully and ~~*exclusively*~~ effectually vested in the general government of the Union~~. *But*~~: but the impropriety of delegating such extensive trust to one body of men is ~~*self*~~ evident~~.~~—Hence results the necessity of a different organization.

It is obviously impracticable ---- in the fœderal government of these States, to secure all rights of independent sovereignty to each, and yet provide for the interest and safety of all~~.~~—Individuals entering into society, must give up a share of liberty to preserve the rest. The magnitude of the sacrifice must depend as well on situation and circumstance~~s~~, as on the object to be obtained. It is at all times difficult to draw with precision the line between those rights which must be surrendered, and those which may be reserved~~*And*~~; and on the present occasion this difficulty was encreased by a difference among the several States as to their situation, extent, habits, and particular interests.

51. The Convention approved the sending of this now somewhat "forgotten" but rather incredible letter from George Washington to the President of Congress (Arthur St. Clair) to accompany the new Constitution. Congress then resolved unanimously that the Constitution (and this letter) be transmitted to the state legislatures for ratification. This letter prepares for difficult ratification debates. Some scholars include it alongside other sources (like the Federalist Papers) to inform an original understanding.

The letter appears in the handwriting of Gouverneur Morris, though some people theorize that the letter was actually authored by Hamilton. Both served on the Committee of Style, which the Convention tasked with drafting the cover letter.

On Sept. 10, 1787, the Convention voted to instruct the Committee of Style to arrange the articles agreed upon and "to prepare an Address to the people." This book tracks the changes between the "draught of a letter to Congress" presented on Sept. 12, and the final, Sept. 17 version (as reported in Farrand's Records), with Gouverneur Morris' last-minute changes in green.

In all our deliberations on this subject we kept steadily in our view, that which appears to us the greatest interest of every true American, the consolidation of our Union, in which is involved our prosperity, felicity, safety, perhaps our national existence. This important consideration, seriously and deeply impressed on our minds, led each State in the Convention to be less rigid on points of inferior magnitude, than might have been otherwise expected~~. *And*~~; and thus the Constitution, which we now present, is the result of a spirit of amity, and of that mutual deference and concession which the peculiarity of our political situation rendered indispens~~i~~able.

That it will meet the full and entire approbation of ~~*any one*~~ every State is not perhaps to be expected~~ *But*~~; but each will doubtless consider, that had her interest~~s *been*~~ alone been consulted, the consequences might have been particularly disagreeable or injurious to others~~. *That*~~; that it is liable to as few exceptions as could reasonably have been expected, we hope and believe~~. *That*~~; that it may promote the lasting welfare of that country so dear to us all, and secure her freedom and happiness, is our most ardent wish.

With great respect,

We have the Honor to be, SIR,

Your Excellency's most

Obedient and humble Servants:

George Washington, *President.*

By unanimous Order of the CONVENTION.

His Excellency

THE PRESIDENT OF CONGRESS.

Resolution from Constitutional Convention Concerning Ratification of the Proposed Constitution[52]

IN CONVENTION Monday September 17th 1787.

Present

The States of New Hampshire, Massachusetts, Connecticut, Mr. Hamilton from New York, New Jersey, Pennsylvania, Delaware, Maryland, Virginia, North Carolina, South Carolina and Georgia.

Resolved, That the proceeding ~~*This*~~ Constitution ~~*shall*~~ be laid before the United States in Congress assembled, ~~*for their approbation;*~~ and that it is the Opinion of this Convention, that it should ~~*be*~~ afterwards be submitted to a Convention of Delegates, chosen in each State by the People thereof, under the Recommendation of its Legislature, ~~*in order to receive the ratification of such Convention.*~~ for their Assent and Ratification; and that each Convention assenting to, and ratifying the Same, should give Notice thereof to the United States in Congress assembled.

~~*To introduce this government, it is the opinion of this Convention, that each assenting convention should notify its assent and ratification to the United States in Congress assembled; that Congress, after receiving the assent and ratification of the Conventions of—States, should appoint and publish a day, as early as may be, and appoint a place, for commencing proceedings under this Constitution;*~~

Resolved, That it is the Opinion of this Convention, that as soon as the Conventions of nine States shall have ratified this Constitution, the United States in Congress assembled should fix a Day on which Electors should be appointed by the States which shall have ratified the same, and a Day on which the Electors should assemble to vote for the President, and the Time and Place for commencing Proceedings under this Constitution. That after such Publication~~*, the Legislatures of the several States should elect members of the Senate and direct the*~~

52. Similar resolutions appear at the end of the Articles of Confederation. *See* p. 117.

These tracked changes show the difference between the text that was referred to the Committee of Style on Sept. 10, 1787, and the final, Sept. 17 version (as reported in Farrand's Records). These were controversial articles "XXII" and "XXIII" of the draft constitution that was sent to the Committee of Style, and the Committee cleverly converted them to resolutions instead of formal articles based on opposition to including them in the text of the Constitution.

~~*election of members of the House of Representatives; and that the members of the Legislature should meet at the time and place assigned by Congress, and should, as soon as may be after their meeting, choose the President of the United States, and proceed to execute this Constitution.*~~ the Electors should be appointed, and the Senators and Representatives elected: That the Electors should meet on the Day fixed for the Election of the President, and should transmit their Votes certified, signed, sealed and directed, as the Constitution requires, to the Secretary of the United States in Congress assembled, that the Senators and Representatives should convene at the Time and Place assigned; that the Senators should appoint a President of the Senate, for the sole Purpose of receiving, opening and counting the Votes for President;

and, that after he shall be chosen, the Congress, together with the President, should, without Delay, proceed to execute this Constitution.

By the Unanimous Order of the Convention

Go WASHINGTON Presidt

W. JACKSON Secretary.

The Amendments

Introduction

Perhaps the greatest flaw in the Articles of Confederation was the inability to amend them (amendments required unanimity), meaning problems with the Articles could not be adequately addressed, nor could the Articles realistically be amended to reflect changing public sentiment. Article V of the Constitution tries to address these shortcomings, which has led to twenty-seven ratified amendments. Amendments must be properly proposed and then ratified. Article V provides two methods of doing each.

1) An amendment can be proposed and sent to the states by
    a. a two-thirds (66%) majority in the House and Senate, or
    b. a national convention called by two-thirds (66%) of the state legislatures (this option has never occurred).
2) Ratification requires approval by
    a. three-fourths (75%) of the state legislatures, or
    b. state ratifying conventions in three-fourths (75%) of the states (this option only occurring for the Twenty-First Amendment (repeal of prohibition)).

Amendments have generally come in waves, beginning with what we now call the "Bill of Rights" (the first ten Amendments), which were needed to secure ratification of the Constitution by enough states. The second wave, the Reconstruction Amendments, reflected what some have called the "Second Founding." These Amendments restructured American laws after the Civil War and addressed what many of the Framers saw as a substantial missed opportunity in the 1787 Constitution (adequately addressing slavery and incorporation of certain rights so that the rights protections apply against state governments, not just the federal government as originally designed). After a few more amendments, a third wave occurred during the Civil Rights Era of the 1960s.

On August 24, 1789, the House voted in favor of presenting seventeen amendments to the states for ratification and forwarded the proposed amendments to the Senate. The Senate made changes and the two proposals underwent reconciliation to arrive at the final versions. Congress approved twelve amendments, but the states only ratified ten. For the Bill of Rights, this book compares the final text with the House version passed on August 24, 1789. It also includes James Madison's proposed language and other proposals so that the reader can compare these versions, the House version, and the ratified text.

For subsequent amendments, the book compares a key draft with the ratified version as transcribed by the National Archives (unless substantial rearranging occurred, which is not tracked).[1] For many amendments, the book also includes other notable proposals so that the reader can compare each to the ratified version. For example, for the Seventeenth Amendment (Popular Election of Senators), changes are tracked between the ratified version and a House joint resolution from the same session of Congress, but Sen. Henry Storrs had proposed the amendment some 85 years before, so that version is also included for reference. Notable proponents and opponents provide commentary in the margin. For Amendments XI–XXVII, the drafts compared are identified in each section, with final transcriptions from the National Archives.

---

1. Like the Constitution (*see* p. 131), there are sometimes variations between different versions of an Amendment—the version that Congress passed, the ones that the states actually ratified, or later printed versions. Typically, variations are in punctuation. This book does not wade into proposing a "correct" final version of every amendment but instead defers to the version transcribed by the National Archives.

Congress of the United States,
begun and held at the City of New-York, on
Wednesday the fourth of March, one thousand seven hundred and eighty nine.

Engrossed Bill of Rights

Amendments I–X (Bill of Rights)

Passed Congress September 25, 1789.
Ratified December 15, 1791.

~~*James Madison Draft (June 8, 1789)*~~

~~*First. That there be prefixed*~~[[1]] ~~*to the Constitution a declaration, that all power is originally vested in, and consequently derived from, the people. That Government is instituted and ought to be exercised for the benefit of the people; which consists in the enjoyment of life and liberty, with the right of acquiring and using property, and generally of pursuing and obtaining happiness and safety. That the people have an indubitable, unalienable, and indefeasible right to reform or change their Government, whenever it be found adverse or inadequate to the purposes of its institution.*~~[2]

[*View Madison's draft language in Annals of Congress*]

Congress of the United States,
begun and held at the City of New-York, on
Wednesday the fourth of March, one thousand seven hundred
and eighty nine.

THE Conventions of a number of the States, having at the time of their adopting the Constitution, expressed a desire, in order to prevent misconstruction or abuse of its powers, that further declaratory and restrictive clauses should be added: And as extending the ground of public confidence in the Government, will best ensure the beneficent ends of its institution.

RESOLVED by the Senate and House of Representatives of the United States of America, in Congress assembled, two thirds of both Houses concurring, that the following Articles be proposed to the Legislatures of the several States, as amendments to the Constitution of the United States, all, or any of which Articles, when ratified by three fourths of the said Legislatures, to be valid to all intents and purposes, as part of the said Constitution; viz.

2. Interestingly, Madison wanted to incorporate a right that was referenced in the Declaration, "that the people have an indubitable, unalienable, and indefeasible right to reform or change their Government, whenever it be found adverse or inadequate to the purposes of its institution," a proposal that failed.

THOMAS JEFFERSON: *[While in France.]* Unquestionably, we need a Bill of Rights. The Constitution does not protect individual freedoms clearly enough against intrusions by the federal government.

JAMES MADISON: I originally didn't think so because the government only has the limited power we gave it, but I've come around to the idea. I've proposed some new language before the Preamble to clarify a few central ideas. But I see that Congress wants to cut this language.[[1]]

ROGER SHERMAN: The existing Preamble is fine. Also isn't it a bit early to be amending the Constitution already? The point of Art. 5 is to correct problems, and we aren't sure whether there are any problems yet.

JAMES MADISON: Many people are dissatisfied with the Constitution, but would be satisfied with these amendments. The Federalists also promised everyone that we'd pass a Bill of Rights.

ARTICLES in addition to, and Amendment of the Constitution of the United States of America, proposed by Congress, and ratified by the Legislatures of the several States, pursuant to the fifth Article of the original Constitution.[3]

Amendment I

[*Religion; Speech and the Press; Assembly; Petition*]

Congress shall make no law ~~*establishing*~~ respecting an establishment of religion, or prohibiting the free exercise thereof~~,~~; or abridging the freedom of speech, or of the press; or the right of the people peaceably to assemble, ~~*and consult for their common good*~~, and to petition the Government for a redress of grievances.~~, *nor shall the rights of Conscience be infringed.*~~ [[2]]

Compared Draft

House Passed Version (August 24, 1789)

Article the Third[4]

Congress shall make no law establishing religion or prohibiting the free exercise thereof, nor shall the rights of Conscience be infringed.

Article the Fourth

The Freedom of Speech, and of the Press, and the right of the People peaceably to assemble, and consult for their common good, and to apply to the Government for a redress of grievances, shall not be infringed.

JAMES MADISON: Congress should not establish a religion, and enforce the legal observation of it by law, nor compel men to worship God in any manner contrary to their conscience. And please do not omit freedom of conscience or of the press. These are the *choicest* privileges of the people and were unguarded in the English constitution.[[2]]

JAMES MADISON: We should weave the amendments into the main text of the Constitution, not just append them to the end.

ELBRIDGE GERRY: Agree, though I also do not think it matters much.

ROGER SHERMAN: Nonsense. That will delegitimize the whole document. Plus, I'm not even sure we could do that. The People passed the Constitution, but only State Governments will ratify amendments. All amendments need to be supplements, at the end.

3. This is the original title of the Amendments, taken from the Sept. 25, 1789 Joint Resolution of Congress Proposing 12 Amendments to the U.S. Constitution. Although Congress initially approved twelve amendments, the first was never ratified, and the second was only ratified in 1992 (Amendment XXVII).

4. People regularly (and incorrectly) contend that because it is listed first, the First Amendment is the most important. As we can see from the prior footnote, Congress passed two other amendments first, which the states failed to ratify.

The final version of the First Amendment combines amendments that were originally separate in the House draft.

Other Selected Drafts

Virginia Convention (June 27, 1788)

All men have an equal, natural and unalienable right to the free exercise of religion according to the dictates of conscience, and that no particular religious sect or society ought to be favored or established by Law in preference to others.

That the people have a right peaceably to assemble together to consult for their common good or to instruct their Representatives; and that every person has a right to petition or apply to the legislature for redress of grievances

New Hampshire Convention (June 21, 1788)

Congress shall make no Laws touching Religion, or to infringe the rights of Conscience.

New York Convention (July 26, 1788)

That the people have a right peaceably to assemble together to consult for their common good, or to instruct their Representatives; and that every Person has a right to Petition or apply to the Legislature for redress of Grievances. That Freedom of the Press ought not to be violated or restrained.

James Madison Draft (June 8, 1789)

Fourthly. That in article 1st, section 9, between clauses 3 and 4, be inserted these clauses, to wit: The civil rights of none shall be abridged on account of religious belief or worship, nor shall any national religion be established,[5] nor shall the full and equal rights of conscience be in any manner, or on any pretext, infringed.

The people shall not be deprived or abridged of their right to speak, or to write, or to publish their sentiments; and the freedom of the press, as one of the great bulwarks of liberty, shall be inviolable. The people shall not be restrained from peaceably assembling and consulting for their common good; nor from applying to the Legislature by petitions, remonstrances, for redress of their grievances.

1689 English Declaration

That it is the right of the subjects to petition the king, and all commitments and prosecutions for such petitioning are illegal.

5. Madison's original proposal included a prohibition of the establishment of any "national religion."

Amendment II[[3]]

[*Right to Bear Arms*]

A well regulated Militia, ~~*composed of the body of the People,*~~ being necessary to the security of a free State, the right of the people to keep and bear Arms, shall not be infringed~~*, but no one religiously scrupulous of bearing arms, shall be compelled to render military service in person*~~.[6]

Compared Draft

House Passed Version (August 24, 1789)

Article the Fifth

A well regulated militia, composed of the body of the People, being the best security of a free State, the right of the People to keep and bear arms, shall not be infringed, but no one religiously scrupulous of bearing arms, shall be compelled to render military service in person.

Other Selected Drafts

James Madison Draft (June 8, 1789)

Fourthly. That in article 1st, section 9, between clauses 3 and 4, . . . The right of the people to keep and bear arms shall not be infringed; a well armed and well

6. In the early United States, citizen militias were drawn from the local community to provide for the common defense. Standing armies were viewed by many with suspicion, so militias could serve that role or, if a standing army were established, militias could counter abuses. The modern debates about the Second Amendment largely turn on whether the focus of this right is on "militia" or "the people" (or at times, "well regulated" vs. "shall not be infringed"). The Articles of Confederation describe arming a militia in Article VI. *See* p. 108. (As does John Dickinson's earlier draft Articles.) The Supreme Court held in *District of Columbia v. Heller* (2008), that the Second Amendment protects an individual right to bear arms for self-defense.

Some have argued that the final, omitted phrase (regarding conscientious objectors) suggests that the amendment focused on militias and not on individual rights. As this book's introduction notes, omission can cut both ways.

While the bill of rights in most states at the time mirrored the federal version of the Second Amendment, some states had narrower protections (clearly only for militias), but Pennsylvania (September 28, 1776) and Vermont (July 8, 1777) had broader protections: "the people have the right to bear arms for the defence of themselves and the State." As shown in the selected drafts, the 1689 English Bill of Rights included a right to bear arms for self-defense, but it was limited to Protestants and could be regulated by Parliament. *See* p. 22.

ELBRIDGE GERRY: These ten amendments, I take it, are intended to secure the people against bad governments.

I am apprehensive, sirs, that this clause would give an opportunity to the people in power to destroy the constitution itself. They can declare who are those religiously scrupulous and prevent them from taking arms.

What, sirs, is the use of a militia?

It is to prevent the establishment of a standing army, the bane of liberty. We saw this in England.[[3]]

JOSHUA SENEY: I'm sorry, but what are you talking about? Do you have a question or a change?

ELBRIDGE GERRY: I am just getting to it. We need to redraft or remove the final sentence.

[Final sentence removed in the Senate.]

regulated militia being the best security of a free country: but no person religiously scrupulous of bearing arms shall be compelled to render military service in person.[7]

Constitutional Amendments Committee Version (June 27, 1788)

17th. That the people have a right to keep and bear arms; that a well-regulated militia, composed of the body of the people trained to arms, is the proper, natural, and safe defence of a free state; that standing armies, in time of peace, are dangerous to liberty, and therefore ought to be avoided, as far as the circumstances and protection of the community will admit; and that, in all cases, the military should be under strict subordination to, and governed by, the civil power.

. . .

19th. That any person religiously scrupulous of bearing arms ought to be exempted, upon payment of an equivalent to employ another to bear arms in his stead.

1689 English Declaration

That the subjects which are Protestants may have arms for their defence suitable to their conditions and as allowed by law.

---

7. The House select committee switched the order of Madison's proposed phrases, placing the militia first. It also tied the importance of the militia to the state rather than to the nation.

Amendment III
[*Quartering Soldiers*]

No Soldier shall, in time of peace be quartered in any house, without the consent of the Owner, nor in time of war, but in a manner to be prescribed by law.[8]

Compared Draft

House Passed Version (August 24, 1789)

Article the Sixth

No soldier shall, in time of peace, be quartered in any house without the consent of the owner, nor in time of war, but in a manner to be prescribed by law.

Other Selected Drafts

New Hampshire Convention (June 21, 1788)

Nor shall soldiers in Time of Peace be Quartered upon private Houses without the consent of the Owners

James Madison Draft (June 8, 1789)

Fourthly. That in article 1st, section 9, between clauses 3 and 4, . . . No soldiers shall in time of peace be quartered in any house without the consent of the owner; nor at any time, but in a manner warranted by law.

PATRICK HENRY: As stated in the Declaration, the quartering of soldiers was one of the principal reasons for dissolving the connection with Great Britain.

8. After the French and Indian War, British soldiers remained in America and Quartering Acts required colonists to house British troops when barracks were full. The Third Amendment is a direct response. In wartime, quartering would be permissible, but only within guidelines set out by law.

Joseph Story, interpreting the Third Amendment in his *Commentaries on the Constitution of the United States* and borrowing from *Semayne's Case* (1604) stated that a person's house was his castle. This "castle doctrine," led to "zones of privacy" that now extend beyond the Third Amendment; it is used in the context of the First, Fourth, Fifth, and Ninth Amendments.

Amendment IV[[4]]

[*Searches and Seizures; Warrants*]

The right of the people to be secure in their persons, houses, papers, and effects, against unreasonable searches and seizures, shall not be violated, and no Warrants shall issue, but upon probable cause, supported by Oath or affirmation, and particularly describing the place to be searched, and the persons or things to be seized.[9]

Compared Draft

House Passed Version (August 24, 1789)

Article the Seventh

The right of the People to be secure in their persons, houses, papers and effects, against unreasonable searches and seizures, shall not be violated, and no warrants shall issue, but upon probable cause supported by oath or affirmation, and particularly describing the place to be searched, and the persons or things to be seized.

Other Selected Drafts

Virginia Convention (June 27, 1788)

That every freeman has a right to be secure from all unreasonable searches and seizures of his person, his papers and his property; all warrants, therefore, to search suspected places, or seize any freeman, his papers or property, without information upon Oath (or affirmation of a person religiously scrupulous of taking an oath) of legal and sufficient cause,[[5]] are grievous and oppressive; and all general Warrants to search suspected places, or to apprehend any suspected person, without specifically naming or describing the place or person, are dangerous and ought not to be granted.[10]

THOMAS JEFFERSON: As I alluded to in the Declaration, the King gave his agents broad authority to search and seize ships, warehouses, and homes using general, unspecific warrants. Let us follow Massachusetts (1756) and others to offer limited protection against general warrants.[[4]]

JAMES WILSON: As *[influential criminal law theorist]* Beccaria says, "let the laws be clear and simple: let the entire force of the nation be united in their defence: let them, and them only, be feared."

JAMES MADISON: I'll tweak Virginia's language; instead of "legal and sufficient cause," let's use "probable cause," the latter being a well-established legal concept.[[5]]

---

9. Colonists endured British ransacking of their homes and arrests without warrants, and knew of famous instances of the same in England like the *Wilkes v. Wood* (1763) case, leading to the Fourth Amendment. This Amendment protects against such abuses and protects privacy rights. "Searches and seizures" must be reasonable, and warrants must be based on probable cause and include specific details.

10. The Virginia Convention revised the language that first appeared in the Virginia Declaration of Rights of 1776, and advocated for its application to the federal government.

James Madison Draft (June 8, 1789)

Fourthly. That in article 1st, section 9, between clauses 3 and 4, . . . The rights of the people to be secured in their persons, their houses, their papers, and their other property, from all unreasonable searches and seizures, shall not be violated by warrants issued without probable cause,[[6]] supported by oath or affirmation, or not particularly describing the places to be searched, or the persons or things to be seized.

ELBRIDGE GERRY:
I'm not sure if "shall not be violated by warrants issued without probable cause" is a typo or what, but it should be changed to "shall not be violated," and then a separate clause covering warrants.[[6]]

ROGER SHERMAN: Most of these are rights enjoyed by Englishmen and can also be found in Virginia's Declaration of Rights (1776). There is not much debate about these. But let us also constitutionalize the traditional protection against double jeopardy.

If a person is acquitted at the first trial, he ought not to be tried a second time.[[7]]

Amendment V
[*Grand Jury; Double Jeopardy; Self-Incrimination; Due Process; Takings*]

No person shall be held to answer for a capital, or otherwise infamous crime, unless on a presentment or indictment of a Grand Jury, except in cases arising in the land or naval forces, or in the Militia, when in actual service in time of War or public danger; nor shall any person be subject~~,~~ ~~*except in case of impeachment, to more than one trial, or one punishment for the same offense,*~~ for the same offence to be twice put in jeopardy of life or limb;[[7]] nor shall be compelled in any criminal case to be a witness against himself, nor be deprived of life, liberty, or property, without due process of law; nor shall private property be taken for public use, without just compensation.[11]

Compared Draft

House Passed Version (August 24, 1789)

Article the Eighth[12]

No person shall be subject, except in case of impeachment, to more than one trial, or one punishment for the same offense, nor shall be compelled in any criminal case, to be a witness against himself, nor be deprived of life, liberty or property, without due process of law; nor shall private property be taken for public use without just compensation.

---

11. This important Amendment (rooted in Magna Carta) is a mixture of provisions affecting both civil and criminal law. The provisions limit the power of the government to take action against the individual. It includes many due-process rights and (somewhat ill-fittingly) prevents the government from taking private property without just compensation. Madison might have had a copy of the Northwest Ordinance nearby when drafting this amendment; the Northwest Ordinance also lumps together procedural rights with a takings clause. *See* p. 126.

12. The final versions of the Fifth and Sixth Amendments (shown with minimal redlines here) move clauses around from earlier drafts. Full texts of drafts are included here for reference. The final version places the "impartial jury" language into the Sixth Amendment and Double Jeopardy into the Fifth Amendment.

Article the Tenth

The trial of all crimes (except in cases of impeachment, and in cases arising in the land or naval forces, or in the militia when in actual service in time of War or public danger) shall be by an Impartial Jury of the Vicinage, with the requisite of unanimity for conviction, the right of challenge, and other accustomed requisites; and no person shall be held to answer for a capital, or otherways infamous crime, unless on a presentment or indictment by a Grand Jury; but if a crime be committed in a place in the possession of an enemy, or in which an insurrection may prevail, the indictment and trial may by law be authorised in some other place within the same State.

Other Selected Drafts

Virginia Convention (June 27, 1788)

In all capital and criminal prosecutions, a man hath a right to demand the cause and nature of his accusation, to be allowed counsel in his favor, and to a fair and speedy trial by an impartial Jury of his vicinage, without whose unanimous consent he cannot be found guilty, (except in the government of the land and naval forces) nor can he be compelled to give evidence against himself.

James Madison Draft (June 8, 1789)

Fourthly. That in article 1st, section 9, between clauses 3 and 4, . . . No person shall be subject, except in cases of impeachment, to more than one punishment or one trial for the same offence; nor shall be compelled to be a witness against himself; nor be deprived of life, liberty, or property, without due process of law; nor be obliged to relinquish his property,[[8]] where it may be necessary for public use, without a just compensation.

JAMES MADISON: I'll modify and add a takings clause to the Virginia Convention's proposal.[[8]]

. . .

Seventhly. That in article 3d, section 2, the third clause be struck out, and in its place be inserted the clauses following, to wit: The trial of all crimes (except in cases of impeachments, and cases arising in the land or naval forces, or the militia when on actual service, in time of war or public danger) shall be by an impartial jury of freeholders of the vicinage, with the requisite of unanimity for conviction, of the right of challenge, and other accustomed requisites; and in all crimes punishable with loss of life or member, presentment or indictment by a grand jury shall be an essential preliminary, provided that in cases of crimes committed within any county which may be in possession of an enemy, or in which a general insurrection may prevail, the trial may by law be authorized in some other county of the same State, as near as may be to the seat of the offence. In cases of crimes committed not within any county, the trial may by law be in such county as the laws shall have prescribed.

1689 English Declaration

That jurors ought to be duly impanelled and returned, and jurors which pass upon men in trials for high treason ought to be freeholders.

That all grants and promises of fines and forfeitures of particular persons before conviction are illegal and void.

Amendment VI
[*Jury Trial for Crimes; Criminal Procedural Rights*]

In all criminal prosecutions, the accused shall enjoy the right to a speedy and public trial, by an impartial jury of the State and district wherein the crime shall have been committed, which district shall have been previously ascertained by law,[13] and [[9]] to be informed of the nature and cause of the accusation; to be confronted with the witnesses against him; to have compulsory process for obtaining witnesses in his favor, and to have the Assistance of Counsel for his defence.[14]

THE HOUSE:
The Committee proposes adding this redline, rewording the vicinage language. This is a special concern in a country the size of the United States where law and judicial practices differ from one place to another. A jury of a man's neighbors is more likely to understand the relevant circumstances and give him a fair trial.[[9]]

Compared Draft

House Passed Version (August 24, 1789)

Article the Ninth

In all criminal prosecutions, the accused shall enjoy the right to a speedy and public trial, to be informed of the nature and cause of the accusation, to be confronted with the witnesses against him, to have compulsory process for obtaining witnesses in his favor, and to have the assistance of counsel for his defence.

Other Selected Drafts

Virginia Convention (June 27, 1788)

In all capital and criminal prosecutions, a man hath a right to demand the cause and nature of his accusation, to be allowed counsel in his favor, and to a fair and

13. Parliament had provided that Americans suspected of certain crimes against the Crown could be transported to Britain for trial (due to juries sometimes refusing to convict offenders who were obviously guilty of violating English law), prompting the requirement of trials in the "district wherein the crime shall have been committed," here and in Art. III, § 2. This amendment was also proposed to protect the right to a fair trial, a traditional right of Englishmen and one that was protected in most state constitutions.

14. The Sixth Amendment is also rooted in rights declared in Magna Carta, including due-process rights. Regarding the right to counsel, the Fifth Amendment right to counsel, first recognized in *Miranda v. Arizona* (1966), refers to the right to have an attorney present during a custodial interrogation; the Sixth Amendment right to counsel refers the right to effective assistance of counsel during critical stages of criminal prosecutions. For drafts, see Fifth Amendment.

speedy trial by an impartial Jury of his vicinage, without whose unanimous consent he cannot be found guilty, (except in the government of the land and naval forces) nor can he be compelled to give evidence against himself.

James Madison Draft (June 8, 1789)

Fourthly. That in article 1st, section 9, between clauses 3 and 4, . . In all criminal prosecutions, the accused shall enjoy the right to a speedy and public trial, to be informed of the cause and nature of the accusation, to be confronted with his accusers, and the witnesses against him; to have a compulsory process for obtaining witnesses in his favor; and to have the assistance of counsel or his defence.

Amendment VII
[*Civil Trial Rights*]

In Suits at common law, where the value in controversy shall exceed twenty dollars, the right of trial by jury shall be preserved, and no fact tried by a jury, shall be otherwise re-examined in any Court of the United States, than according to the rules of the common law.[15]

Selected Drafts

House Passed Version (August 24, 1789)

Article the Eleventh

No appeal to the Supreme Court of the United States, shall be allowed, where the value in controversy shall not amount to one thousand dollars,[[10]] nor shall any fact, triable by a Jury according to the course of the common law, be otherwise re-examinable, than according to the rules of common law.

Article the Twelfth

In suits at common law, the right of trial by Jury shall be preserved.[16]

New Hampshire Convention (June 21, 1788)

All Common Law Cases between Citizens of different States shall be commenced in the Common Law Courts of the respective States and no appeal shall be allowed to the Federal court in such Cases unless the sum or value of the thing in Controversy amount to three Thousand Dollars.

JAMES MADISON: There is little danger that any federal court will admit an appeal where the matter in dispute is under a thousand dollars, but as the possibility of it happening has excited in the minds of many citizens, the greatest apprehension that persons of opulence would carry a cause from the extremities of the union to the Supreme Court, and therefore prevent the due administration of justice, it ought to be guarded against.[[10]]

---

15. The Seventh Amendment guarantees a jury trial in civil cases at law in federal court. Some Framers wanted to include the right (rooted in English common law) in the main text of the Constitution (for example, in Article III, § 2), but those efforts failed. In colonial times, when sympathetic local juries acquitted fellow colonialists accused of evading British duties or taxes, British authorities created special courts to try and convict them. This amendment ensured that the new federal government protected the right to jury trials and made a distinction between the facts of a case, which were to be determined by juries, and the interpretation of law, which judges determine.

16. This amendment was proposed to correct a perceived defect in the Constitution. Article III, Section 2 of the Constitution guaranteed the right of jury trial to criminal defendants but said nothing about civil cases. *See* p. 154.

In civil actions between Citizens of different States every issue of fact arising in actions at common law shall be tried by jury, if the parties, or either of them request it.

Virginia Convention (June 27, 1788)

That in controversies respecting property, and in suits between man and man, the ancient trial by jury is one of the greatest Securities to the rights of the people, and ought to remain sacred and inviolable.

New York Convention (July 26, 1788)

In all other cases to which the Judicial Power of the United States extends, and in which the Supreme Court of the United States has not original Jurisdiction, the Causes shall be heard, tried, and determined in some one of the State Courts, with the right of Appeal to the Supreme Court of the United States. . . .

James Madison Draft (June 8, 1789)

Sixthly. That, in article 3d, section 2, be annexed to the end of clause 2d, these words, to wit: But no appeal to such court shall be allowed where the value in controversy shall not amount to ___ dollars: nor shall any fact triable by jury, according to the course of common law, be otherwise re-examinable than may consist with the principles of common law.

Amendment VIII
[*Excessive Bail; Cruel and Unusual Punishment*]

Excessive bail shall not be required, nor excessive fines imposed, nor cruel and unusual punishments inflicted.[17]

Compared Draft

House Passed Version (August 24, 1789)

Article the Thirteenth

Excessive bail shall not be required, nor excessive fines imposed, nor cruel and unusual punishments inflicted.

Other Selected Drafts

Virginia Convention (June 27, 1788)

That excessive Bail ought not to be required; nor excessive Fines imposed; nor Cruel or unusual Punishments inflicted.

James Madison Draft (June 8, 1789)

Fourthly. That in article 1st, section 9, between clauses 3 and 4, . . . Excessive bail shall not be required, nor excessive fines imposed, nor cruel and unusual punishments inflicted.

1689 English Declaration of Rights

That excessive bail ought not to be required, nor excessive fines imposed, nor cruel and unusual punishments inflicted.

JAMES MADISON: There is consensus that this is an important right, dating back to at least the English Bill of Rights.

17. Beccaria's treatise *On Crimes and Punishment* (1764) informed many of the Framers' views on proportional punishment. There was little debate over the need for or language of this amendment.

Amendment IX
[*Unenumerated Rights*]

The enumeration in the Constitution, of certain rights, shall not be construed to deny or disparage[[11]] others retained by the people.[18]

ELBRIDGE GERRY: This should probably be "impair" instead of "disparage." The latter is not very clear. *[Proposal fails.]* [[11]]

Compared Draft

House Passed Version (August 24, 1789)

Article the Fifteenth

The enumeration in the Constitution of certain rights, shall not be construed to deny or disparage others retained by the people.

Other Selected Drafts

Virginia Convention (June 27, 1788)

There are certain natural rights of which men, when they form a social compact cannot deprive or divest their posterity, among which are the enjoyment of life and liberty, with the means of acquiring, possessing and protecting property, and pursuing and obtaining happiness and safety.

New York Convention (July 26, 1788)

That the Powers of Government may be reassumed by the People, whensoever it shall become necessary to their Happiness; that every Power, Jurisdiction and Right, which is not by the said Constitution clearly delegated to the Congress of the United States, or to the departments of the Government thereof, remains to

18. The Ninth Amendment was included to address fears that expressly protecting certain rights might be misinterpreted to allow the infringement of rights that exist but were not explicitly listed in the text of the new Constitution. The Amendment clarified that just because a right is enumerated, that should not be construed to mean that the Constitution does not protect other rights that are not enumerated.

This Amendment can be traced in part to the Declaration of Independence, recognizing natural rights: "That to secure these rights, Governments are instituted among Men, deriving their just powers from the consent of the governed. . . ." The House adopted part of Madison's language, which the Senate revised. Akhil Amar posits a "close triangular interrelation among the Preamble and the Ninth and Tenth Amendments," the core theme being popular sovereignty—"We the People" retaining the ultimate power.

the People of the several States or to their respective State Governments to whom they may have granted the same. . . .

James Madison Draft (June 8, 1789)

Fourthly. That in article 1st, section 9, between clauses 3 and 4, . . . The exceptions here or elsewhere in the Constitution, made in favor of particular rights, shall not be so construed as to diminish the just importance of other rights retained by the people, or as to enlarge the powers delegated by the Constitution; but either as actual limitations of such powers, or as inserted merely for greater caution.

Amendment X
[*Rights Reserved to the States and the People*]

The powers not [[12]] delegated to the United States by the Constitution, nor prohibited by it~~,~~ to the States, are reserved to the States respectively, or to the people.[19] [[13]]

Compared Draft

House Passed Version (August 24, 1789)

Article the Seventeenth

The powers not delegated by the Constitution, nor prohibited by it, to the States, are reserved to the States respectively.

Other Selected Drafts

Massachusetts Convention (February 6, 1788)

That it be explicitly declared that all Powers not expressly delegated by the aforesaid Constitution are reserved to the several States to be by them exercised.

James Madison Draft (June 8, 1789)

Eighthly. That immediately after article 6th, be inserted, as article 7th, the clauses following, to wit: . . . The powers not delegated by this Constitution, nor prohibited by it to the States, are reserved to the States respectively.

PATRICK HENRY: We need this amendment. For example, in Great Britain, for every possible right that is not reserved to the people by some express provision or compact, it is within the king's prerogative.

THOMAS TUDOR TUCKER: We should add "expressly" before "delegated," as stated in the Articles of Confederation.[[12]] *[See p. 104.]*

JAMES MADISON: No, there are *implied* powers of government that we haven't expressly enumerated. We don't want to cause confusion.

ROGER SHERMAN: I agree with Mr. Madison.

DANIEL CARROLL: We should add "or to the people" at the end to emphasize the idea that ultimate power resides with the people.[[13]]

---

19. The Ninth Amendment tries to guard against an inference that the only rights that exist are enumerated rights. In contrast, the Tenth Amendment tries to guard against using the new Constitution to infer powers in the national government that were not granted. The Tenth Amendment expresses a federalism principle—that powers not given to the federal government are reserved to each state or to the People.

The Supreme Court's Tenth Amendment jurisprudence has varied over time. At times it has been interpreted as an affirmative federalism limitation used to invalidate federal statutes as infringing on power reserved to the states or the People. At other times, it is interpreted as the Ninth Amendment is sometimes interpreted—less substantively and more as a rule of construction.

ATTEST,

Frederick Augustus Muhlenberg, Speaker of the House of Representatives

John Adams, Vice-President of the United States, and President of the Senate

John Beckley, Clerk of the House of Representatives.

Sam. A Otis, Secretary of the Senate

Rejected from the Bill of Rights[20]

Selective Incorporation of Parts of the Bill of Rights to the States[21]

House Passed Version (August 24, 1789)

Article the Fourteenth

No State shall infringe the right of trial by Jury in criminal cases, nor the rights of conscience, nor the freedom of speech, or of the press.

James Madison Draft (June 8, 1789)

Fifthly.[[14]] That in article 1st, section 10, between clauses 1 and 2, be inserted this clause, to wit: No State shall violate the equal rights of conscience, or the freedom of the press, or the trial by jury in criminal cases.[[15]]

JAMES MADISON: This is the most valuable amendment on the whole list. If we restrain the federal government from infringing on these rights, we should do so against the states. The people want these protections.[[14]]

THOMAS TUDOR TUCKER: We should leave these protections to states, not govern this nationally.[[15]]

[Senate ultimately strikes.]

Separation of Powers[22]

House Passed Version (August 24, 1789)

Article the Sixteenth

The powers delegated by the Constitution to the government of the United States, shall be exercised as therein appropriated, so that the Legislative shall never exercise the powers vested in the Executive or Judicial; nor the Executive the powers vested in the Legislative or Judicial; nor the Judicial the powers vested in the Legislative or Executive.

---

20. James Madison proposed these additional amendments (in addition to the reapportionment amendment on p. 222), but these failed in the Senate.

21. Madison and the House wanted to incorporate parts of the Bill of Rights to apply to the states (not just to the federal government). This was rejected. However, the Supreme Court has since held that most of the provisions of the Bill of Rights apply to the states through the Fourteenth Amendment's Due Process Clause.

22. Madison proposed an entirely new article of the Constitution. The House splits these into two proposed amendments (sixteenth and seventeenth). The seventeenth survived, becoming the Tenth Amendment; his sixteenth failed.

James Madison Draft (June 8, 1789)

Eighthly.[[16]] That immediately after article 6th, be inserted, as article 7th, the clauses following, to wit: The powers delegated by this Constitution are appropriated to the departments to which they are respectively distributed: so that the Legislative Department shall never exercise the powers vested in the Executive or Judicial, nor the Executive exercise the powers vested in the Legislative or Judicial, nor the Judicial exercise the powers vested in the Legislative or Executive Departments.

Ninthly. That article 7th be numbered as article 8th.

JAMES MADISON:
The people will love this amendment. It helps explain the Constitution and guarantees that the powers are separate and distinct.[[16]]

ROGER SHERMAN:
This is wholly unnecessary, and others agree. The text of the Constitution already provides for this clearly enough.

JAMES MADISON:
It will do no harm to adopt it.

[Senate defeats this amendment on September 7, 1789.]

CALEB STRONG: The Supreme Court just ruled in *Chisholm v. Georgia* (1793) that people can sue states, based on the text of Article III. We need to pass an amendment clarifying that this is not permitted. We are accustomed to states having sovereign immunity based on English tradition. This amendment will advance state autonomy, and these young states also might not survive financially if they continue to incur lawsuits.

Amendment XI
[*Suits Against States*]

[Passed Congress March 4, 1794. Ratified February 7, 1795.]

The Judicial power of the United States~~, *except in cases arising under treaties made under the authority of the United States,*~~ shall not be construed to extend to any suit in law or equity, commenced or prosecuted against one of the United States by Citizens of another State, or by Citizens or Subjects of any Foreign State.

Compared Draft

Senator Albert Gallatin Proposed Amendment (January 14, 1794):

The judicial power of the United States, except in cases arising under treaties, made under the authority of the United States, shall not be construed to extend to any suit in law or equity, commenced or prosecuted against one of the United States, by citizens of another state, or by citizens or subjects of any foreign state. [*View Senate Journal*][23]

Other Selected Drafts

Proposed Amendment to Senator Albert Gallatin Proposed Amendment (January 14, 1794):

The Judicial power of the United States extends to all cases in law and equity in which one of the United States is a party; but no suit shall be prosecuted against one of the United States by citizens of another State, or by citizens of subjects of a foreign State, where the cause of action shall have arisen before the ratification of this amendment. [*View Senate Journal*]

23. Note for eBook readers: currently, government-supported links for later amendments only link to entire documents (not individual pages). However, the information can be located within those documents using the dates that are provided.

Amendment XII
[*Election of President*]

[Passed Congress December 9, 1803. Ratified June 15, 1804.][24]

The Electors shall meet in their respective states and vote by ballot for President and Vice-President, one of whom, at least, shall not be an inhabitant of the same state with themselves; they shall name in their ballots the person voted for as President, and in distinct ballots the person voted for as Vice-President, and they shall make distinct lists of all persons voted for as President, and of all persons voted for as Vice-President, and of the number of votes for each, which lists they shall sign and certify, and transmit sealed to the seat of the government of the United States, directed to the President of the Senate; the President of the Senate shall, in the presence of the Senate and House of Representatives, open all the certificates and the votes shall then be counted; The person having the greatest number of votes for President, shall be the President, if such number be a majority of the whole number of Electors appointed; and if no person have such majority, then from the persons having the highest numbers not exceeding three on the list of those voted for as President, the House of Representatives shall choose immediately, by ballot, the President. But in choosing the President, the votes shall be taken by states, the representation from each state having one vote; a quorum for this purpose shall consist of a member or members from two-thirds of the states, and a majority of all the states shall be necessary to a choice. And if the House of Representatives shall not choose a President whenever the right of choice shall devolve upon them, before the fourth day of March next following, then the Vice-President shall act as President, as in case of the death or other constitutional disability of the President.[25]

---

24. As discussed on p. 149, the Twelfth Amendment was designed to avoid a repeat of the contested election of 1800.

25. **Twentieth Amendment § 3** [Presidential Term and Succession]: If, at the time fixed for the beginning of the term of the President, the President elect shall have died, the Vice President elect shall become President. If a President shall not have been chosen before the time fixed for the beginning of his term, or if the President elect shall have failed to qualify, then the Vice President elect shall act as President until a President shall have qualified; and the Congress may by law provide for

The person having the greatest number of votes as Vice-President, shall be the Vice-President, if such number be a majority of the whole number of Electors appointed, and if no person have a majority, then from the two highest numbers on the list, the Senate shall choose the Vice-President; a quorum for the purpose shall consist of two-thirds of the whole number of Senators, and a majority of the whole number shall be necessary to a choice. But no person constitutionally ineligible to the office of President shall be eligible to that of Vice-President of the United States.

Selected Drafts

House Select Committee of Seventeen Draft (October 22, 1803)

In all future elections of President and Vice President, the Electors shall name in their ballots the person voted for as President, and in distinct ballots the person voted for as Vice President, of whom one at least shall not be an inhabitant of the same State with themselves. The person having a majority of all the Electors for President shall be the President; and if there shall be no such majority, the President shall be chosen from the highest numbers, not exceeding three, on the list for President, by the House of Representatives, in the manner directed by the Constitution. The person having the greatest number of votes as Vice President shall be the Vice President, and in case of an equal number of votes for two or more persons for Vice President, they being the highest on the list, the Senate shall choose the Vice President from those having such equal number, in the manner directed by the Constitution. [*View House Journal*]

the case wherein neither a President elect nor a Vice President elect shall have qualified, declaring who shall then act as President, or the manner in which one who is to act shall be selected, and such person shall act accordingly until a President or Vice President shall have qualified.

Amendment XIII
[*Abolition of Slavery*]

[Passed Congress January 31, 1865. Ratified December 6, 1865.]

Section 1. [*Prohibition on Slavery and Involuntary Servitude*][26]

Neither slavery nor involuntary servitude, except as a punishment for crime whereof the party shall have been duly convicted,[27] shall exist within the United States, or any place subject to their jurisdiction.

Section 2. [*Enforcement*]

Congress shall have power to enforce this article by appropriate legislation.

Selected Drafts

Northwest Ordinance (1787)

There shall be neither slavery nor involuntary servitude in the said territory, otherwise than in the punishment of crimes whereof the party shall have been duly convicted.

Rep. Ashley (Dec 14, 1863)

Slavery or involuntary servitude, except in punishment of crime, whereof the party shall have been duly convicted, is hereby forever prohibited in all the States of this Union, and in all Territories now owned, or which may hereafter be acquired by the United States.

Rep. Wilson (Dec 14, 1863)

Slavery, being incompatible with a free government, is forever prohibited in the United States; and involuntary servitude shall be permitted only as a punishment for crime. Congress shall have power to enforce the foregoing section of this article by appropriate legislation.

ABRAHAM LINCOLN: If slavery is not wrong, nothing is wrong. But I have done as much as I can do with my powers as President and we need a constitutional amendment.

LYMAN TRUMBULL: Completely agree, Mr. President.

JAMES ASHLEY: I agree with James Madison *[see p. 147]* that there cannot be such a thing as property in man. A majority in a republic cannot rightfully enslave the minority, nor can the accumulated decrees of courts or the musty precedents of governments make oppression just. It is a system at war with human nature, revolting and brutal. Some slave barons justify it with scripture, but it is at variance with the precepts of Christianity and every idea of justice. It is absolutely indefensible in itself, a terrible barbarism of indescribable villainy.

---

26. The Thirteenth Amendment was the first of three "Reconstruction Amendments," rebuilding America after the Civil War.

27. Notice that the Thirteenth Amendment closely mirrors language from the Northwest Ordinance (1787). *See also* p. 121. Some states exploited the language "except as a punishment for crime whereof the party shall have been duly convicted," by passing broad criminal laws aimed at former slaves so that they could be convicted of crimes and re-enslaved.

Sen. Henderson (Jan 11, 1864)

Slavery or involuntary servitude, except as a punishment for crime, shall not exist in the United States.

Sen. Sumner (Feb 8, 1864)

Everywhere within the limits of the United States, and of each State or Territory thereof, all persons are equal before the law, so that no person can hold another as a slave; and the Congress shall have power to make all laws necessary and proper to carry this declaration into effect everywhere in the United States.

Rep. Thomas Corwin (March 2, 1861)[28]

No amendment shall be made to the Constitution which will authorize or give to Congress the power to abolish or interfere, within any State, with the domestic institutions thereof, including that of persons held to labor or service by the laws of said State.

28. After Lincoln prevailed in the 1860 election, to placate the South and to prevent a civil war, President Buchanan and congressmen rushed to enact the opposite of today's Thirteenth Amendment. The Corwin Amendment actually passed in Congress in 1861. Although Lincoln opposed slavery, he stated in his first inaugural address that he had "no objection" to the Corwin Amendment (likely because it did not expand slavery) and Congress sent it to the states. Although a few states ratified it, the Civil War prevented full ratification.

Amendment XIV
[*Equal Protection and Other Rights*]

[Passed Congress June 13, 1866. Ratified July 9, 1868.][29]

Section 1. *[Rights]*[[17]]

All persons born or naturalized in the United States, and subject to the jurisdiction thereof, are citizens of the United States and of the State wherein they reside. No State shall make or enforce any law which shall abridge the privileges or immunities[[18]] of citizens of the United States; nor shall any State deprive any person of life, liberty, or property, without due process of law; nor deny to any person within its jurisdiction the equal protection of the laws.[[19]]

Section 2. *[Apportionment of Representation]*[30]

Representatives shall be apportioned among the several States according to their respective numbers, counting the whole number of persons in each State, excluding Indians not taxed. But when the right to vote at any election for the choice of electors for President and Vice-President of the United States, Representatives in Congress, the Executive and Judicial officers of a State, or the members of the Legislature thereof, is denied to any of the male inhabitants of such State, being twenty-one years of age, and citizens of the United States, or in any way abridged, except for participation in rebellion, or other crime, the basis of representation therein shall be reduced in the proportion which the number of such male citizens shall bear to the whole number of male citizens twenty-one years of age in such State.

29. Many Southern states tried to rescind their ratification of the Fourteenth Amendment after federal troops were withdrawn from the South (Georgia, North Carolina, South Carolina, and Kentucky). Congress did not recognize these attempts to rescind. The Fourteenth Amendment combined several drafts, so changes are not tracked.

30. Section 2 amends the Three-Fifths Clause.

JOHN BINGHAM: Some contend that the Bill of Rights only applies to the *federal* government. The great object of the first section of this amendment is to restrain the power of the *states* and compel them at all times to respect the great fundamental guarantees of the Bill of Rights. As the Declaration of Independence says *[see p. 97]*, the sacred rights of persons are dear to freemen and formidable only to tyrants.[[17]]

THADDEUS STEVENS: All citizens are entitled to privileges, immunities, and equal protection under law, and the federal government has a duty to step in when states fail to uphold these rights.[[18]]

MARTIN LUTHER KING, JR: *[In 1963]* When the architects of our Republic wrote the magnificent words of the Constitution and the Declaration of Independence, they were signing a promissory note to which every American was to fall heir. This note was a promise that all men would be guaranteed the inalienable rights of life, liberty, and the pursuit of happiness.[[19]]

Section 3. [*Disqualification from Holding Office for Insurrection/Rebellion*][31]

No person shall be a Senator or Representative in Congress, or elector of President and Vice-President, or hold any office, civil or military, under the United States, or under any State, who, having previously taken an oath, as a member of Congress, or as an officer of the United States, or as a member of any State legislature, or as an executive or judicial officer of any State, to support the Constitution of the United States, shall have engaged in insurrection or rebellion against the same, or given aid or comfort to the enemies thereof. But Congress may by a vote of two-thirds of each House, remove such disability.

Section 4. [*Public Debt*]

The validity of the public debt of the United States, authorized by law, including debts incurred for payment of pensions and bounties for services in suppressing insurrection or rebellion, shall not be questioned. But neither the United States nor any State shall assume or pay any debt or obligation incurred in aid of insurrection or rebellion against the United States, or any claim for the loss or emancipation of any slave; but all such debts, obligations and claims shall be held illegal and void.

Section 5. [*Enforcement*]

The Congress shall have the power to enforce, by appropriate legislation, the provisions of this article.

Selected Drafts

H.R. 543: Joint Committee on Reconstruction Draft (April 30, 1866)[[20]]

Section 1: No State shall make or enforce any law which shall abridge the privileges or immunities of citizens of the United States; nor shall any State deprive

THADDEUS STEVENS: One flaw in the April 30 draft is that Section 3 does not go far enough.[[20]]

JACOB HOWARD: Agreed.

31. Section 3 was at issue in ***Trump v. Anderson* (2024)**, with challengers seeking to disqualify Donald Trump from the 2024 presidential race under Section 3 for his alleged involvement in the January 6, 2021, Capitol Breach.

any person of life, liberty, or property without due process of law; nor deny to any person within its jurisdiction the equal protection of the laws.

Section 2. Representatives shall be apportioned among the several States, which may be included within this Union, according to their respective numbers, counting the whole number of persons in each State, excluding Indians not taxed. But whenever in any State the elective franchise shall be denied to any portion of its male citizens not less than twenty-one years of age, or in any way abridged, except for participation in rebellion or other crime, the basis of representation in such State shall be reduced in the proportion which the number of such male citizens shall bear to the whole number of male citizens not less than twenty-one years of age.

Section 3. Until the fourth day of July, in the year one thousand eight hundred and seventy, all persons who voluntarily adhered to the late insurrection,[32] giving it aid and comfort, shall be excluded from the right to vote for representatives in Congress and for electors for the President and Vice President of the United States.

Section 4. Neither the United States nor any State shall assume or pay any debt or obligation already incurred, or which may hereafter be incurred, in aid of insurrection or of war against the United States, or any claim for compensation for loss of involuntary service or labor.

Section 5. The Congress shall have power to enforce, by appropriate legislation, the provisions of this article. *[View Congressional Record]*

Jacob Howard Proposed Addition (May 30, 1866)

All persons born in the United States and subject to the jurisdiction thereof are citizens[[21]] of the United States and of the States wherein they reside. No person shall be a Senator or Representative in Congress, or an elector of President and Vice President, or hold any office, civil or military, under the United States, or under any State, who, having previously taken an oath as a member of Congress,

JACOB HOWARD: The committee's draft is missing a citizenship clause. Citizenship is a hotly debated issue, and clarification is particularly needed to protect many rights after ***Dred Scott***. I have added some proposed language.[[21]]

[This language was added as the first sentence of the Amendment.]

32. This phrase is an opportunity to analyze changes to drafts. In the 2024 disqualification proceedings against Donald Trump seeking to prevent him from running or holding office for his purported involvement in the January 6, 2021, Capitol Breach (arguing that Section 3 of the Fourteenth Amendment applies), some argued that Section 3 only applied to insurrectionists from the Civil War. One response is that this earlier draft limited the reach of Section 3 to the "late insurrection" (the Civil War), and that limitation was removed in the final version. (The ratified version does not reference the "late insurrection.") This omission supports an argument that the drafters did not want to limit Section 3 to only the Civil War—it applies to future insurrections as well.

or as an officer of the United States, or as a member of any State Legislature, or as an executive or judicial officer of any State, to support the Constitution of the United States, shall have engaged in insurrection or rebellion against the same, or given aid or comfort to the enemies thereof; but Congress may, by a vote of two thirds of each House, remove such disability. The obligations of the United States incurred in suppressing insurrection, or in defense of the Union or for payment of bounties or pensions incident thereto, shall remain inviolate. *[View Congressional Record]*

Amendment XV [[22]]

[*Right to Vote Not Denied by Race*]

[Passed Congress February 26, 1869. Ratified February 3, 1870.]

Section 1. [*Right to Vote*][33]

The right of citizens of the United States to vote shall not be denied or abridged by the United States or by any State on account of race, color, or previous condition of servitude.

Section 2. [*Enforcement*]

The Congress shall have the power to enforce this article by appropriate legislation.

CHARLES SUMNER: As Alexander Hamilton said in *Federalist 54*, once slaves are free, they are entitled to full rights. This includes equal suffrage. We are mechanics, and the machine we are constructing has for its object the conservation of equal rights.[[22]]

JOHN BINGHAM: Agreed.

Selected Drafts

Sen. Sumner Proposal (February 9, 1869)

That the right to vote, to be voted for, and to hold office shall not be defiled or abridged anywhere in the United States under any pretence of race or color; and all provisions in any State constitutions, or in any laws, State, territorial, or municipal, inconsistent herewith, are hereby declared null and void.

Sec. 2. And be it further enacted, That any person who, under any pretence of race or color, wilfully hinders or attempts to hinder any citizen of the United States from being registered, or from voting, or from being voted for, or from holding office, or who attempts by menaces to deter any such citizen from the exercise or enjoyment of the rights of citizenship above mentioned, shall be punished by a fine not less than one hundred nor more than three thousand dollars, or by imprisonment in the common jail for not less than thirty days nor more than one year.

33. This amendment prohibits the federal government and each state from denying or abridging a citizen's right to vote based on race. But notably, the Supreme Court interpreted this amendment narrowly and many Southern states effectively ignored it for decades. Laws were enacted that required people (targeting Blacks) to demonstrate literacy, prove their good character, pay voting taxes, or overcome other hurdles before being allowed to vote. These discriminatory laws were the target of federal civil-rights reforms in the 1960s and 1970s.

Sec. 3. And be it further enacted, That every person legally engaged in preparing a register of voters, or in holding or conducting an election, who wilfully refuses to register the name or to receive, count, return, or otherwise give the proper legal effect to the vote of any citizen under any pretence of race or color, shall be punished by a fine not less than five hundred nor more than four thousand dollars, or by imprisonment in the common jail for not less than three calendar months nor more than two years.

Sec. 4. And be it further enacted, That the district courts of the United States shall have exclusive jurisdiction of all offences against this act; and the district attorneys, marshals and deputy marshals, the commissioners appointed by the circuit and territorial courts of the United States, with powers of arresting, imprisoning, or bailing offenders, and every other officer specially empowered by the President of the United States, shall be, and they are hereby, required, at the expense of the United States, to institute proceedings against any person who violates this act, and cause him to be arrested and imprisoned or bailed, as the case may be, for trial before such court as by this act has cognizance of the offence.

Sec. 5. And be it further enacted, That every citizen unlawfully deprived of any of the rights of citizenship secured by this act under any pretence of race or color, may maintain a suit against any person so depriving him, and recover damages in the district court of the United States for the district in which such person may be found. *[View drafts in Congressional Record]*

Sen. Fowler Proposal (February 9, 1869):

All the male citizens of the United States, residents of the several States now or hereafter comprehended in the Union, of the age of twenty-one years and upward, shall be entitled to an equal vote in all elections in the State wherein they shall reside, the period of such residence as a qualification for voting to be decided by each State, except such citizens as shall engage in rebellion or insurrection, or shall be duly convicted of treason or other infamous crime.

Sen. Stewart Proposal (February 9, 1869):

No discrimination shall be made in any State among the citizens of the United States in the exercise of the elective franchise, or in the right to hold office in any State, on account of race, color, nativity, property, education, or creed.

Rep. Boutwell Proposal (February 15, 1869):

No discrimination shall be made in any State among citizens of the United Status in the exercise of the elective franchise or in the right to hold office in any State on account of race, color, nativity, property, education or creed.

Rep. Bingham Proposal (February 20, 1869):

The right of citizens of the United States to vote and hold office shall not be denied or abridged by any State on account of race, color, nativity, property, creed, or previous condition of servitude.

Amendment XVI
[*Income Tax*]

[Passed Congress July 2, 1909. Ratified February 3, 1913.]

The Congress shall have power to lay and collect ~~*direct*~~ taxes on incomes, from whatever source derived, without apportionment among the several States ~~*to population*~~, and without regard to any census or enumeration.

Compared Draft

Sen. Bristow Substitute for Joint Resolution 39 (July 5, 1909):

The Congress shall have power to lay and collect direct taxes on incomes without apportionment among the several States according to population. *[View Congressional Record]*

Other Selected Drafts

Joint Resolution 25 (April 28, 1909)

The Congress shall have power to lay and collect taxes on incomes and inheritances.

WILLIAM HOWARD TAFT:
We need this amendment to overturn the Supreme Court's terrible decision in ***Pollock v. Farmers' Loan & Trust Co.*** (1895), finding that income taxes on rents, dividends, and interest were direct taxes and thus had to be apportioned among the states on the basis of population. As we learned under the Articles of Confederation, the federal government needs a stable income source.

Amendment XVII
[*Popular Election of Senators*]

[Passed Congress May 13, 1912. Ratified April 8, 1913.]

The Senate of the United States shall be composed of two Senators from each State, elected by the people thereof, for six years; and each Senator shall have one vote. The electors in each State shall have the qualifications requisite for electors of the most numerous branch of the State legislatures.

~~*The times, places, and manner of holding elections for Senators shall be as prescribed in each State by the legislature thereof.*~~ [[23]]

When vacancies happen in the representation of any State in the Senate, the executive authority of such State shall issue writs of election to fill such vacancies: Provided, That the legislature of any State may empower the executive thereof to make temporary appointments until the people fill the vacancies by election as the legislature may direct.

This amendment shall not be so construed as to affect the election or term of any Senator chosen before it becomes valid as part of the Constitution.

SEN. JOSEPH BRISTOW: Many see the need for this amendment to respond to corruption in state legislatures *[who previously elected senators, see Art. I, § 3, p. 139]* and state gridlock electing senators.

But this race-rider clause would allow states to discriminate and would not allow Congress to intervene. My amendment simply strikes the sentence.[[23]]

Compared Draft

House Joint Resolution 39, (May 1, 1911)

The Senate of the United States shall be composed of two Senators from each State, elected by the people thereof, for six years; and each Senator shall have one vote. The electors in each State shall have the qualifications requisite for electors of the most numerous branch of the State legislatures.

The times, places, and manner of holding elections for Senators shall be as prescribed in each State by the legislature thereof.

When vacancies happen in the representation of any State in the Senate, the executive authority of such State shall issue writs of election to fill such vacancies: Provided, That the legislature of any State may empower the executive thereof to make temporary appointments until the people fill the vacancies by election as the legislature may direct. This amendment shall not be so construed as to affect the election or term of any Senator chosen before it becomes valid as part of the Constitution.

Other Selected Drafts

Sen. Storrs Resolution (February 14, 1826)

Resolved, That it is expedient that the Constitution of the United States be so amended, that the Senators from the several States shall not be appointed by the Legislatures of the States, but shall be chosen by the electors, in each State, having the qualifications requisite for electors of the most numerous branch of the State Legislature. *[View Image]*

Amendment XVIII
[*Prohibition of Liquor*]

[Passed Congress December 18, 1917. Ratified January 16, 1919.]

Section 1. [*Prohibition*][34]

After one year from the ratification of this article the manufacture, sale, or transportation of intoxicating liquors within, the importation thereof into, or the exportation thereof from the United States and all territory subject to the jurisdiction thereof for beverage purposes is hereby prohibited.[35]

Section 2. [*Enforcement*][[24]]

The Congress and the several States shall have concurrent power to enforce this article by appropriate legislation.

Section 3. [*Ratification Deadline*]

This article shall be inoperative unless it shall have been ratified as an amendment to the Constitution by the legislatures of the several States, as provided in the Constitution, within seven years from the date of the submission hereof to the States by the Congress.

ANDREW VOLSTEAD: Consistent with Section 2, now we need a set of strong laws to enforce this wonderful amendment. I'll start drafting.[[24]]

WOODROW WILSON: I will veto your laws, Volstead. They purport to be based on both *wartime* prohibition and prohibition under the Eighteenth Amendment. I'm fine with the latter but the war is over so there is no basis for the former.

ANDREW VOLSTEAD: Congress will override your veto. You don't have the votes.

34. The temperance movement led to this short-lived amendment. Consumption, possession, and self-production for personal consumption were not prohibited. Connecticut and Rhode Island rejected the amendment.

35. **Twenty-First Amendment §1** [Repeal of Prohibition]: The eighteenth article of amendment to the Constitution of the United States is hereby repealed.

AARON SARGENT: The Supreme Court has repeatedly rejected attempts to recognize voting rights for women in the Constitution (for example, the Fourteenth or Fifteenth Amendments), so we can clarify this once and for all with an amendment that is directly on point.[[25]]

Amendment XIX[[25]]
[*Women's Suffrage*]

[Passed Congress June 4, 1919. Ratified August 18, 1920.]

The right of citizens of the United States to vote shall not be denied or abridged by the United States or by any State on account of sex.

Congress shall have power to enforce this article by appropriate legislation.

Compared Draft

Sen. Sargent Proposed Amendment, (January 10, 1878) ("Susan B. Anthony Amendment"):

The right of citizens of the United States to vote shall not be denied or abridged by the United States or by any State on account of sex. Congress shall have power to enforce this article by appropriate legislation. *[View Congressional Record]*

Other Selected Drafts

Sen. Pomeroy Proposed Amendment (S.R. No. 260) December 8, 1870:

The basis of suffrage in the United States shall be that of citizenship; and all native or naturalized citizens shall enjoy the same rights and privileges of the elective franchise; but each State shall determine by law the age of the citizen and the time of the residence required for the exercise of the right of suffrage, which shall apply equally to all citizens; and also shall make all laws concerning the time, places, and manner of holding elections for all State and municipal officers. *[View Congressional Record]*

Senate Bill 1, 39th Congress (December 4, 1865) (Sen. Cowan Amendment—Dec. 12, 1866)

Be it enacted by the Senate and House of Representatives of the United States of America in Congress assembled, That, from and after the passage of this act, each and every *~~male~~*[36] person, of the age of twenty-one years and upwards, who has not been convicted of any infamous crime or offence, and who shall have been born or naturalized in the United States, and who shall have resided in the said District for the period of six months previous to any election therein, shall be entitled to the elective franchise and shall be deemed an elector and entitled to vote at any election in said District without any distinction on account of color, race, or nationality. *[View Congressional Record]*

---

36. Notice the date—60 years before the Nineteenth Amendment. As an early attempt at women's suffrage, Sen. Cowan moved to amend a D.C. voting bill by striking "male" in the bill. The vote failed 37 to 9.

Amendment XX[[26]]

[*"Lame Duck" Amendment*]

[Passed Congress March 2, 1932. Ratified January 23, 1933.]

Section 1. [*Terms*]

The terms of the President and the Vice President ~~*elected after the adoption of this amendment*~~ shall end at noon on the 20th day of January ~~*commence at noon on the third Monday in January following their election*~~, and the terms of Senators and Representatives ~~*elected after the adoption of this amendment*~~ at noon on the 3d day of January ~~*shall commence at noon on the first Monday in January following their election*~~, of the years in which such terms would have ended if this article had not been ratified; and the terms of their successors shall then begin.

Section 2. [*Meetings of Congress*]

The Congress shall assemble at least once in every year, and such meeting shall begin at noon on the 3d day of January ~~*first Monday in January*~~, unless they shall by law appoint a different day.

Section 3. [*Succession*][37]

If, at the time fixed for the beginning of the term of the President, the President elect shall have died, the Vice President elect shall become President. If a President shall not have been chosen before the time fixed for the beginning of his term, or if the President elect shall have failed to qualify, then the Vice President elect shall act as President until a President shall have qualified; and the Congress may by law provide for the case wherein neither a President elect nor a Vice President elect shall have qualified, declaring who shall then act as President, or the manner in which one who is to act shall be selected, and such person shall act accordingly until a President or Vice President shall have qualified.

37. Section 3 clarifies that the Vice President becomes President if the President dies before Inauguration Day, and it gives Congress the authority to determine who should be acting President if no President is declared by Inauguration Day. (See disputed elections of 1800 and 1876.)

ELLISON SMITH: Section 1 reduces the "lame-duck period" between election and inauguration. But why do we use specific dates for these? It could land on a Sunday.[[26]]

GEORGE NORRIS: Our committee spent a lot of time on this exact point. We're not changing the constitutional term length, and if we don't specify precise dates, these elected officials could serve longer or shorter than their specified term.

ALBEN BARKLEY: I was reared in an old-fashioned school of thought which took the position that it is better to work on Sunday when the ox is in the ditch than to deliberately put him in the ditch in order that we might work on Sunday.

GEORGE NORRIS: Do you think that the ox is more liable to be in the ditch on the last day of the session than on the first day?

ALBEN BARKLEY: Yes, probably so. I'll still vote on your bill, just sayin'. A good story is like fine Kentucky bourbon; it improves with age and, if you don't use it too much, it will never hurt anyone.

[This is a summary of some of the actual (bipartisan) discussion of the amendment.]

Section 4. [*Congress and Presidential Succession*]

The Congress may by law provide for the case of the death of any of the persons from whom the House of Representatives may choose a President whenever the right of choice shall have devolved upon them, and for the case of the death of any of the persons from whom the Senate may choose a Vice President whenever the right of choice shall have devolved upon them.

Section 5. [*Effective Date*]

Sections 1 and 2 shall take effect on the 15th day of October following the ratification of this article.

Section 6. [*Ratification Deadline*]

This article shall be inoperative unless it shall have been ratified as an amendment to the Constitution by the legislatures of three-fourths of the several States within seven years from the date of its submission.

Compared Draft

Senate Joint Resolution 253, 67th Congress, (Feb. 23, 1923)[38]

SECTION 1. That the terms of the President and Vice President of the United States elected after the adoption of this amendment shall commence at noon on the third Monday in January following their election.

Sec. 2. That the terms of Senators and Representatives elected after the adoption of this amendment shall commence at noon on the first Monday in January following their election.

Sec. 3. That the Congress shall assemble at least once in every year and such meetings shall be on the first Monday in January, unless they shall by law appoint a different day. *[View Congressional Record]*

38. S.J. Res. 253 is an early version of this amendment, shepherded through Congress over 10 years by Sen. Norris. This is an example of how long amendments can take to work through Congress.

SEN. EDWARD EDWARDS:
The Eighteenth Amendment is one of the most brazen infringements upon personal liberty that has ever been perpetrated on a free people. Since its enactment, the people have also had to wallow through years of corruption, violence, and a system that incentivizes crime by opening golden avenues of wealth by bootlegging and breaking the law. And much of the liquor out there now contains poison, often put there by our own government to discourage consumption![[27]]

SEN. ROBERT WAGNER:
We should strike section three. It gives too much power to the federal government, and this should be an issue left to the states.[[28]]

[Subsequent motion to strike Section 3 passed 33 to 32.]

Amendment XXI[[27]]
[*Repeal of Prohibition*]

[Passed Congress February 20, 1933. Ratified December 5, 1933.]

Section 1. [*Repeal of Eighteenth Amendment*][39]

The eighteenth article of amendment to the Constitution of the United States is hereby repealed.

Section 2. [*Importation, Transportation, and Sale of Liquor*]

The transportation or importation into any State, Territory, or possession of the United States for delivery or use therein of intoxicating liquors, in violation of the laws thereof, is hereby prohibited.

~~*Section 3. Congress shall have concurrent power to regulate or prohibit the sale of intoxicating liquors to be drunk on the premises where sold.*~~[[28]]

Section ~~4~~ 3. [*Ratification Deadline*]

This article shall be inoperative unless it shall have been ratified as an amendment to the Constitution by conventions in the several States, as provided in the Constitution, within seven years from the date of the submission hereof to the States by the Congress.

Compared Draft

Senate Joint Resolution 211 (Jan. 12, 1933)

[Same as final version but Section 3 stricken from Judiciary Committee draft.]
[View Congressional Record]

39. Many people and law-enforcement authorities ignored prohibition under the Eighteenth Amendment, which undermined respect for the law and increased contempt for authority. Additionally, public outrage grew as organized and dangerous mobs capitalized on prohibition.

Amendment XXII
[*Presidential Term Limits*]

[Passed Congress March 21, 1947. Ratified February 27, 1951.]

Section 1. [*Two-Term Limit*]

~~*Any person who has served as*~~ No person shall be elected to the office of the President ~~*of the United States during all or portions of any two terms shall thereafter be Ineligible to hold*~~ more than twice, and no person who has held the office of President, or acted as President, for more than two years of a term to which some other person was elected President shall be elected to the office of the President more than once. But this Article shall not apply to any person holding the office of President when this Article was proposed by the Congress, and shall not prevent any person who may be holding the office of President, or acting as President, during the term within which this Article ~~*is ratified*~~ becomes operative from holding ~~*such*~~ the office of President or acting as President during the remainder of such term.

Section 2. [*Ratification Deadline*]

This article shall be inoperative unless it shall have been ratified as an amendment to the Constitution by the legislatures of three-fourths of the several States within ~~7~~ seven years from the date of its submission to the States by the Congress.

REP. EARL MICHENER: We should enshrine George Washington's two-term legacy.

REP. ESTES KEFAUVER: I am against this amendment. You are only even considering it because FDR continues to be reelected. Do we not trust the wisdom of the American people when electing a President? Hamilton, Morris, Sherman, Wilson, and many others certainly thought we should—we are departing from what the Founders wanted. *[See p. 149.]*

SEN. ROBERT TAFT: *[Son of President and Justice Taft.]* This is getting held up in the Senate; I have proposed some compromise language in Section 1.

Compared Draft

House Joint Resolution No. 27, February 6, 1947

Any person who has served as President of the United States during all or portions of any two terms shall thereafter be Ineligible to hold the office of President. But this article shall not prevent any person who may hold the office of President during the term within which this article is ratified from holding such office for the remainder of such term.

This article shall be inoperative unless It shall have been ratified as an amendment to the Constitution by the legislatures of three-fourths of the several States within 7 years from the date of its submission to the States by the Congress. *[View Congressional Record]*

Amendment XXIII
[*District of Columbia Electors*]

[Passed Congress June 16, 1960. Ratified March 29, 1961.]

Section 1. [*Electors*]

The District constituting the seat of Government of the United States shall appoint in such manner as the Congress may direct:

A number of electors of President and Vice President equal to the whole number of Senators and Representatives in Congress to which the District would be entitled if it were a State, but in no event more than the least populous State; they shall be in addition to those appointed by the States, but they shall be considered, for the purposes of the election of President and Vice President, to be electors appointed by a State; and they shall meet in the District and perform such duties as provided by the twelfth article of amendment.

Section 2. [*Enforcement*]

The Congress shall have power to enforce this article by appropriate legislation.

Compared Draft

House Joint Resolution 757, June 14, 1960

[No change in final version]

Other Selected Drafts

Senate Joint Resolution 39, June 14, 1960[40]

ARTICLE—On any date that the total number of vacancies in the House of Representatives exceeds half of the authorized membership thereof, and for a period of sixty days there—after, the executive authority of each State shall have power to make temporary appointments to fill any vacancies, including those happening during such period, in the representation from his State in the House

40. S.J. Res. 39 contained more robust voting protections, including abolishing a poll tax (see Twenty-Fourth Amendment, p. 216) and property qualifications.

of Representatives. Any person temporarily appointed to fill any such vacancy shall serve until the people fill the vacancy by election as provided for by article I, section 2, of the Constitution.

ARTICLE—

Section 1. The right of citizens of the United States to vote in any primary or other election for electors for President or Vice President, or for Senator or Representative in Congress, shall not be denied or abridged by the United States or any State by reason of failure to pay any poll tax or other tax or to meet any property qualification.

SEC. 2. Nothing in this article shall be construed to invalidate any provision of law denying the right to vote to paupers or persons supported at public expense or by charitable institutions.

SEC. 3. The Congress shall have power to enforce this article by appropriate legislation.

ARTICLE—

The people of the District constituting the seat of the Government of the United States shall elect, in such manner and under such regulations as the Congress shall provide by law—

a number of Delegates to the House of Representatives equal to the number of Representatives to which they would be entitled if the District were a State with such powers as the Congress, by law, shall determine; and

a number of electors of President and Vice President equal to the whole number of Senators and Representatives in the Congress to which the District would be entitled if it were a State; such electors shall possess the qualifications required by article II of this Constitution; they shall be In addition to those appointed by the States, but they shall be considered, for the purposes of the election of President and Vice President, to be electors appointed by a State; and they shall meet in the District and cast their ballots as provided by the twelfth article of amendment. *[View Congressional Record]*

SEN. SPESSARD HOLLAND:
Although I do not oppose discriminating against Blacks based on race, I do have a problem with poll taxes because I care about voting and wealth discrimination. Poll taxes make voting more difficult for poor Whites and Blacks.

Amendment XXIV
[*Abolition of Poll Tax*][41]

[Passed Congress August 27, 1962. Ratified January 23, 1964.]

Section 1. [*No Poll Tax*]

The right of citizens of the United States to vote in any primary or other election for President or Vice President, for electors for President or Vice President, or for Senator or Representative in Congress, shall not be denied or abridged by the United States or any State by reason of failure to pay any poll tax or other tax. ~~or other tax or to meet any property qualification.~~

~~SEC. 2. Nothing in this article shall be construed to invalidate any provision of law denying the right to vote to paupers or persons supported at public expense or by charitable institutions.~~

Section 2. [*Enforcement*]

The Congress shall have power to enforce this article by appropriate legislation.

Compared Draft

Senate Joint Resolution 39, June 14, 1960

. . .

Section 1. The right of citizens of the United States to vote in any primary or other election for electors for President or Vice President, or for Senator or Representative in Congress, shall not be denied or abridged by the United States or any State by reason of failure to pay any poll tax or other tax or to meet any property qualification.

SEC. 2. Nothing in this article shall be construed to invalidate any provision of law denying the right to vote to paupers or persons supported at public expense or by charitable institutions.

SEC. 3. The Congress shall have power to enforce this article by appropriate legislation. *[View Congressional Record]*

41. By 1902, all states of the former Confederacy had enacted a poll tax, largely an effort to disenfranchise Black voters without running afoul of the Fifteenth Amendment.

Amendment XXV
[*Presidential Vacancy*][42]

[Passed Congress July 6, 1965. Ratified February 10, 1967.]

Section 1. [*Presidential Vacancy*]

In case of the removal of the President from office or of his death or resignation, the Vice President shall become President.

Section 2. [*Vice-Presidential Vacancy*]

Whenever there is a vacancy in the office of the Vice President, the President shall nominate a Vice President who shall take office upon confirmation by a majority vote of both Houses of Congress.

Section 3. [*Declaration by President*]

Whenever the President transmits to the President pro tempore of the Senate and the Speaker of the House of Representatives his written declaration that he is unable to discharge the powers and duties of his office, and until he transmits to them a written declaration to the contrary, such powers and duties shall be discharged by the Vice President as Acting President.

Section 4. [*Declaration by Vice President and Others*]

Whenever the Vice President~~,~~ and a majority of either the principal officers of the executive departments or of such other body as Congress may by law provide, transmit to the President pro tempore of the Senate and the Speaker of the House of Representatives their written declaration that the President is unable to discharge the powers and duties of his office, the Vice President shall immediately assume the powers and duties of the office as Acting President.

~~*Whenever*~~ Thereafter, when the President transmits to the President pro tempore of the Senate and the Speaker of the House of Representatives

42. Art. I, §1 tries to account for presidential vacancies but is ambiguous. America had a long history of confusion regarding presidential powers during illness or incapacity, and the assassination of John F. Kennedy in 1963 prompted serious calls for reform. The Twenty-Fifth Amendment clarifies the role of the Vice President (they "become President"), accounts for vice-presidential vacancies, and provides a mechanism for determining whether the President is unable to discharge the powers and duties of office.

his written declaration that no inability exists, he shall resume the powers and duties of his office unless the Vice President~~,~~ and a majority of either the principal officers of the executive department~~s~~ or of such other body as Congress may by law provide, transmit within ~~*two*~~ four days to the President pro tempore of the Senate and the Speaker of the House of Representatives their written declaration that the President is unable to discharge the powers and duties of his office. Thereupon Congress shall ~~*immediately proceed to decide the issue. If the*~~ decide the issue, assembling within forty-eight hours for that purpose if not in session. If the Congress, within twenty-one days after receipt of the latter written declaration, or, if Congress is not in session, within twenty-one days after Congress is required to assemble, determines by two-thirds vote of both Houses that the President is unable to discharge the powers and duties of ~~*the*~~ his office, the Vice President shall continue to discharge the same as Acting President; otherwise, the President shall resume the powers and duties of his office.

Compared Draft

Senate Joint Resolution 1, February 19, 1965

Section 1. In case of the removal of the President from office or of his death or resignation, the Vice President shall become President.

Section 2. Whenever there Is a vacancy in the office of the Vice President, the President shall nominate a Vice President who shall take office upon confirmation by a majority vote of both Houses of Congress.

Section 3. Whenever the President transmits to the President of the Senate and the Speaker of the House of Representatives his written declaration that he is unable to discharge the powers and duties of his office, such powers and duties shall be discharged by the Vice President as Acting President.

Section 4. Whenever the Vice President, and a majority of the principal officers of the executive departments or such other body as Congress may by law provide, transmit to the President of the Senate and the Speaker of the House of Representatives their written declaration that the President is unable to discharge the powers and duties of his office, the Vice President shall immediately assume the powers and duties of the office as Acting President.

Section 5. Whenever the President transmits to the President of the Senate and the Speaker of the House of Representatives his written declaration that no inability exists, he shall resume the powers and duties of his office unless the Vice President, and a majority of the principal officers of the executive departments or such other body as Congress may by law provide, transmit within two days to the President of the Senate and the Speaker of the House of Representatives their written declaration that the President is unable to discharge the powers and duties of his office. Thereupon Congress shall immediately proceed to decide the issue. If the Congress determines by two-thirds vote of both Houses that the President is unable to discharge the powers and duties of the office, the Vice President shall continue to discharge the same as Acting President; otherwise the President shall resume the powers and duties of his office. *[View Congressional Record]*

Other Selected Drafts

Senate Joint Resolution 35 (Keating-Kefauver Proposal), February 5, 1963

In case of the removal of the President from office or of his death or resignation, the said office shall devolve on the Vice President. In case of the inability of the President to discharge the powers and duties of the said office, the said powers and duties shall devolve on the Vice President, until the inability be removed. The Congress may by law provide for the case of removal, death, resignation or inability, both of the President and Vice President, declaring what officer shall then be President, or in case of inability, act as President, and such officer shall be or act as President accordingly, until a President shall be elected or, in case of inability, until the Inability shall be earlier removed. The commencement and termination of any inability shall be determined by such method as Congress shall by law provide.

SEN. ESTES KEFAUVER: *[Now a senator, see p. 213.]* I would have the Congress pass a law to regulate when the President or Vice President cannot discharge their duties, rather than trying to spell it out in a constitutional amendment.

SEN. BIRCH BAYH: Draftees for the war in Vietnam are old enough to be drafted but not old enough to vote on the politicians sending them there. The youth also deserve the opportunity to influence the future of our Nation through the ballot box.

Amendment XXVI
[*Reduction of Voting Age*]

[Passed Congress March 23, 1971. Ratified July 1, 1971.]

Section 1. [*Eighteen Years of Age*]

The right of citizens of the United States, who are eighteen years of age or older, to vote shall not be denied or abridged by the United States or by any State on account of age.

Section 2. [*Enforcement*]

The Congress shall have power to enforce this article by appropriate legislation.

~~*This article shall be inoperative unless it shall have been ratified as an amendment to the Constitution by the legislatures of three-fourths of the several States within seven years from the date of its submission to the States by the Congress.*~~

Compared Draft

Senate Joint Resolution 53, June 2, 1953

Section 1. The right of citizens of the United States, who are eighteen years of age or older, to vote shall not be denied or abridged by the United States or by any State on account of age. The Congress shall have power to enforce this article by appropriate legislation.

Sec. 2. This article shall be inoperative unless it shall have been ratified as an amendment to the Constitution by the legislatures of three-fourths of the several States within seven years from the date of its submission to the States by the Congress. *[View Document (Hein Online)]*

Amendment XXVII
[*Congressional Compensation*]

[Originally proposed Sept. 25, 1789. Ratified May 7, 1992.]

No law, varying the compensation for the services of the Senators and Representatives, shall take effect, until an election of Representatives shall have intervened.[43]

Compared Draft

House Passed Version (August 24, 1789)

Article the Second

No law, varying the compensation for the services of the Senators and Representatives, shall take effect, until an election of Representatives shall have intervened.

Other Selected Drafts

James Madison Draft (June 8, 1789)

Thirdly. That in article 1st, section 6, clause 1, there be added to the end of the first sentence, these words, to wit: "But no law varying the compensation last ascertained shall operate before the next ensuing election of Representatives." *[View in Annals of Congress]*

JAMES MADISON: *[From his grave in Montpelier, VA.]*

I (along with some state ratifying conventions) proposed this in my original Bill of Rights in 1789. *[See p. 170.]* Some people fear that politicians will be greedy and raise their own salaries, while other people fear the opposite—only the rich will serve and then set pay so low that those of modest means can never afford to serve.

43. This amendment fell one vote short of ratification when the rest of the Bill of Rights was being ratified. It was revived in 1982 when a college sophomore wrote a paper arguing that the amendment could still be ratified. The student, Gregory Watson, started a grassroots effort to ratify the amendment. (He received a "C" on the paper but the university retroactively awarded him an "A" after enough states ratified the amendment.)

Unratified Amendments[44]

Reapportionment Amendment (1789)[45]

After the first enumeration required by the first article of the Constitution, there shall be one Representative for every thirty thousand, until the number shall amount to one hundred, after which the proportion shall be so regulated by Congress, that there shall be not less than one hundred Representatives, nor less than one Representative for every forty thousand persons, until the number of Representatives shall amount to two hundred; after which the proportion shall be so regulated by Congress, that there shall not be less than two hundred Representatives, nor more than one Representative for every fifty thousand persons.

Titles of Nobility Amendment (1810)[46]

If any citizen of the United States shall accept, claim, receive or retain, any title of nobility or honour, or shall, without the consent of Congress, accept and retain any present, pension, office or emolument of any kind whatever, from any emperor, king, prince or foreign power, such person shall cease to be a citizen of the United States, and shall be incapable of holding any office of trust or profit under them, or either of them.

Preservation of Slavery (Corwin Amendment) (1861)[47]

No amendment shall be made to the Constitution which will authorize or give to Congress the power to abolish or interfere, within any State, with the domestic institutions thereof, including that of persons held to labor or service by the laws of said State.

---

44. These amendments passed Congress, but not enough states ratified them.

45. Certain state ratifying conventions proposed this idea to ensure that the House expanded with population growth, while not creating an unwieldy number of representatives. Madison included it in his draft and it passed in Congress, but only ten of the needed eleven states voted to ratify it.

46. This proposed amendment sought to prevent U.S. citizens from accepting titles of nobility or honors from foreign governments without the consent of Congress. It provided that anyone who accepted such titles would lose their U.S. citizenship.

47. *See* p. 196.

Regulating Child Labor (1924)[48]

Section 1. The Congress shall have power to limit, regulate, and prohibit the labor of persons under eighteen years of age.

Section 2. The power of the several States is unimpaired by this article except that the operation of State laws shall be suspended to the extent necessary to give effect to legislation enacted by the Congress.

Equal Rights Amendment (1972)[49]

Equality of rights under the law shall not be denied or abridged by the United States or by any state on account of sex. The Congress shall have the power to enforce, by appropriate legislation, the provisions of this article. This amendment shall take effect two years after the date of ratification.

D.C. Voting Rights Amendment (1978)[50]

Section 1. For purposes of representation in the Congress, election of the President and Vice President, and article V of this Constitution, the District constituting the seat of government of the United States shall be treated as though it were a State.

Section 2. The exercise of the rights and powers conferred under this article shall be by the people of the District constituting the seat of government, and as shall be provided by the Congress.

---

48. Congress obtained federal protection for working children in 1938, when it passed the Fair Labor Standards Act.

49. This amendment is designed to guarantee equal legal rights for all American citizens regardless of sex, with the goal of preventing gender discrimination. First introduced in 1923 and passed by Congress in 1972, it has gained significant support. Thirty-eight states have now ratified the amendment, but there are debates about the validity of some ratifications that occurred after a 1982 ratification deadline that Congress set (extended from 1979).

50. This proposed amendment aimed to grant the District of Columbia full representation in Congress, including two Senators and a proportionate number of Representatives, as well as participation in the Electoral College for presidential elections. The amendment failed to achieve ratification by the necessary three-fourths (38) of the state legislatures within the seven-year deadline and thus did not become part of the Constitution.

Section 3. The twenty-third article of amendment to the Constitution of the United States is hereby repealed.

Section 4. This article shall be inoperative, unless it shall have been ratified as an amendment to the Constitution by the legislatures of three-fourths of the several States within seven years from the date of its submission.

Comparing the Constitution of the United States with that of the Confederate States

(MARCH 11, 1861)

Introduction

Just before the Civil War, the seven seceding Southern states (South Carolina, Mississippi, Florida, Alabama, Georgia, Louisiana, and Texas) drafted a Provisional Constitution and then signed the Permanent Constitution of the Confederate States of America in 1861. The Confederate States of America ("CSA") used the U.S. Constitution as a template, maintaining the structure and a majority of the language. In effect, the CSA "redlined" the U.S. Constitution. By recreating these redlines through a modern lens, we can quickly and concisely analyze the changes that they made. By this book's general calculation based on the number of words changed or added, the CSA changed around 38% of the U.S. Constitution and kept around 62% (though not all of the changes were substantive).

Why devote time to a constitution from the losing side of the Civil War? The substantive changes shed an obvious light on the South's deepest grievances against the Union and the U.S. Constitution. The Confederate Constitution made many substantive changes including explicit protections for slavery, expanded states' rights (including the ability for states to impeach their federal officials), a single-subject rule for all laws, more restrictions on federal spending, and eliminating diversity jurisdiction in federal courts. By identifying the substantive changes, we can analyze what specific parts of the U.S. Constitution they considered most inadequate in 1861. Additionally, other than slavery, the merits of many of these changes are still debated today.

With its focus on a confederation of states, in many ways the Confederate Constitution has obvious parallels to the Articles of Confederation. The CSA did not foresee that the Confederacy would soon be managing a war of much greater magnitude than even the American Revolution, and some of the difficulties of the Articles resurfaced under the Constitution of the CSA (like government funding and inflexible war spending).

The less substantive changes are also enlightening. Many scholars have offered their own, updated U.S. Constitutions to resolve purported flaws in the U.S. Constitution. The CSA had this precise opportunity in 1861. By then, the U.S. Constitution had existed for seventy years, and there was a body of legal analyses and Supreme Court precedents examining the U.S. Constitution. That meant, and the tracked changes in this book reveal, that the CSA could clarify ambiguities (*e.g.*, Article V), address purported inadequacies, and make stylistic updates. Some changes fall somewhere in the middle (like changes to punctuation, or requiring federal taxes and duties be "necessary" and "for revenue" in Art. I, § 8).

Finally, we can also learn from what the seceding states *did not* change. For such provisions and language, it can be telling that when secessionists had the opportunity to start completely anew, they elected to copy most of the U.S. Constitution. These include many powerful provisions like the Supremacy Clause, the Necessary and Proper Clause, and the entire Bill of Rights.

We the People of the United States, in Order to form a more perfect Union, establish Justice, insure domestic Tranquility, provide for the common defence, promote the general Welfare, and secure the Blessings of Liberty to ourselves and our Posterity, do ordain and establish this Constitution for the United States of America.

Article. I.

Section. 1. All legislative Powers herein granted shall be vested in a Congress of the United States, which shall consist of a Senate and House of Representatives.

Section. 2. The House of Representatives shall be composed of Members chosen every second Year by the People of the several States, and the Electors in each State shall have the Qualifications requisite for Electors of the most numerous Branch of the State Legislature.

No Person shall be a Representative who shall not have attained to the Age of twenty five Years, and been seven Years a Citizen of the United States, and who shall not, when elected, be an Inhabitant of that State in which he shall be chosen.

Representatives and direct Taxes shall be apportioned among the several States which may be included within this Union, according to their respective Numbers, which shall be determined by adding to the whole Number of free Persons, including those bound to Service for a Term of Years, and excluding Indians not taxed, three fifths of all other Persons. The actual Enumeration shall be made within three Years after the first Meeting of the Congress of the United States, and within every subsequent Term of ten Years, in such Manner as they shall by Law direct. The Number of Representatives shall not exceed one for every thirty Thousand, but each State shall have at Least one Representative; and until such enumeration shall be made, the State of New Hampshire shall be entitled to chuse three, Massachusetts eight, Rhode Island and Providence Plantations one, Connecticut five, New York six, New Jersey four, Pennsylvania eight, Delaware one, Maryland six, Virginia ten, North Carolina five, South Carolina five, and Georgia three.

When vacancies happen in the Representation from any State, the Executive Authority thereof shall issue Writs of Election to fill such Vacancies.

The House of Representatives shall chuse their Speaker and other Officers; and shall have the sole Power of Impeachment.

Section. 3. The Senate of the United States shall be composed of two Senators from each State, chosen by the Legislature thereof for six Years; and each Senator shall have one Vote.

Immediately after they shall be assembled in Consequence of the first Election, they shall be divided as equally as may be into three Classes. The Seats of the Senators of the first Class shall be vacated at the Expiration of the second Year, of the second Class at the Expiration of the fourth Year, and of the third Class at the Expiration of the sixth Year, so that one third may be chosen every second Year; and if Vacancies happen by Resignation, or otherwise, during the Recess of the Legislature of any State, the Executive thereof may make temporary Appointments until the next Meeting of the Legislature, which shall then fill such Vacancies.

... shall not have attained to the Age of thirty Years, and been nine Years a Citizen of the United States, and who shall

Excerpt from Engrossed Constitution of the United States of America (1787)

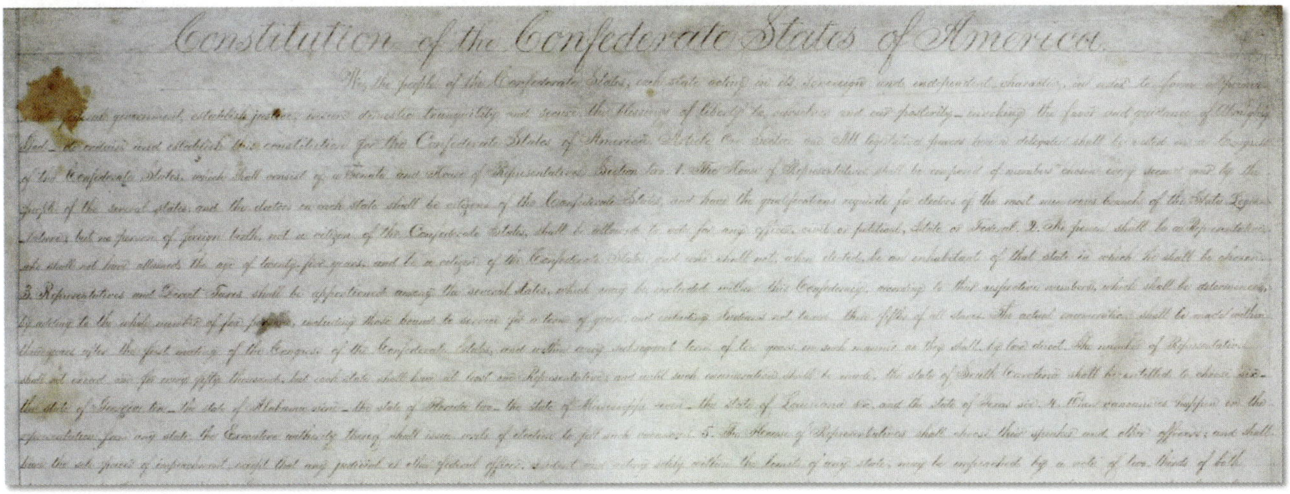

Constitution of the Confederate States of America

We, the people of the Confederate States, each state acting in its sovereign and independent character, in order to form a permanent federal government, establish justice, insure domestic tranquility and secure the blessings of liberty to ourselves and our posterity—invoking the favor and guidance of Almighty God—do ordain and establish this constitution for the Confederate States of America. Article One. Section One. All legislative powers herein delegated shall be vested in a Congress of the Confederate States, which shall consist of a Senate and House of Representatives. Section Two. 1. The House of Representatives shall be composed of members chosen every second year by the people of the several states, and the electors in each state shall be citizens of the Confederate States, and have the qualifications requisite for electors of the most numerous branch of the State Legislature; but no person of foreign birth, not a citizen of the Confederate States, shall be allowed to vote for any officer, civil or political, State or Federal. 2. No person shall be a Representative who shall not have attained the age of twenty-five years, and be a citizen of the Confederate States, and who shall not, when elected, be an inhabitant of that state in which he shall be chosen. 3. Representatives and direct taxes shall be apportioned among the several states, which may be included within this Confederacy, according to their respective numbers, which shall be determined by adding to the whole number of free persons, including those bound to service for a term of years, and excluding Indians not taxed, three fifths of all slaves. The actual enumeration shall be made within three years after the first meeting of the Congress of the Confederate States, and within every subsequent term of ten years, in such manner as they shall by law direct. The number of Representatives shall not exceed one for every fifty thousand, but each state shall have at least one Representative, and until such enumeration shall be made, the State of South Carolina shall be entitled to choose six; the State of Georgia ten; the State of Alabama nine; the State of Florida two; the State of Mississippi seven; the State of Louisiana six, and the State of Texas six. 4. When vacancies happen in the representation from any state, the Executive authority thereof shall issue writs of election to fill such vacancies. 5. The House of Representatives shall choose their Speaker and other officers; and shall have the sole power of impeachment, except that any judicial or other federal officer, resident and acting solely within the limits of any state, may be impeached by a vote of two thirds of both

Excerpt from Engrossed Constitution of the Confederate States of America (1861)

[*Preamble*]

We, the people of the ~~*United*~~ Confederate States, each state acting in its sovereign and independent character, in order to form a ~~*more perfect Union*~~ permanent federal government, establish justice, insure domestic tranquillity ~~*provide for the common defence, promote the general Welfare*~~, and secure the blessings of liberty to ourselves and our Posterity~~,~~ invoking the favor and guidance of Almighty God-do ordain and establish this Constitution for the ~~*United*~~ Confederate States of America.[1]

Article one
[*Legislative Branch*]

Section one. [Legislative Vesting Clause]

All legislative powers herein ~~*granted*~~ delegated shall be vested in a Congress of the ~~*United*~~ Confederate States, which shall consist of a Senate and House of Representatives.

Section two. [House of Representatives]

1.[2] The House of Representatives shall be composed of members chosen every second year by the people of the several states~~,~~; and the electors in each state shall be citizens of the Confederate States, and have the qualifications requisite for electors of the most numerous branch of the State Legislature~~.~~; but no person of foreign birth, not a citizen of the Confederate States, shall be allowed to vote for any officer, civil or political, State or Federal.

2. No person shall be a Representative who shall not have attained ~~*to*~~ the age of twenty-five years, and ~~*been seven Years*~~ be a citizen of the ~~*United*~~ Confederate States, and who shall not, when elected, be an inhabitant of that state in which he shall be chosen.

---

1. This preamble, compared to that of the U.S. Constitution, frames a constitution that is much more focused on state sovereignty and states' rights. As the name reflects, it is a confederation of states rather than a union, with rights more associated with the sovereignty of states and local communities.

2. Numbering and capitalization of headings follow the engrossed 1861 version.

3. Representatives and Direct Taxes shall be apportioned among the several states, which may be included within this ~~*Union*~~ Confederacy, according to their respective numbers, which shall be determined by adding to the whole number of free persons, including those bound to service for a term of years, and excluding Indians not taxed, three-fifths of all ~~*other Persons*~~ slaves. The actual enumeration shall be made within three years after the first meeting of the Congress of the ~~*United*~~ Confederate States, and within every subsequent term of ten years, in such manner as they shall by law direct. The number of Representatives shall not exceed one for every ~~*thirty Thousand*~~ fifty thousand, but each state shall have at least one Representative; and until such enumeration shall be made, the state of ~~*New Hampshire*~~ South Carolina shall be entitled to ~~*chuse three, Massachusetts eight, Rhode-Island and Providence Plantations one, Connecticut five, New-York six, New Jersey four, Pennsylvania eight, Delaware one, Maryland*~~ choose six; the state of Georgia ten; the state of Alabama nine; the state of Florida two; the state of Mississippi seven; the state of Louisiana six~~*, Virginia ten, North Carolina five, South Carolina five,*~~; and ~~*Georgia three*~~ the state of Texas six.

4. When vacancies happen in the representation from any state, the Executive authority thereof shall issue writs of election to fill such vacancies.

5. The House of Representatives shall ~~*chuse*~~ choose their speaker and other officers; and shall have the sole power of impeachment; except that any judicial or other federal officer, resident and acting solely within the limits of any State, may be impeached by a vote of two-thirds of both branches of the Legislature thereof.[3]

Section three. [Senate]

1. The Senate of the ~~*United*~~ Confederate States shall be composed of two Senators from each state, chosen for six years by the legislature thereof, ~~*for six Years*~~ at the regular session next immediately preceding the commencement of the term of service; and each Senator shall have one vote.

2. Immediately after they shall be assembled, in consequence of the first election, they shall be divided as equally as may be into three classes. The seats of the Senators of the first class shall be vacated at the expiration of the second year~~,~~; of the second class at the expiration of the fourth year~~,~~; and of the third class at the expiration of the sixth year~~,~~; so that one-third may be chosen every second year; and

3. The addition in Clause 5 allows state legislatures to impeach their federal judges or officers.

if vacancies happen by resignation, or otherwise, during the recess of the Legislature of any State, the Executive thereof may make temporary appointments until the next meeting of the Legislature, which shall then fill such vacancies.

3. No person shall be a Senator who shall not have attained ~~*to*~~ the age of thirty years ~~*and been nine Years a Citizen of the United States*~~, and be a citizen of the Confederate States; and who shall not, when elected, be an inhabitant of ~~*that*~~ the state for which he shall be chosen.

4. The Vice President of the ~~*United*~~ Confederate States shall be president of the Senate, but shall have no vote, unless they be equally divided.

5. The Senate shall ~~*chuse*~~ choose their other officers~~,~~; and also a president pro tempore~~,~~ in the absence of the Vice President, or when he shall exercise the office of President of the ~~*United*~~ Confederate states.

6. The Senate shall have the sole power to try all impeachments. When sitting for that purpose, they shall be on oath or affirmation. When the President of the ~~*United*~~ Confederate States is tried, the Chief Justice shall preside~~:~~; and no person shall be convicted without the concurrence of two-thirds of the members present.

7. Judgment in cases of impeachment shall not extend further than to removal from office, and disqualification to hold and enjoy any office of honor, trust or profit under the ~~*United*~~ Confederate States~~:~~; but the party convicted shall, nevertheless, be liable and subject to indictment, trial, judgment and punishment according to law.

Section four. [Election and Assembly of Congress]

1. The times, places and manner of holding elections for Senators and Representatives, shall be prescribed in each state by the legislature thereof, subject to the provisions of this Constitution; but the Congress may, at any time, by law, make or alter such regulations, except as to the times and places of ~~*chusing*~~ choosing Senators.

2. The Congress shall assemble at least once in every year~~,~~; and such meeting shall be on the first Monday in December, unless they shall, by law, appoint a different day.

Section five. [Congressional Proceedings]

1. Each House shall be the judge of the elections, returns and qualifications of its own members, and a majority of each shall constitute a quorum to do business; but a smaller number may adjourn from day to day, and may be authorized to compel the attendance of absent members, in such manner~~,~~ and under such penalties as each House may provide.

2. Each House may determine the rules of its proceedings, punish its members for disorderly behavio~~u~~r, and, with the concurrence of two-thirds of the whole number, expel a member.

3. Each House shall keep a journal of its proceedings, and from time to time publish the same, excepting such parts as may in their judgment require secrecy; and the yeas and nays of the members of either House, on any question, shall, at the desire of one-fifth of those present, be entered on the journal.

4. Neither House, during the session of Congress, shall, without the consent of the other, adjourn for more than three days, nor to any other place than that in which the two Houses shall be sitting.

Section six. [Congressional Pay, Privileges, Immunities, Bar on Holding Federal Office]

1. The Senators and Representatives shall receive a compensation for their services, to be ascertained by law, and paid out of the Treasury of the ~~*United*~~ Confederate States. They shall, in all cases, except treason, felony, and breach of the peace, be privileged from arrest during their attendance at the session of their respective Houses, and in going to and returning from the same; and for any speech or debate in either House, they shall not be questioned in any other place.

2. No Senator or Representative shall, during the time for which he was elected, be appointed to any civil office under the authority of the ~~*United*~~ Confederate States, which shall have been created, or the emoluments whereof shall have been ~~e~~increased during such time; and no person holding any office under the ~~*United*~~ Confederate States, shall be a member of either House during his continuance in office. But Congress may, by law, grant to the principal officer in each of the Executive Departments a seat upon the floor of either House, with the privilege of discussing any measures appertaining to his department.[4]

---

4. This addition allows some degree of executive participation in the Confederate Congress, furthering checks-and-balances and oversight.

Section seven. [Legislation]

1. All bills for raising revenue shall originate in the House of Representatives; but the Senate may propose or concur with amendments as on other bills.

2. Every bill which shall have passed ~~*the House of Representatives and the Senate*~~ both Houses, shall, before it becomes a law, be presented to the President of the ~~*United*~~ Confederate States; if he approve, he shall sign it~~,~~; but if not, he shall return it~~,~~ with his objections to that House in which it shall have originated, who shall enter the objections at large on their journal, and proceed to reconsider it. If, after such reconsideration, two-thirds of that House shall agree to pass the bill, it shall be sent, together with the objections, to the other House, by which it shall likewise be reconsidered, and if approved by two-thirds of that House, it shall become a law. But in all such cases, the votes of both Houses shall be determined by yeas and nays~~,~~ and the names of the persons voting for and against the bill shall be entered on the journal of each House respectively. If any bill shall not be returned by the President within ten days (Sundays excepted) after it shall have been presented to him, the same shall be a law, in like manner as if he had signed it, unless the Congress, by their adjournment, prevent its return~~,~~; in which case it shall not be a law. The President may approve any appropriation and disapprove any other appropriation in the same bill. In such case he shall, in signing the bill, designate the appropriations disapproved; and shall return a copy of such appropriations, with his objections, to the House in which the bill shall have originated; and the same proceedings shall then be had as in case of other bills disapproved by the President.[5]

3. Every order, resolution, or vote, to which the concurrence of ~~*the Senate and House of Representatives*~~ both Houses may be necessary (except on a question of adjournment) shall be presented to the President of the ~~*United*~~ Confederate States; and before the same shall take effect, shall be approved by him~~,~~; or being disapproved by him, shall be repassed by two-thirds of ~~*the Senate and House of Representatives*~~ both Houses, according to the rules and limitations prescribed in ~~*the*~~ case of a bill.

5. This addition gave the president a line-item veto.

Section eight. [Enumerated Powers]

The Congress shall have power—

1. To lay and collect taxes, duties, imposts, and excises, for revenue necessary to pay the debts, *and* provide for the common defense, ~~*and general Welfare of the United States;*~~[6] and carry on the Government of the Confederate States; but no bounties shall be granted from the Treasury; nor shall any duties or taxes on importations from foreign nations be laid to promote or foster any branch of industry; and all duties, imposts, and excises shall be uniform throughout the ~~*United*~~ Confederate States~~;~~:

2. To borrow money on the credit of the ~~*United*~~ Confederate States~~;~~:

3. To regulate commerce with foreign nations, and among the several states, and with the Indian tribes; but neither this, nor any other clause contained in the constitution, shall ever be construed to delegate the power to Congress to appropriate money for any internal improvement intended to facilitate commerce; except for the purpose of furnishing lights, beacons, and buoys, and other aids to navigation upon the coasts, and the improvement of harbors and the removing of obstructions in river navigation, in all which cases, such duties shall be laid on the navigation facilitated thereby, as may be necessary to pay the costs and expenses thereof~~;~~:[7]

4. To establish ~~*an*~~ uniform ~~*Rule*~~ laws of naturalization, and uniform laws on the subject of bankruptcies, throughout the ~~*United States;*~~ Confederate States; but no law of Congress shall discharge any debt contracted before the passage of the same~~;~~:

5. To coin money, regulate the value thereof~~,~~ and of foreign coin, and fix the standard of weights and measures~~;~~:

---

6. Section eight, Clause 1 removes "general welfare," and adds that taxes, duties, etc. must be "for revenue" and "necessary," substantially limiting the broad original spending clause. Many scholars have argued that the inflexibility of the CSA's Constitution made it much harder to fund and fight the Civil War.

7. The CSA heavily edited the Commerce Clause. Changes to Clause 3 prohibit the Confederate Congress from appropriating money for "internal improvements" (public works/infrastructure) to "facilitate commerce" other than for navigation. Internal improvements were hotly debated at the time, and the CSA wanted to leave most of them to the states. (The Northern states favored investing in internal improvements, while the more agrarian Southern states thought that this federal spending disproportionately benefitted the North.) This is consistent with striking "promote the general Welfare" from the preamble and Section 8, Clause 1. To the CSA, it was generally the states' job to promote the general welfare, not the federal government.

6. To provide for the punishment of counterfeiting the securities and current coin of the ~~*United*~~ Confederate States~~;~~:

7. To establish post offices and post ~~*roads*~~ routes; but the expenses of the Post Office Department, after the first day of March in the year of our Lord eighteen hundred and sixty-three, shall be paid out of its own revenues~~;~~:[8]

8. To promote the progress of science and useful arts, by securing for limited times to authors and inventors the exclusive right to their respective writings and discoveries~~;~~:

9. To constitute tribunals inferior to the Supreme Court~~;~~:

10. To define and punish piracies and felonies committed on the high seas, and offenses against the law of nations~~;~~:

11. To declare war, grant letters of marque and reprisal, and make rules concerning captures on land and water~~;~~:

12. To raise and support armies~~,~~; but no appropriation of money to that use shall be for a longer term than two years~~;~~:

13. To provide and maintain a navy~~;~~:

14. To make rules for the government and regulation of the land and naval forces~~;~~:

15. To provide for calling forth the militia to execute the laws of the ~~*Union*~~ Confederate States, suppress insurrections, and repel invasions~~;~~:

16. To provide for organizing, arming, and disciplining~~,~~ the militia, and for governing such part of them as may be employed in the service of the ~~*United*~~ Confederate States~~,~~; reserving to the states, respectively, the appointment of the officers, and the authority of training the militia according to the discipline prescribed by Congress~~;~~:

17. To exercise exclusive legislation, in all cases whatsoever, over such district (not exceeding ten miles square) as may, by cession of ~~*particular*~~ one or more States~~,~~ and the acceptance of Congress, become the seat of the Government of the ~~*United*~~ Confederate States~~,~~; and to exercise like authority over all places purchased by the consent of the legislature of the State in which the same shall

8. Clause 7 requires the Post Office Department to eventually be self-sufficient. This was likely in response to perceived inefficiencies in the United States postal system at the time and reflected the Confederacy's broader emphasis on states' rights and limited central government.

be, for the erection of forts, magazines, arsenals, dockyards, and other needful buildings~~;~~: and

18. To make all laws which shall be necessary and proper for carrying into execution the foregoing powers, and all other powers vested by this Constitution in the Government of the ~~*United*~~ Confederate States, or in any department or officer thereof.

Section nine. [Powers Denied Congress]

~~*The Migration or Importation of such Persons as any of the States now existing shall think proper to admit, shall not be prohibited by the Congress prior to the Year one thousand eight hundred and eight, but a Tax or duty may be imposed on such Importation, not exceeding ten dollars for each Person.*~~

1. The importation of negroes of the African race, from any foreign country, other than the slaveholding States or Territories of the United States of America, is hereby forbidden; and Congress is required to pass such laws as shall effectually prevent the same.[9]

2. Congress shall also have power to prohibit the introduction of slaves from any State not a member of, or Territory not belonging to, this Confederacy.

3. The privilege of the writ of habeas corpus shall not be suspended, unless when in cases of rebellion or invasion the public safety may require it.[10]

4. No bill of attainder, ~~*or*~~ ex post facto law, or law denying or impairing the right of property in negro slaves shall be passed.

5. No capitation or other direct tax shall be laid, unless in proportion to the census or enumeration ~~*herein before*~~ hereinbefore directed to be taken.

6. No tax or duty shall be laid on articles exported from any State~~.~~, except by a vote of two-thirds of both Houses.

---

9. Clause 1 continues the U.S. Constitution's ban on importing foreign slaves (after 1808, see Art. I, §.9), but protects the slave trade within the United and Confederate States. By limiting the market, this ban increases the value of domestic slaves. Unlike the U.S. Constitution, which took great efforts to avoid directly referencing slavery, the Confederates' Constitution is clear about the topic.

10. Like the Union, the Confederacy also suspended the writ of habeas corpus during the Civil War (allowing for detention based on suspicion only, not probable cause that a crime has been committed or some other valid reason for detention.).

7. No preference shall be given by any regulation of commerce or revenue to the ports of one State over those of another~~: nor shall Vessels bound to, or from, one State, be obliged to enter, clear, or pay Duties in another~~.[11]

8. No money shall be drawn from the Treasury, but in consequence of appropriations made by law; and a regular statement and account of the receipts and expenditures of all public money shall be published from time to time.

9. Congress shall appropriate no money from the Treasury except by a vote of two-thirds of both Houses, taken by yeas and nays, unless it be asked and estimated for by some one of the heads of department, and submitted to Congress by the President; or for the purpose of paying its own expenses and contingencies; or for the payment of claims against the Confederate States, the justice of which shall have been judicially declared by a tribunal for the investigation of claims against the Government, which it is hereby made the duty of Congress to establish.[12]

10. All bills appropriating money shall specify in federal currency the exact amount of each appropriation and the purposes for which it is made; and Congress shall grant no extra compensation to any public contractor, officer, agent, or servant, after such contract shall have been made or such service rendered.

11. No title of nobility shall be granted by the ~~United~~ Confederate States~~:~~; and no person holding any office of profit or trust under them, shall, without the consent of the Congress, accept of any present, emolument, office~~,~~ or title~~,~~ of any kind whatever~~,~~ from any king, prince~~,~~ or foreign State.

12. Congress shall make no law respecting an establishment of religion, or prohibiting the free exercise thereof; or abridging the freedom of speech, or of the press; or the right of the people peaceably to assemble~~,~~ and ~~to~~ petition the Government for a redress of grievances.[13]

---

11. This change allows states to manage port usage and fees, giving states greater control over commerce.

12. This substantial addition in Clause 9 requires a two-thirds vote for most spending.

13. The CSA (borrowing from Madison's desires seventy years earlier) placed the first eight amendments to the U.S. Constitution in Article one, Section 9, largely with only changes to punctuation.

The CSA placed the Ninth and Tenth Amendments into Article six. The Eleventh Amendment is included in Article three, and the Twelfth Amendment is incorporated into Article two.

13. A well-regulated militia, being necessary to the security of a free State, the right of the people to keep and bear arms, shall not be infringed.

14. No soldier shall, in time of peace, be quartered in any house, without the consent of the owner,; nor in time of war, but in a manner to be prescribed by law.

15. The right of the people to be secure in their persons, houses, papers, and effects, against unreasonable searches and seizures, shall not be violated,; and no warrants shall issue, but upon probable cause, supported by oath or affirmation, and particularly describing the place to be searched, and the persons or things to be seized.

16. No person shall be held to answer for a capital, or otherwise infamous crime, unless on a presentment or indictment of a grand jury, except in cases arising in the land or naval forces, or in the militia, when in actual service, in time of war or public danger; nor shall any person be subject for the same offence to be twice put in jeopardy of life or limb; nor *shall* be compelled, in any criminal case, to be a witness against himself,; nor be deprived of life, liberty, or property, without due process of law; nor shall private property be taken for public use, without just compensation.

17. In all criminal prosecutions, the accused shall enjoy the right to a speedy and public trial, by an impartial jury of the State and district wherein the crime shall have been committed, which district shall have been previously ascertained by law, and to be informed of the nature and cause of the accusation; to be confronted with the witnesses against him; to have compulsory process for obtaining witnesses in his favor,; and to have the assistance of counsel for his defence.

18. In suits at common law, where the value in controversy shall exceed twenty dollars, the right of trial by jury shall be preserved,; and no fact so tried by a jury, shall be otherwise re-examined in any court of the *United States* Confederacy, than according to the rules of *the* common law.

19. Excessive bail shall not be required, nor excessive fines imposed, nor cruel and unusual punishments inflicted.

20. Every law, or resolution having the force of law, shall relate to but one subject, and that shall be expressed in the title.[14]

14. The Confederate Constitution included a single-subject rule for legislation, which most state constitutions have today. This is intended to prevent overly complex laws covering a wide array of subjects, and to avoid hidden or unpopular provisions being attached to more popular bills.

Section ten. [Powers Denied States]

1. No state shall enter into any treaty, alliance, or confederation; grant letters of marque and reprisal; coin money; ~~*emit Bills of Credit;*~~ make any-thing but gold and silver coin a tender in payment of debts; pass any bill of attainder, or ex post facto law, or law impairing the obligation of contracts; or grant any title of nobility.

2. No state shall, without the consent of the Congress, lay any imposts or duties on imports or exports, except what may be absolutely necessary for executing its inspection laws~~:~~; and the net produce of all duties and imposts, laid by any State on imports or exports~~,~~ shall be for the use of the Treasury of the ~~*United*~~ Confederate States; and all such laws shall be subject to the revision and contro~~*u*~~l of ~~*the*~~ Congress.

3. No state shall, without the consent of Congress, lay any duty on tonnage, except on seagoing vessels, for the improvement of its rivers and harbors navigated by the said vessels; but such duties shall not conflict with any treaties of the Confederate States with foreign nations; and any surplus revenue, thus derived, shall, after making such improvement, be paid into the common treasury. Nor shall any state keep troops~~,~~ or ships of war in time of peace, enter into any agreement or compact with another state, or with a foreign power, or engage in war, unless actually invaded, or in such imminent danger as will not admit of delay. But when any river divides or flows through two or more states, they may enter into compacts with each other to improve the navigation thereof.

Article two
[*Executive Branch*]

Section one. [Vesting Clause, President's Role, Election, Qualifications, Succession, Pay, Oath]

1. The executive power shall be vested in a President of the ~~*United*~~ Confederate States of America. He ~~*shall hold his Office during the Term of four Years, and, together with the*~~ and the Vice President~~,~~ ~~*chosen for the same Term, be*~~ shall hold their offices for the term of six years; but the President shall not be re-eligible. The President and Vice President shall be elected~~,~~ as follows:[15]

2. Each State shall appoint, in such manner as the legislature thereof may direct, a number of electors~~,~~ equal to the whole number of Senators and Representatives to which the State may be entitled in the Congress~~:~~; but no Senator, or Representative, or person holding an office of trust or profit under the ~~*United*~~ Confederate States, shall be appointed an elector.

3.[16] The electors shall meet in their respective States~~,~~ and vote by ballot for ~~*two Persons,*~~ President and Vice President, one of whom ~~*one*~~, at least, shall not be an inhabitant of the same state with themselves~~.~~ ~~*And*~~; they shall name in their ballots the person voted for as President, and in distinct ballots the person voted for as Vice President, and they shall make ~~*a List*~~ distinct lists of all ~~*the*~~ persons voted for as President, and of ~~*the Number*~~ all persons voted for as Vice President, and of ~~*Votes*~~ the number of votes for each~~;~~, which lists they shall sign and certify, and transmit, sealed, to the seat of the Government of the ~~*United*~~ Confederate States, directed to the President of the Senate~~.~~; the President of the Senate shall, in the presence of the Senate and House of Representatives, open all the certificates, and the votes shall then be counted~~.~~; the person having the greatest number of votes for President shall be the President, if such number be a majority of the whole number of electors appointed; and if ~~*there be more than one who*~~ no person have such majority, ~~*and have an equal Number of Votes*~~ then from the persons having the highest numbers, not exceeding three, on the list of those voted for

15. Rather than unlimited four-year terms, the CSA allowed the president one, six-year term, and incorporated the Twelfth Amendment to the U.S. Constitution.

16. Clause 3 adopts the Twelfth Amendment almost verbatim. Thus, these tracked changes essentially show how the Twelfth Amendment changed Art. II, § 1 of the U.S. Constitution.

as President, the House of Representatives shall choose immediately, ~~*chuse by Ballot one of them for President; and if no Person have a Majority, then from the five highest on the List the said House shall in like Manner chuse the President. But in chusing the President, the Votes*~~ by ballot, the President. But in choosing the President, the votes shall be taken by states, the representation from each state having one vote; a quorum for this purpose shall consist of a member or members from two-thirds of the states, and a majority of all the states shall be necessary to a choice. And if the House of Representatives shall not choose a President, whenever the right of choice shall devolve upon them, before the fourth day of March next following, then the Vice President shall act as President, as in case of the death, or other constitutional disability of the President.

4. ~~*In every Case, after the Choice of the President, the*~~ The person having the greatest number of ~~*Votes of the Electors*~~ votes as Vice President shall be the Vice President, ~~*. But*~~ if ~~*there should remain*~~ such number be a majority of the whole number of electors appointed; and if no person have a majority, then, from the two ~~*or more who have equal Votes*~~ highest numbers on the list, the Senate shall ~~*chuse from them by Ballot the Vice President*~~ choose the Vice President; a quorum for the purpose shall consist of two-thirds of the whole number of Senators, and a majority of the whole number shall be necessary to a choice.

5. But no person constitutionally ineligible to the office of President shall be eligible to that of Vice President of the Confederate States.

6. The Congress may determine the time of ~~*chusing*~~ choosing the electors, and the day on which they shall give their votes; which day shall be the same throughout the ~~*United*~~ Confederate States.

7. No person except a natural-born ~~*Citizen, or a Citizen*~~ citizen~~,~~ of the ~~*United*~~ Confederate States, or a citizen thereof, at the time of the adoption of this Constitution, or a citizen thereof born in the United States prior to the twentieth of December, eighteen hundred and sixty, shall be eligible to the office of President; neither shall any person be eligible to that office who shall not have attained ~~*to*~~ the age of thirty-five years, and been fourteen years a resident within the ~~*United States*~~ limits of the Confederate States, as they may exist at the time of his election.

8. In case of the removal of the President from office, or of his death, resignation, or inability to discharge the powers and duties of the said office, the same shall devolve on the Vice President~~,~~; and the Congress may, by law, provide for the

case of removal, death, resignation, or inability, both of the President and Vice President, declaring what officer shall then act as President, and such officer shall act accordingly~~,~~ until the disability be removed~~,~~ or a President shall be elected.

9. The President shall, at stated times, receive for his services~~,~~ a compensation, which shall neither be ~~e~~increased nor diminished during the period for which he shall have been elected~~,~~; and he shall not receive within that period any other emolument from the ~~*United*~~ Confederate States, or any of them.

10. Before he enters on the execution of his office, he shall take the following oath or affirmation: "I do solemnly swear (or affirm) that I will faithfully execute the Office of President of the ~~*United*~~ Confederate States, and will to the best of my ability, preserve, protect, and defend the Constitution thereof ~~*the United States*~~."

Section two. [President's Powers]

1. The President shall be commander-in-chief of the army and navy of the ~~*United*~~ Confederate States, and of the militia of the several states, when called into the actual service of the ~~*United*~~ Confederate States; he may require the opinion, in writing, of the principal officer in each of the Executive Departments, upon any subject relating to the duties of their respective offices~~,~~; and he shall have power to grant reprieves and pardons for offences against the ~~*United*~~ Confederate States, except in cases of impeachment.

2. He shall have power, by and with the advice and consent of the Senate, to make treaties, provided two-thirds of the Senators present concur; and he shall nominate, and by and with the advice and consent of the Senate, shall appoint, ambassadors, other public ministers and consuls, judges of the Supreme Court, and all other officers of the ~~*United*~~ Confederate States, whose appointments are not herein otherwise provided for, and which shall be established by law~~:~~; but the Congress may, by law, vest the appointment of such inferior officers, as they think proper, in the President alone, in the courts of law, or in the heads of departments.

3. The principal officer in each of the Executive Departments, and all persons connected with the diplomatic service, may be removed from office at the pleasure of the President. All other civil officers of the Executive Departments may be removed at any time by the President, or other appointing power, when their services are unnecessary, or for dishonesty, incapacity. inefficiency, miscon-

duct, or neglect of duty; and when so removed, the removal shall be reported to the Senate, together with the reasons therefor.[17]

4. The President shall have power to fill ~~*up*~~ all vacancies that may happen during the recess of the Senate, by granting commissions which shall expire at the end of their next session; but no person rejected by the Senate shall be reappointed to the same office during their ensuing recess.

Section three. [President's Duties]

1. ~~*He*~~ The President shall, from time to time, give to the Congress information of the state of the ~~*Union*~~ Confederacy, and recommend to their consideration such measures as he shall judge necessary and expedient; he may, on extraordinary occasions, convene both Houses, or either of them~~,~~; and in case of disagreement between them, with respect to the time of adjournment, he may adjourn them to such time as he shall think proper; he shall receive ambassadors and other public ministers; he shall take care that the laws be faithfully executed, and shall commission all the officers of the ~~*United*~~ Confederate States.

Section four. [Impeachment]

1. The President, Vice President, and all civil officers of the ~~*United*~~ Confederate States, shall be removed from office on impeachment for, and conviction of, treason, bribery, or other high crimes and misdemeanors.

---

17. This addition clarified that the Confederate president had the ability to terminate virtually any person working within the Executive Branch for any reason. Some people argue today that this power implicitly exists in Article II, Sec. 1, of the U.S. Constitution. *See* p. 148. In 1789, the U.S. Congress considered requiring Senate approval for removing Cabinet members, and Vice President John Adams **broke a 9–9 tie**, defeating the proposal. When the CSA had the opportunity to revise the Constitution, they gave the president this express power. This raises an interesting question: If Confederates felt the need to add this clause, how clearly does the "unitary Executive" power exist in the U.S. Constitution?

Article three
[*Judicial Branch*]

Section one. [Vesting Clause]

1. The judicial power of the ~~*United*~~ Confederate States~~,~~ shall be vested in one Supreme Court,[18] and in such inferior courts as the Congress may from time to time ordain and establish. The judges, both of the Supreme and inferior courts, shall hold their offices during good behavio~~u~~r, and shall, at stated times, receive for their services~~,~~ a compensation, which shall not be diminished during their continuance in office.

Section two. [Justiciability, Supreme Court Jurisdiction, Jury Trials]

1. The judicial power shall extend to all cases~~, *in Law and Equity,*~~ arising under this Constitution, the laws of the ~~*United*~~ Confederate States, and treaties made~~,~~ or which shall be made~~,~~ under their authority; to all cases affecting ambassadors, other public ministers and consuls; to all cases of admiralty and maritime jurisdiction; to controversies to which the ~~*United*~~ Confederate States shall be a party; to controversies between two or more States; between a State and citizens of another State where the State is plaintiff; ~~*between Citizens of different States;*~~[19] between citizens ~~*of the same state*~~ claiming lands under grants of different States; and between a State~~,~~ or the citizens thereof, and foreign states, citizens~~,~~ or subjects; but no State shall be sued by a citizen or subject of any foreign state.[20]

2. In all cases affecting ambassadors, other public ministers, and consuls, and those in which a State shall be a party, the supreme court shall have original jurisdiction. In all the other cases before mentioned, the Supreme Court shall have appellate jurisdiction, both as to law and fact, with such exceptions, and under such regulations, as the Congress shall make.

---

18. Although there were many interesting proposals (including a Supreme Court comprised of each district judge) the CSA never constituted a Supreme Court.

19. The CSA eliminated diversity jurisdiction for federal courts. This limited the number of cases that could be heard in federal court, forcing many matters into state courts.

20. Other changes incorporate the Eleventh Amendment to the U.S. Constitution. Notably, the final clause prevents suits by citizens of the Union (including property seized during the Civil War), as they would be citizens of a foreign state.

3. The trial of all crimes, except in cases of impeachment, shall be by jury;, and such trial shall be held in the state where the said crimes shall have been committed; but when not committed within any state, the trial shall be at such place or places as the Congress may by law have directed.

Section three. [Definition and Punishment for Treason]

1. Treason against the ~~*United*~~ Confederate States, shall consist only in, levying war against them, or in adhering to their enemies, giving them aid and comfort. No person shall be convicted of treason unless on the testimony of two witnesses to the same overt act, or on confession in open court.

2. The Congress shall have power to declare the punishment of treason,; but no attainder of treason shall work corruption of blood, or forfeiture, except during the life of the person attainted.

Article four
[*Relationships Between the States*]

Section one. [Full Faith and Credit]

1. Full faith and credit shall be given in each state to the public acts, records, and judicial proceedings of every other state. And the Congress may, by general laws, prescribe the manner in which such acts, records, and proceedings shall be proved, and the effect thereof.

Section two. [Interstate Comity: Privileges and Immunities, Extradition, Slavery]

1. The citizens of each state shall be entitled to all the privileges and immunities of citizens in the several states., and shall have the right of transit and sojourn in any state of this Confederacy, with their slaves and other property; and the right of property in said slaves shall not be thereby impaired.[21]

21. Section 2, Clause 1 adds to privileges and immunities the protection of a person's interest in slaves and other property as they move between states. This provision also prepares for the possibility of new states that are not slave states.

2. A person charged in any State with treason, felony, or other crime against the laws of such state, who shall flee from justice, and be found in another state, shall, on demand of the Executive authority of the state from which he fled, be delivered up, to be removed to the state having jurisdiction of the crime.

3. No ~~*Person*~~ slave or other person held to service or labo~~*u*~~r in ~~*one*~~ any State or territory of the Confederate States, under the laws thereof, escaping or lawfully carried into another, shall, in consequence of any law or regulation therein, be discharged from such service or labo~~*ur,*~~; but shall be delivered up on claim of the party to whom such ~~*Service or Labour*~~ slave belongs, or to whom such service or labor may be due.

Section three. [Addition of New States and Territories]

1. ~~*New*~~ Other states may be admitted ~~*by the Congress into this Union*~~ into this Confederacy by a vote of two-thirds of the whole House of Representatives, and two-thirds of the Senate, the Senate voting by states; but no new state shall be formed or erected within the jurisdiction of any other state; nor any state be formed by the junction of two or more states, or parts of states, without the consent of the Legislatures of the states concerned as well as of the Congress.

2. The Congress shall have power to dispose of and make all needful rules and regulations ~~*respecting*~~ concerning the ~~*Territory or other*~~ property of the ~~*United*~~ Confederate States, including the lands thereof.~~*; and nothing in this Constitution shall be so construed as to Prejudice any Claims of the United States, or of any particular State.*~~

3. The Confederate States may acquire new territory; and Congress shall have power to legislate and provide governments for the inhabitants of all territory belonging to the Confederate States, lying without the limits of the several States; and may permit them, at such times, and in such manner as it may by law provide, to form States to be admitted into the Confederacy. In all such territory, the institution of negro slavery, as it now exists in the Confederate States, shall be recognized and protected by Congress, and by the territorial government: and the inhabitants of the several Confederate States and Territories shall have the right to take to such territory any slaves lawfully held by them in any of the states or territories of the Confederate States.[22]

22. Clause 3 reflects a pivotal issue in the 1860 presidential race—slavery in new territories. The CSA expressly protected (but did not require) the slave trade in new territories.

Section four. [Republican Form of Government]

The ~~*United*~~ Confederate States shall guarantee to every state ~~*in this Union*~~ that now is or hereafter may become a member of this Confederacy, a republican form of government,~~;~~ and shall protect each of them against invasion; and on application of the legislature~~,~~ (or of the Executive ~~(~~when the legislature ~~*cannot be convened*~~ is not in session) against domestic violence.

Article five
[*Amending the Constitution*]

Section one.

1. Upon the demand of any three states, legally assembled in their several conventions, the Congress shall summon a convention of all the states, to take into consideration such amendments to the Constitution as the said states shall concur in suggesting at the time when the said demand is made; and should any of the proposed amendments to the Constitution be agreed on by the said convention—voting by states—and the same be ratified by the legislatures of two-thirds of the several states, or by conventions in two-thirds thereof—as the one or the other mode of ratification may be proposed by the general convention—they shall thenceforward form a part of this Constitution. But no state shall, without its consent, be deprived of its equal representation in the Senate.[23]

~~*The Congress, whenever two thirds of both Houses shall deem it necessary, shall propose Amendments to this Constitution, or, on the Application of the Legislatures of two thirds of the several States, shall call a Convention for proposing Amendments, which, in either Case, shall be valid to all Intents and Purposes, as Part of this Constitution, when ratified by the Legislatures of three fourths of the several States, or by Conventions in three fourths thereof, as the one or the other Mode of Ratification may be proposed by the Congress; Provided that no Amendment which may be made prior to the Year One thousand eight hundred and eight shall in any Manner affect the first and fourth Clauses in the Ninth Section of the first Article; and that no State, without its Consent, shall be deprived of it's equal Suffrage in the Senate.*~~

23. The CSA made amending the constitution easier (ratification by only two-thirds or 66% of states instead of three-fourths or 75%) and clarified an ambiguity in Article V of the U.S. Constitution (a national convention can only propose amendments that were suggested by state conventions).

Article six

[*Supreme Law; No Religious Tests*]

1. The Government established by this Constitution is the successor of the Provisional Government of the Confederate States of America, and all the laws passed by the latter shall continue in force until the same shall be repealed or modified; and all the officers appointed by the same shall remain in office until their successors are appointed and qualified, or the offices abolished.

2. All debts contracted and engagements entered into~~,~~ before the adoption of this Constitution~~,~~ shall be as valid against the ~~*United*~~ Confederate States under this Constitution, as under the ~~*Confederation*~~ Provisional Government.

3. This Constitution, and the laws of the ~~*United*~~ Confederate States ~~*which shall be*~~ made in pursuance thereof~~;~~, and all treaties made, or which shall be made~~,~~ under the authority of the ~~*United*~~ Confederate States, shall be the supreme law of the land; and the judges in every state shall be bound thereby, ~~*any Thing*~~ anything in the constitution or laws of any state to the contrary notwithstanding.

4. The Senators and Representatives before mentioned, and the members of the several state legislatures, and all executive and judicial officers, both of the ~~*United*~~ Confederate States, and of the several states, shall be bound by oath or affirmation, to support this Constitution; but no religious test shall ever be required as a qualification to any office or public trust under the ~~*United*~~ Confederate States.

5. The enumeration, in the Constitution, of certain rights, shall not be construed to deny or disparage others retained by the people of the several states.[24]

6. The powers not delegated to the ~~*United*~~ Confederate States by the Constitution, nor prohibited by it to the states, are reserved to the states, respectively, or to the people thereof.

24. The CSA placed their versions of the Ninth and Tenth Amendments to the U.S. Constitution here. The additions of "of the several states" and "thereof" reinforce state citizenship rather than citizenship in a national entity.

Article seven
[*Ratification*]

1. The ratification of the conventions of ~~*nine*~~ five states~~,~~ shall be sufficient for the establishment of this Constitution between the states so ratifying the same.

2. When five states shall have ratified this Constitution, in the manner before specified, the Congress under the Provisional Constitution, shall prescribe the time for holding the election of President and Vice President; and for the meeting of the Electoral College; and for counting the votes, and inaugurating the President. They shall, also, prescribe the time for holding the first election of members of Congress under this Constitution, and the time for assembling the same. Until the assembling of such Congress, the Congress under the Provisional Constitution shall continue to exercise the legislative powers granted them; not extending beyond the time limited by the Constitution of the Provisional Government.

Adopted unanimously by the Congress of the Confederate States of South Carolina, Georgia, Florida, Alabama, Mississippi, Louisiana and Texas, sitting in convention at the capitol, the city of Montgomery, Alabama, on the Eleventh day of March, in the year Eighteen Hundred and Sixty one.

HOWELL COBB, President of the Congress.

1. South Carolina: R. Barnwell Rhett, C. G. Memminger, Wm. Porcher Miles, James Chesnut, Jr., R. W. Barnwell, William W. Boyce, Lawrence M. Keitt, T. J. Withers.

2. Georgia: Francis S. Bartow, Martin J. Crawford, Benjamin H. Hill, Thos. R. R. Cobb.

3. Florida: Jackson Morton, J. Patton Anderson, Jas. B. Owens.

4. Alabama: Richard W. Walker, Robt. H. Smith, Colin J. McRae, William P. Chilton, Stephen F. Hale, David P. Lewis, Tho. Fearn, Jno. Gill Shorter, J. L. M. Curry.

5. Mississippi: Alex. M. Clayton, James T. Harrison, William S. Barry, W. S. Wilson, Walker Brooke, W. P. Harris, J. A. P. Campbell.

6. Louisiana: Alex. de Clouet, C. M. Conrad, Duncan F. Kenner, Henry Marshall.

7. Texas: John Hemphill, Thomas N. Waul, John H. Reagan, Williamson S. Oldham, Louis T. Wigfall, John Gregg, William Beck Ochiltree.[25]

25. Ultimately, the Confederate States were: Alabama, Arkansas, Florida, Georgia, Louisiana, Mississippi, North Carolina, South Carolina, Tennessee, Texas, and Virginia. The Confederacy also recognized Kentucky and Missouri as members.

Conclusion

History is not just what we *recall*, it also includes what we intentionally or unintentionally *forget*. We use this curated history to develop and maintain governments. Lasting governments build and improve on past experiments that have proved beneficial (like due-process protections and voting rights) and abandon those that have failed (such as slavery and ex post facto laws). Throughout these pages, we have traced the iterative and adaptive journey of the documents that define the American experiment. By examining documents like Magna Carta, the English Declaration of Rights, the Articles of Confederation, the United States Constitution, and the Confederate Constitution, we have delved deep into the layers of historical context and the thought processes of the drafters. Studying redlined versions of the founding documents *in context* has hopefully facilitated unique and enlightening insights into the Framers' calculus of inclusion and exclusion.

One theme is solidified by analyzing the drafting record and debates in this book: the Constitution is truly a "bundle of compromises." Primary compromises include:

- The nature of the bicameral legislature (the House based on state population, and each state equally represented in the Senate);
- The three-fifths compromise (three-fifths of the slave population is counted for purposes of determining the number of seats in the House, the number of presidential electoral votes for each state would be allocated, and how much money the states would pay in taxes);
- The "Madisonian Compromise" (that Congress has the power to create lower federal courts but is not required to);
- Compromise on the importation of slaves (guaranteed for at least 20 years, but Congress can regulate interstate commerce and impose tariffs on imports);
- The electoral college for presidential elections (voting for electors instead of direct elections).

Similarly, reviewing the vote count for these compromises, and indeed for most of the revisions shown in this book, reveals that there was rarely unanimity. As the drafters themselves explained, the survival of the convention, and by extension the Nation, depended on the delegates' willingness to subordinate their individual preferences to the collective enterprise. This spirit of pragmatic compromise, born of necessity, is perhaps the most vital and least appreciated element of the Founders' legacy.

This book tracked changes within documents and also *between* documents. The need for the Constitution can be directly traced to the inadequacies of the Articles of Confederation. It follows that comprehending the strengths and weaknesses of the Articles is crucial to truly understanding the Constitution. The Constitution borrowed several clauses from the Articles and filled in many of the Articles' gaps. Among others, the Framers of the Constitution carried over from the Articles: privileges and immunities, full faith and credit, extradition, speech and debate immunity, protection of many rights of states, and providing for the general welfare and common defense. The revised Preamble also mirrors much of Article III of the Articles.

To understand the Articles and the Constitution, we must understand the Declaration of Independence, and the Declaration of Independence owes many of its most important themes to earlier documents like the Articles of Association (1774) and the Stamp Act Congress's 1765 Declarations of Rights and Grievances. The 1765 Declaration borrows heavily from the 1689 English Declaration of Rights, which declared fundamental rights based on Magna Carta (1215). The Constitution and Declaration of Independence view these rights and protections through a new lens of "We the People," but the existence of the rights themselves had been pondered long before. This journey of revision did not end in 1787. The process of amendment, interpretation, and societal debate has continued to adapt the American charter for over two centuries. The addition of the Bill of Rights was the first great revision. The Reconstruction Amendments represented a "Second Founding," a radical attempt to redraft the Nation's commitment to equality after the Civil War.

Understanding the iterative journey of the Constitution equips you with several practical tools. Studies suggest that most Americans have not even read the Constitution and only vaguely know details about its contents. Hopefully this book's more engaging medium begins to change that story. Knowledge of constitutional history and the Framers' true design empowers citizens to engage more thoughtfully and accurately in legal and political discourse in our own time, aiding in distinguishing historical and constitutional reality from political myth.

By tracing the Constitution's development and comparing it with other historical documents, this book offers a unique lens through which to view the past and its ongoing influence on the present and future. To borrow from George Washington (*see* p. 164), it is my ardent wish that this book, and your diligent study, contribute to promoting "the lasting Welfare of that Country so dear to us all and secure her Freedom and Happiness."

Declaration of Independence

(JULY 4, 1776)

In Congress, July 4, 1776
The unanimous Declaration of the thirteen united States of America

When in the Course of human events, it becomes necessary for one people to dissolve the political bands which have connected them with another, and to assume among the powers of the earth, the separate and equal station to which the Laws of Nature and of Nature's God entitle them, a decent respect to the opinions of mankind requires that they should declare the causes which impel them to the separation.

We hold these truths to be self-evident, that all men are created equal, that they are endowed by their Creator with certain unalienable Rights, that among these are Life, Liberty and the pursuit of Happiness.—That to secure these rights, Governments are instituted among Men, deriving their just powers from the consent of the governed,—That whenever any Form of Government becomes destructive of these ends, it is the Right of the People to alter or to abolish it, and to institute new Government, laying its foundation on such principles and organizing its powers in such form, as to them shall seem most likely to effect their Safety and Happiness. Prudence, indeed, will dictate that Governments long established should not be changed for light and transient causes; and accordingly all experience hath shewn, that mankind are more disposed to suffer, while evils are sufferable, than to right themselves by abolishing the forms to which they are accustomed. But when a long train of abuses and usurpations, pursuing invariably the same Object evinces a design to reduce them under absolute Despotism, it is their right, it is their duty, to throw off such Government, and to provide new Guards for their future security.—Such has been the patient sufferance of these Colonies; and such is now the necessity which constrains them to alter their former Systems of Government. The history of the present King of Great Britain is a history of repeated injuries and usurpations, all having in direct object the establishment of an absolute Tyranny over these States. To prove this, let Facts be submitted to a candid world.

He has refused his Assent to Laws, the most wholesome and necessary for the public good.

He has forbidden his Governors to pass Laws of immediate and pressing importance, unless suspended in their operation till his Assent should be obtained; and when so suspended, he has utterly neglected to attend to them.

He has refused to pass other Laws for the accommodation of large districts of people, unless those people would relinquish the right of Representation in the Legislature, a right inestimable to them and formidable to tyrants only.

He has called together legislative bodies at places unusual, uncomfortable, and distant from the depository of their public Records, for the sole purpose of fatiguing them into compliance with his measures.

He has dissolved Representative Houses repeatedly, for opposing with manly firmness his invasions on the rights of the people.

He has refused for a long time, after such dissolutions, to cause others to be elected; whereby the Legislative powers, incapable of Annihilation, have returned to the People at large for their exercise; the State remaining in the mean time exposed to all the dangers of invasion from without, and convulsions within.

He has endeavoured to prevent the population of these States; for that purpose obstructing the Laws for Naturalization of Foreigners; refusing to pass others to encourage their migrations hither, and raising the conditions of new Appropriations of Lands.

He has obstructed the Administration of Justice, by refusing his Assent to Laws for establishing Judiciary powers.

He has made Judges dependent on his Will alone, for the tenure of their offices, and the amount and payment of their salaries.

He has erected a multitude of New Offices, and sent hither swarms of Officers to harrass our people, and eat out their substance.

He has kept among us, in times of peace, Standing Armies without the Consent of our legislatures.

He has affected to render the Military independent of and superior to the Civil power.

He has combined with others to subject us to a jurisdiction foreign to our constitution, and unacknowledged by our laws; giving his Assent to their Acts of pretended Legislation:

For Quartering large bodies of armed troops among us:

For protecting them, by a mock Trial, from punishment for any Murders which they should commit on the Inhabitants of these States:

For cutting off our Trade with all parts of the world:

For imposing Taxes on us without our Consent:

For depriving us in many cases, of the benefits of Trial by Jury:

For transporting us beyond Seas to be tried for pretended offences

For abolishing the free System of English Laws in a neighbouring Province, establishing therein an Arbitrary government, and enlarging its Boundaries so as to render it at once an example and fit instrument for introducing the same absolute rule into these Colonies:

For taking away our Charters, abolishing our most valuable Laws, and altering fundamentally the Forms of our Governments:

For suspending our own Legislatures, and declaring themselves invested with power to legislate for us in all cases whatsoever.

He has abdicated Government here, by declaring us out of his Protection and waging War against us.

He has plundered our seas, ravaged our Coasts, burnt our towns, and destroyed the lives of our people.

He is at this time transporting large Armies of foreign Mercenaries to compleat the works of death, desolation and tyranny, already begun with circumstances of Cruelty & perfidy scarcely paralleled in the most barbarous ages, and totally unworthy the Head of a civilized nation.

He has constrained our fellow Citizens taken Captive on the high Seas to bear Arms against their Country, to become the executioners of their friends and Brethren, or to fall themselves by their Hands.

He has excited domestic insurrections amongst us, and has endeavoured to bring on the inhabitants of our frontiers, the merciless Indian Savages, whose known rule of warfare, is an undistinguished destruction of all ages, sexes and conditions.

In every stage of these Oppressions We have Petitioned for Redress in the most humble terms: Our repeated Petitions have been answered only by repeated injury. A Prince whose character is thus marked by every act which may define a Tyrant, is unfit to be the ruler of a free people.

Nor have We been wanting in attentions to our Brittish brethren. We have warned them from time to time of attempts by their legislature to extend an unwarrantable jurisdiction over us. We have reminded them of the circumstances of our emigration and settlement here. We have appealed to their native justice and magnanimity, and we have conjured them by the ties of our common kindred to disavow these usurpations, which, would inevitably interrupt our connections and correspondence. They too have been deaf to the voice of justice and of consanguinity. We must, therefore, acquiesce in the necessity, which denounces our Separation, and hold them, as we hold the rest of mankind, Enemies in War, in Peace Friends.

We, therefore, the Representatives of the united States of America, in General Congress, Assembled, appealing to the Supreme Judge of the world for the rectitude of our intentions, do, in the Name, and by Authority of the good People of these Colonies, solemnly publish and declare, That these United Colonies are, and of Right ought to be Free and Independent States; that they are Absolved from all Allegiance to the British Crown, and that all political connection between them and the State of Great Britain, is and ought to be totally dissolved; and that as Free and Independent States, they have full Power to levy War, conclude Peace, contract Alliances, establish Commerce, and to do all other Acts and Things which Independent States may of right do. And for the support of this Declaration, with a firm reliance on the protection of divine Providence, we mutually pledge to each other our Lives, our Fortunes and our sacred Honor.

[Signatures omitted. See p. 99*]*

Articles of Confederation

(NOVEMBER 15, 1777)

Articles of Confederation

To all to whom these Presents shall come, we the under signed Delegates of the States affixed to our Names send greetings. Where as the Delegates of the United States of America in Congress assembled did on the fifteenth day of November is the Year of our Lord One Thousand Seven Hundred and Seventy seven, and in the Second Year of the Independence of America agree to certain articles of Confederation and perpetual Union between the States of New hampshire, Massachusetts-bay, Rhodeisland and Providence Plantations, Connecticut, New York, New Jersey, Pennsylvania, Delaware, Maryland, Virginia, North Carolina, South Carolina and Georgia in the Words following viz

"Articles of Confederation and perpetual Union between the States of Newhampshire, Massachusettsbay, Rhodeisland and Providence Plantations, Connecticut, New-York, New Jersey, Pennsyl-vania, Delaware, Maryland, Virginia, North Carolina, South Carolina and Georgia.

Article I.

The Style of the confederacy shall be "The United States of America."

Article II.

Each state retains its Sovereignty, freedom and independence, and every Power, Jurisdiction and right, which is not by this confederation expressly delegated to the United States, in Congress assembled.

Article III.

The said States hereby severally enter into a firm league of friendship with each other, for their common defence, the security of their Liberties, and their mutual and general welfare, binding them-selves to assist each other, against all force offered to, or attacks made upon them, or any of them, on account of religion, Sovereignty, trade, or any other pretence what[so]ever.

Article IV.

The better to secure and perpetuate mutual friendship and intercourse among the people of the different States in this union, the free inhabitants of each of these States, paupers, vagabonds and fugitives from Justice excepted, shall be entitled to all privileges and immunities of free citizens in the Several States; and the people of each State shall have free ingress and regress to and from any other state, and shall enjoy therein all the privileges of trade and commerce, subject to the same duties, impositions and restrictions as the inhabitants thereof respectively, provided that such restriction shall not extend so far as to prevent the removal of property imported into any State, to any other State of which the Owner is an inhabitant; provided also that no imposition, duties or restriction shall be laid by any State, on the property of the united States, or either of them.

If any Person guilty of, or charged with treason, felony, or other high misdemeaner in any State, shall flee from Justice, and be found in any of the United States, he shall upon demand of the Governor or executive power, of the State from which he fled, be delivered up and re-moved to the State having jurisdiction of his offences.

Full faith and Credit shall be given in each of these States to the records, acts and judicial proceedings of the courts and magistrate of every other State.

Article V.

For the more convenient management of the general interests of the United States, delegates shall be annually appointed in such manner as the legislature of each State shall direct, to meet in Congress on the first Monday in November, in every year, with a power reserved to each State, to recal its delegates, or any of them, at any time within the year, and to send others in their stead, for the remainder of the Year.

No state shall be represented in Congress by less than two, nor by more than Seven Members; and no person shall be capable of being a delegate for more than three years in any term of six years; nor shall any person, being a delegate, be capable of holding any office under the United States, for which he, or another for his benefit receives any salary, fees or emolument of any kind.

Each state shall maintain its own delegates in a meeting of the States, and while they act as members of the committee of the States.

In determining questions in the united States, in Congress assembled, each State shall have one vote.

Freedom of Speech and debate in Congress shall not be impeached or questioned in any Court, or place out of Congress, and the members of congress shall be protected in their persons from arrests and imprisonments, during the time of their going to and from, and attendance on congress except for treason, felony, or breach of the peace.

Article VI.

No State without the Consent of the United States in congress assembled, shall send any embassy to, or receive any embassy from, or enter into any conferrence, agreement, alliance or treaty with any King prince or State; not shall any person holding any office of profit or trust under the united States, or any of them, accept of any present, emolument, office or title of any kind whatever from any king, prince or foreign State; nor shall the united States in congress assembled, or any of them, grant any title of nobility.

No two or more States shall enter into any treaty, confederation or alliance whatever between them, without the consent of the united States in congress assembled, specifying accurately the purposes for which the same is to be entered into, and how long it shall continue.

No State shall lay any imposts or duties, which may inter-fere with any Stipulations in treaties, entered into by the united States in congress assembled, with any king, prince or State, in pursuance of any treaties already proposed by congress, to the courts of France and Spain.

No vessels of war shall be kept up in time of peace by any State, except such number only, as shall be deemed necessary by the united States in congress assembled, for the defence of such state, or its trade; nor shall any body of forces be kept up by any State, in time of peace, except such number only, as in the judgment of the united States, in congress assembled, shall be deemed requisite to garrison the forts necessary for the defence of such state; but every State shall always keep up a well regulated and disciplined militia, sufficiently armed and accoutred, and shall provide and constantly have ready for use, in public stores, a due number of field pieces and tents, and a proper quantity of arms, ammunition and camp equipage.

No state shall engage in any war without the consent of the united States in congress assembled, unless such State be actually invaded by enemies, or shall have received certain advice of a resolution being formed by some nation of Indians to invade such state, and the danger is so imminent as not to admit of a delay, till the united States in congress assembled can be consulted: nor shall any state grant commissions to any ships or vessels of war, nor letters of marque or reprisal, except it be after a declaration of war by the united States in congress assembled, and then only against the kingdom or state and the subjects thereof, against which war has been so declared, and under such regulations as shall be established by the united States in congress assembled, unless such state be infested by pirates, in which case vessels of war may be fitted out for that occasion, and kept so long as the danger shall continue, or until the united States in congress assembled shall determine otherwise.

Article VII.

When land-forces raised by any State for the common defence, all officers of or under the rank of colonel, shall be appointed by the legislature of each state respectively by whom such forces shall be raised, or in such manner as such state shall direct, and all vacancies shall be filled up by the State which first made the appointment.

Article VIII.

All charges of war, and all other expences that shall be incurred for the common defence or general welfare, and allowed by the united States in congress assembled, shall be defrayed out of a common treasury, which shall be supplied by the several states, in proportion to the value of all land within each state, granted to or surveyed for any Person, as such land and the buildings and improvements thereon shall be estimated according to such mode as the united States in congress assembled, shall from time to time direct and appoint. The taxes for paying that proportion shall be laid and levied by the authority and direction of the legislatures of the several states within the time agreed upon by the united States in congress assembled.

Article IX.

The united States in congress assembled, shall have the sole and exclusive right and power of determining on peace and war, except in the cases mentioned in the Sixth article ___ of sending and receiving ambassadors ___ entering into treaties and alliances, provided that no treaty of commerce shall be made whereby the legislative power of the respective States shall be restrained from imposing such imposts and duties on foreigners, as their own people are subjected to, or from prohibiting the exportation or importation of any species of goods or commodities whatsoever ___ of establishing rules for deciding in all cases, what captures on land or water shall be legal, and in what manner prizes taken by land or naval forces in the service of the united States shall be divided or appropriated ___ of granting letters of marque and reprisal in times of peace ___ appointing courts for the trial of piracies and felonies committed on the high seas and establishing courts for receiving and determining finally appeals in all cases of captures, provided that no member of congress shall be appointed a judge of any of the said courts.

The united States in congress assembled shall also be the last resort on appeal in all disputes and differences now subsisting or that hereafter may arise between two or more states concerning boundary, jurisdiction or any other cause whatever; which authority shall always be exercised in the manner following. Whenever the legislative or executive authority or lawful agent of any state in controversy with another shall present a petition to congress stating the matter in question and praying for a hearing, notice thereof shall be given by order of congress to the legislative or executive authority of the other state in controversy, and a day assigned for the appearance of the parties by their lawful agents, who shall then be directed to appoint by joint consent, commissioners or judges to constitute a court for hearing and determining the matter in question: but if they cannot agree, congress shall name three persons out of each of the united States, and from the list of such persons each party shall alternately strike out one, the petitioners beginning, until the number shall be reduced to thirteen; and from that number not less than seven, nor more than nine names as congress shall direct, shall in the presence of congress be drawn out by lot, and the persons whose names shall be so drawn or any five of them, shall be commissioners or judges, to hear and finally determine the controversy, so always as a major part of the judges who shall hear the cause shall agree in the determination: and if either party shall neglect to attend at the day appointed, without showing reasons, which congress shall judge sufficient, or being present shall refuse to strike, the congress shall proceed to nominate three persons out of each state, and the secretary of congress shall strike on behalf of such party absent or refusing; and the judgment and sentence of the court to be appointed, in the manner before prescribed, shall be final and conclusive; and if any of the parties shall refuse to submit to the authority of such court, or to appear or defend their claim or cause; the court shall nevertheless proceed to pronounce sentence, or judgment, which shall in like manner be final and decisive, the judgment or sentence and other proceedings being in either case transmittted to congress, and lodged among the acts of congress for the security of the parties concerned: provided that every commissioner, before he sits in judgment, shall take an oath to be administred by one of the judges of the Supreme or Superior court of the State, where the cause shall be tried, "well and truly to hear and determine the matter in question, according to the best of his judgment, without favour, affection or hope of reward:" provided also that no state shall be deprived of territory for the benefit of the united States.

All controversies concerning the private right of soil claimed under different grants of two or more states, whose jurisdictions as they may respect such lands, and the states which passed such grants are adjusted, the said grants or either of them being at the same time claimed to have originated ante-cedent to such settlement of jurisdiction, shall on the petition of either party to the congress of the united States, be finally determined as near as maybe in the same manner as is before prescribed for deciding disputes respecting territorial jurisdiction between different States.

The united States in congress assembled shall also have the sole and exclusive right and power of regulating the alloy and value of coin struck by their own authority, or by that of the respective states ___ fixing the standard of weights and measures throughout the united States ___ regulating the trade and managing all affairs with the Indians, not members of any of the States, provided that the legislative right of any State within its own limits be not in-fringed or violated ___ establishing and regulating post-offices from one state to another, throughout all the united States, and exacting such postage on the papers passing thro' the same as may be requisite to defray the expences of the said office ___ appointing all officers of the land forces, in the service of the united States, excepting regimental officers ___ appointing all the officers of the naval forces, and commissioning all officers whatever in the service of the united States ___ making rules for the government and regulation of the said land and naval forces, and directing their operations.

The united States in congress assembled shall have authority to appoint a committee, to sit in the recess of congress, to be denominated "A Committee of the States," and to consist of one delegate from each state; and to appoint such other committees and civil officers as may be necessary for managing the general affairs of the united States under their direction ___ to appoint one of their number to preside, provided that no person be allowed to serve in the office of president more than one year in any term of three years; to ascertain the necessary sum of Money to be raised for the Service of the united States, and to appropriate and apply the same for defraying the public expences ___ to borrow money, or emit bills on the credit of the united States, transmitting every half year to the respective states an account of the sums of money so borrowed or emitted, ___ to build and equip a navy ___ to agree upon the number of land forces, and to make requisitions from each state for its quota, in proportion to the number of white inhabitants in such state; which requisition shall be binding, and there upon the legislature of each state shall appoint the regimental officers, raise the men and cloath, arm, and equip them in a soldier like manner, at the expence of the united States, and the officers and men so cloathed, armed and equipped shall [march to the place] appointed, and within the time agreed on by the united States in [congress assembled]. But if the united States in congress assembled shall, on consideration of circumstances judge proper that any state should not raise men, or should raise a smaller number than its quota, and that any other state should raise a greater number of men than the quota thereof, such extra number shall be raised, officered, cloathed, armed and equipped in the same manner as the quota of such state, unless the legislature of such state shall judge that such extra number cannot be safely spared out of the same, in which case they shall raise officer, cloath, arm and equip as many of such extra number as they judge can be safely spared. And the officers and men so cloathed, armed and equipped, shall march to the place appointed, and within the time agreed on by the united States in congress assembled.

The united States in congress assembled shall never engage in a war nor grant letters of marque and reprisal in time of peace, nor enter into any treaties or alliances, nor coin money, nor regulate the value thereof, nor ascertain the sums and expences necessary for the defence and welfare of the united States, or any of them, nor emit bills, nor borrow money on the credit of the united States, nor appropriate money, nor agree upon the number of vessels of war, to be built or purchased, or the number of land or sea forces to be raised, nor appoint a commander in chief of the army or navy, unless nine states assent to the same nor shall a question on any other point, except for adjourning from day to day be determined, unless by the votes of a majority of the united States in congress assembled.

The congress of the united States shall have power to adjourn to any time within the year, and to any place within the united States, so that no period of adjournment be for a longer duration than the space of six Months, and shall publish the Journal of their proceedings monthly, except such parts thereof relating to treaties, alliances or military operations, as in their judgment require secresy; and the yeas and nays of the delegates of each state on any question shall be entered on the Journal, when it is desired by any delegate; and the delegates of a state, or any of them, at his or their request shall be furnished with a transcript of the said Journal, except such parts as are above excepted, to lay before the legislatures of the several states.

Article X.

The committee of the States, or any nine of them, shall be authorised to execute, in the recess of congress, such of the powers of congress as the united States in congress assembled, by the consent of nine States, shall from time to time think expedient to vest them with; provided that no power be delegated to the said committee, for the exercise of which, by the articles of con-federation, the voice of nine states in the congress of the united States assembled is requisite.

Article XI.

Canada acceding to this confederation, and joining in the measures of the united States, shall be admitted into, and entitled to all the advantages of this union: but no other colony shall be admitted into the same, unless such admission be agreed to by nine states.

Article XII.

All bills of credit emitted, monies borrowed and debts contracted by, or under the authority of congress, before the assembling of the united states, in pursuance of the present confederation, shall be deemed and considered as a charge against the united States, for payment and satisfaction whereof the said united States, and the public faith are hereby solemnly pledged.

Article XIII.

Every state shall abide by the determinations of the united States in congress assembled, on all questions which by this confederation are submitted to them. And the Articles of this confederation shall be inviolably observed by every state, and the union shall be perpetual; nor shall any alteration at any time hereafter be made in any of them; unless such alteration be agreed to in a congress of the united states, and be afterwards con-firmed by the legislatures of every state.

And Whereas it hath pleased the Great Governor of the World to incline the hearts of the legislatures we respectively represent in congress, to approve of, and to authorize us to ratify the said articles of confederation and perpetual union, know Ye that we the undersigned delegates, by virtue of the power and authority to us given for that purpose, do by these presents, in the name and in behalf of our respective constituents, fully and entirely ratify and confirm each and every of the said articles of confederation and perpetual union, and all and singular the matters and things therein contained. And we do further solemnly plight and engage the faith of our respective constituents, that they shall abide by the determinations of the united States in congress assembled, on all questions, which by the said confederation are submitted to them.

And that the articles thereof shall be inviolably observed by the states we respectively represent, and that the union shall be perpetual. In Witness whereof we have hereunto set our hands in Congress. Done at Philadelphia in the state of Pennsylvania the ninth Day of July in the Year of our Lord one Thousand seven Hundred and Seventy-eight, and in the third year of the independence of America.

[Signatures omitted. See p. 118*]*

Constitution of the United States

(SEPTEMBER 28, 1787)

Preamble

WE the People of the United States, in order to form a more perfect Union, establish Justice, insure domestic Tranquility, provide for the Common Defence, promote the general Welfare, and secure the Blessings of Liberty to ourselves and our Posterity, do ordain and establish this CONSTITUTION for the United States of America.

Article I.

Sect. 1 All legislative powers herein granted shall be vested in a Congress of the United States, which shall consist of a Senate and House of Representatives.

Sect. 2. The House of Representatives shall be composed of members chosen every second year by the people of the several states, and the electors in each state shall have the qualifications requisite for electors of the most numerous branch of the state legislature.

No person shall be a representative who shall not have attained to the age of twenty-five years, and been seven years a citizen of the United States, and who shall not, when elected, be an inhabitant of that state in which he shall be chosen.

Representatives and direct taxes shall be apportioned among the several states which may be included within this Union, according to their respective numbers, which shall be determined by adding to the whole number of free persons, including those bound to service for a term of years, and excluding Indians not taxed, three-fifths of all other persons. The actual enumeration shall be made within three years after the first meeting of the Congress of the United States, and within every subsequent term of ten years, in such manner as they shall by law direct. The number of representatives shall not exceed one for every thirty thousand, but each State shall have at least one representative; and until such enumeration shall be made, the state of NewHampshire shall be entitled to chuse three, Massachusetts eight, Rhode-Island and Providence Plantations one, Connecticut five, New-York six, New-Jersey four, Pennsylvania eight, Delaware one, Maryland six, Virginia ten, NorthCarolina five, SouthCarolina five, and Georgia three.

When vacancies happen in the representation from any state, the Executive authority thereof shall issue writs of election to fill such vacancies.

The House of Representatives shall chuse their Speaker and other officers; and shall have the sole power of impeachment.

Sect. 3. The Senate of the United States shall be composed of two senators from each state, chosen by the legislature thereof, for six years; and each senator shall have one vote.

Immediately after they shall be assembled in consequence of the first election, they shall be divided as equally as may be into three classes. The seats of the senators of the first class shall be vacated at the expiration of the second year, of the second class at the expiration of the fourth year, and of the third class at the expiration of the sixth year, so that one-third may be chosen every second year; and if vacancies happen by resignation, or otherwise, during the recess of the legislature of any state, the Executive thereof may make temporary appointments until the next meeting of the legislature, which shall then fill such vacancies.

No person shall be a senator who shall not have attained to the age of thirty years, and been nine years a citizen of the United States, and who shall not, when elected, be an inhabitant of that state for which he shall be chosen.

The Vice-President of the United States shall be President of the senate, but shall have no vote, unless they be equally divided.

The Senate shall chuse their other officers, and also a President *pro tempore,* in the absence of the Vice-President, or when he shall exercise the office of President of the United States.

The Senate shall have the sole power to try all impeachments. When sitting for that purpose, they shall be on oath or affirmation. When the President of the United States is tried, the Chief Justice shall preside: And no person shall be convicted without the concurrence of two-thirds of the members present.

Judgment in cases of impeachment shall not extend further than to removal from office, and disqualification to hold and enjoy any office of honor, trust or profit under the United States; but the party convicted shall nevertheless be liable and subject to indictment, trial, judgment and punishment, according to law.

Sect. 4. The times, places and manner of holding elections for senators and representatives, shall be prescribed in each State by the legislature thereof: but the Congress may at any time by law make or alter such regulations, except as to the places of chusing Senators.

The Congress shall assemble at least once in every year, and such meeting shall be on the first Monday in December, unless they shall by law appoint a different day.

Sect. 5. Each house shall be the judge of the elections, returns and qualifications of its own members, and a majority of each shall constitute a quorum to do business; but a smaller number may adjourn from day to day, and may be authorised to compel the attendance of absent members, in such manner, and under such penalties as each house may provide.

Each house may determine the rules of its proceedings, punish its members for disorderly behaviour., and, with the concurrence of two-thirds, expel a member.

Each house shall keep a journal of its proceedings, and from time to time publish the same, excepting such parts as may in their judgment require secrecy; and the yeas and nays of the members of either house on any question shall, at the desire of one-fifth of those present, be entered on the journal.

Neither house, during the session of Congress, shall without the consent of the other, adjourn for more than three days, nor to any other place than that in which the two houses shall be sitting.

Sect. 6. The senators and representatives shall receive a compensation for their services, to be ascertained by law, and paid out of the treasury of the United States. They shall in all cases, except treason, felony and breach of the peace, be privileged from arrest during their attendance at the session of their respective houses, and in going to and returning from the same; and for any speech or debate in either house, they shall not be questioned in any other place.

No senator or representative shall, during the time for which he was elected, be appointed to any civil office under the authority of the United States, which shall have been created, or the emoluments whereof shall have been encreased during such time; and no person holding any office under the United States, shall be a member of either house during his continuance in office.

Sect. 7. All bills for raising revenue shall originate in the house of representatives; but the senate may propose or concur with amendments as on other bills.

Every bill which shall have passed the house of representatives and the senate, shall, before it become a law, be presented to the president of the United States; if he approve he shall sign it, but if not he shall return it, with his objections to that house in which it shall have originated, who shall enter the objections at large on their journal, and proceed to reconsider it. If after such reconsideration two-thirds of that house shall agree to pass the bill, it shall be sent, together with the objections, to the other house, by which it shall likewise be reconsidered, and if approved by two-thirds of that house, it shall become a law. But in all such cases the votes of both houses shall be determined by yeas and nays, and the names of the persons voting for and against the bill shall be entered on the journal of each house respectively. If any bill shall not be returned by the President within ten days (Sundays excepted) after it shall have been presented to him, the same shall be a law, in like manner as if he had signed it, unless the Congress by their adjournment prevent its return, in which case it shall not be a law.

Every order, resolution, or vote to which the concurrence of the Senate and House of Representatives may be necessary (except on a question of adjournment) shall be presented to the President of the United States; and before the same shall take effect, shall be approved by him, or, being disapproved by him, shall be re-passed by two-thirds of the Senate and House of Representatives, according to the rules and limitations prescribed in the case of a bill.

Sect. 8. The Congress shall have power

To lay and collect taxes, duties, imposts and excises, to pay the debts and provide for the common defence and general welfare of the United States; but all duties, imposts and excises shall be uniform throughout the United States:

To borrow money on the credit of the United States:

To regulate commerce with foreign nations, and among the several states, and with the Indian tribes:

To establish an uniform rule of naturalization, and uniform laws on the subject of bankruptcies throughout the United States:

To coin money, regulate the value thereof, and of foreign coin, and fix the standard of weights and measures:

To provide for the punishment of counterfeiting the securities and current coin of the United States:

To establish post-offices and post-roads:

To promote the progress of science and useful arts,

by securing for limited times to authors and inventors the exclusive right to their respective writings and discoveries:

To constitute tribunals inferior to the supreme court:

To define and punish piracies and felonies committed on the high seas, and offences against the law of nations:

To declare war, grant letters of marque and reprisal, and make rules concerning captures on land and water:

To raise and support armies, but no appropriation of money to that use shall be for a longer term than two years:

To provide and maintain a navy:

To make rules for the government and regulation of the land and naval forces:

To provide for calling forth the militia to execute the laws of the union, suppress insurrections and repel invasions:

To provide for organizing, arming, and disciplining the militia, and for governing such part of them as may be employed in the service of the United States, reserving to the States respectively, the appointment of the officers, and the authority of training the militia according to the discipline prescribed by Congress:

To exercise exclusive legislation in all cases whatsoever, over such district (not exceeding ten miles square) as may, by cession of particular states, and the acceptance of Congress, become the seat of the government of the United States, and to exercise like authority over all places purchased by the consent of the legislature of the state in which the same shall be, for the erection of forts, magazines, arsenals, dock-yards, and other needful buildings:—And

To make all laws which shall be necessary and proper for carrying into execution the foregoing powers, and all other powers vested by this constitution in the government of the United States, or in any department or officer thereof.

Sect. 9. The migration or importation of such persons as any of the States now existing shall think proper to admit, shall not be prohibited by the Congress prior to the year one thousand eight hundred and eight, but a tax or duty may be imposed on such importation, not exceeding ten dollars for each person.

The privilege of the writ of *habeas corpus* shall not be suspended, unless when in cases of rebellion or invasion the public safety may require it.

No bill of attainder or ex post facto law shall be passed.

No capitation, or other direct, tax shall be laid, unless in proportion to the *census* or enumeration herein before directed to be taken.

No tax or duty shall be laid on articles exported from any state. No preference shall be given by any regulation of commerce or revenue to the ports of one state over those of another: nor shall vessels bound to, or from, one State, be obliged to enter, clear, or pay duties in another.

No money shall be drawn from the treasury, but in consequence of appropriations made by law; and a regular Statement and account of the receipts and expenditures of all public money shall be published from time to time.

No title of nobility shall be granted by the United States: And no person holding any office of profit or trust under them, shall, without the consent of the Congress, accept of any present, emolument, office, *or* title, of any kind whatever, from any king, prince or foreign state.

Sect. 10. No state shall enter into any treaty, alliance, or confederation; grant letters of marque and reprisal; coin money; emit bills of credit; make any thing but gold and silver coin a tender in payment of debts; pass any bill of attainder, *ex post facto law*, or law impairing the obligation of contracts, or grant any title of nobility.

No state shall, without the consent of the Congress, lay any imposts or duties on imports or exports, except what may be absolutely necessary for executing its inspection laws; and the net produce of all duties and imposts, laid by any state on imports or exports, shall be for the use of the Treasury of the United States; and all such laws shall be subject to the revision and controul of the Congress. No state shall, without the consent of Congress, lay any duty of tonnage, keep troops, or ships of war in time of peace, enter into any agreement or compact with another state, or with a foreign power, or engage in war, unless actually invaded, or in such imminent danger as will not admit of delay.

Article II.

Sect. 1. The executive power shall be vested in a President of the United States of America. He shall hold his office during the term of four years, and, together with the Vice-President, chosen for the same term, be elected as follows:—

Each state shall appoint, in such manner as the legislature thereof may direct, a number of electors, equal to the whole number of senators and representatives to which the state may be entitled in the Congress: but no senator or representative, or person holding an office of trust or profit under the United States, shall be appointed an elector.

The electors shall meet in their respective states, and vote by ballot for two persons, of whom one at least shall not be an inhabitant of the same state with themselves. And they shall make a list of all the persons voted for, and of the number of votes for each; which list they shall sign and certify, and transmit sealed to the seat of the government of the United States, directed to the President of the Senate. The president of the Senate shall, in the presence of the Senate and House of Representatives, open all the certificates, and the votes shall then be counted. The person having the greatest number of votes shall be the President, if such number be a majority of the whole number of electors appointed; and if there be more than one who have such majority, and have an equal number of votes, then the House of Representatives shall immediately chuse by ballot one of them for President; and if no person have a majority, then from the five highest on the list the said House shall in like manner chuse the President. But in chusing the President, the votes shall be taken by states, the representation from each state having one vote; a quorum for this purpose shall consist of a member or members from two-thirds of the states, and a majority of all the states shall be necessary to a choice. In every case, after the choice of the President, the person having the Greatest number of votes of the electors shall be the Vice-President. But if there should remain two or more who have equal votes, the Senate shall chuse from them by ballot the Vice-President.

The Congress may determine the time of chusing the electors, and the day on which they shall give their votes; which day shall be the same throughout the United States.

No person except a natural born citizen, or a citizen of the United States, at the time of the adoption of this constitution, shall be eligible to the office of President; neither shall any person be eligible to that office who shall not have attained to the age of thirty-five years, and been fourteen years a resident within the United States.

In case of the removal of the President from office, or of his death, resignation, or inability to discharge the powers and duties of the said office, the same shall devolve on the Vice-President, and the Congress may by law provide for the case of removal, death, resignation, or inability, both of the President and Vice-President, declaring what officer shall then act as President, and such officer shall act accordingly, until the disability be removed, or a President shall be elected.

The President shall, at stated times, receive for his services, a compensation, which shall neither be encreased nor diminished during the period for which he shall have been elected, and he shall not receive within that period any other emolument from the United States, or any of them.

Before he enter on the execution of his office, he shall take the following oath or affirmation:—

"I do solemnly swear (or affirm) that I will faithfully execute the office of President of the United States, and will to the best of my ability, preserve, protect and defend the constitution of the United States."

Sect. 2. The President shall be commander in chief of the army and navy of the United States, and of the militia of the several states, when called into the actual service of the United States; he may require the opinion, in writing, of the principal officer in each of the executive departments, upon any subject relating to the duties of their respective offices, and he shall have power to grant reprieves and pardons for offences against the United States, except in cases of impeachment.

He shall have power, by and with the advice and consent of the Senate, to make treaties, provided two-thirds of the Senators present concur; and he shall nominate, and by and with the advice and consent of the Senate, shall appoint ambassadors, other public ministers and consuls, judges of the supreme court, and all other officers of the United States, whose appointments are not herein otherwise provided for, and which shall be established by law. But the Congress may by law vest the appointment of such inferior officers, as they think proper in the President alone, in the courts of law, or in the heads of departments.

The President shall have power to fill up all vacancies that may happen during the recess of the Senate, by granting commissions which shall expire at the end of their next Session.

Sect. 3. He shall from time to time give to the Congress information of the state of the union, and recommend to their consideration such measures as he shall judge necessary and expedient; he may, on extraordinary occasions, convene both houses, or either of them, and in case of disagreement between them, with respect to the time of adjournment, he may adjourn them to such time as he shall think proper; he shall receive ambassadors and other public ministers; he shall take care that the laws be faithfully executed, and shall commission all the officers of the United States.

Sect. 4. The president, vice-president and all civil officers of of the United States shall be removed from office on impeachment for, and conviction of, treason, bribery, or other high crimes and misdemeanors.

Article III.

Sect. 1. The judicial power of the United States, shall be vested in one supreme court, and in such inferior courts as the Congress may from time to time ordain and establish. The judges, both of the supreme and inferior court, shall hold their offices during good behaviour, and shall, at stated times, receive for their services, a compensation, which shall not be diminished during their continuance in office.

Sect. 2. The judicial power shall extend to all cases, in law and equity, arising under this constitution, the laws of the United States, and treaties made, or which shall be made, under their authority; to all cases affecting ambassadors, other public ministers and consuls; to all cases of admiralty and maritime jurisdiction; to controversies to which the United States shall be a party; to controversies between two or more states, between a state and citizens of another State, between citizens of different states, between citizens of the same state claiming lands under grants of different states, and between a state, or the citizens thereof, and foreign States, citizens or subjects.

In all cases affecting ambassadors, other public ministers and consuls, and those in which a state shall be party, the supreme court shall have original jurisdiction. In all the other cases before mentioned, the supreme court shall have appellate jurisdiction, both as to law and fact, with such exceptions, and under such regulations as the Congress shall make.

The trial of all crimes, except in cases of impeachment, shall be by jury; and such trial shall be held in the state where the said crimes shall have been committed; but when not committed within any state, the trial shall be at such place or places as the Congress may by law have directed.

Sect. 3. Treason against the United States, shall consist only in levying war against them, or in adhering to their enemies, giving them aid and comfort. No person shall be convicted of treason unless on the testimony of two witnesses to the same overt act, or on confession in open court.

The Congress shall have power to declare the punishment of treason, but no attainder of treason shall work corruption of blood, or forfeiture, except during the life of the person attained.

Article IV.

Sect. 1. Full faith and credit shall be given in each state to the public acts, records and judicial proceedings of every other state. And the Congress may by general laws prescribe the manner in which such acts, records and proceedings shall be proved, and the effect thereof.

Sect. 2. The citizens of each state shall be entitled to all privileges and immunities of citizens in the several states.

A person charged in any state with treason, felony, or other crime, who shall flee from justice, and be found in another state, shall, on demand of the executive authority of the state from which he fled, be delivered up, to be removed to the state having jurisdiction of the crime.

No person held to service or labour in one state, under the laws thereof, escaping into another, shall, in consequence of any law or regulation therein, be discharged from such service or labour, but shall be delivered up on claim of the party to whom such service or labour may be due.

Sect. 3. New states may be admitted by the Congress into this union; but no new state shall be formed or erected within the jurisdiction of any other state; nor any state be formed by the junction of two or more states, or parts of states, without the consent of the legislatures of the states concerned as well as of the Congress.

The Congress shall have power to dispose of and make all needful rules and regulations respecting the territory or other property belonging to the United States; and nothing in this constitution shall be so construed as to prejudice any claims of the United States, or of any particular state.

Sect. 4. The United States shall guarantee to every state in this union a Republican form of government, and shall protect each of them against invasion; and on application of the legislature, or of the executive (when the legislature cannot be convened) against domestic violence.

Article V.

The Congress, whenever two-thirds of both Houses shall deem it necessary, shall propose amendments to this constitution, or, on the application of the legislatures of two-thirds of the several states, shall call a convention for proposing amendments, which, in either case, shall be valid to all intents and purposes, as part of this constitution, when ratified by the legislatures of three-fourths of the several States, or by conventions in three-fourths thereof, as the one or the other mode of ratification may be proposed by the Congress: Provided, that no amendment which may be made prior to the year one thousand eight hundred and eight shall in any manner affect the first and fourth clauses in the ninth section of the first article; and that no state, without its consent, shall be deprived of its equal suffrage in the Senate.

Article VI.

All debts contracted and engagements entered into, before the adoption of this constitution, shall be as valid against the United States under this constitution, as under the confederation.

This constitution, and the laws of the United States which shall be made in pursuance thereof; and all treaties made, or which shall be made, under the authority of the United States, shall be the supreme law of the land; and the judges in every state shall be bound thereby, any thing in the constitution or laws of any state to the contrary notwithstanding.

The senators and representatives before mentioned, and the members of the several state legislatures, and all executive and judicial officers, both of the United States and of the several states, shall be bound by oath or affirmation, to support this constitution; but no religious test shall ever be required as a qualification to any office or public trust under the United States.

Article VII.

The ratification of the conventions of nine states, shall be sufficient for the establishment of this constitution between the states so ratifying the same.

DONE in Convention, by the unanimous consent of the States present, the seventeenth day of September, in the year of our Lord one thousand seven hundred and eighty-seven, and of the Independence of the United States of America the twelfth. In witness whereof we have hereunto subscribed our Names.

[Signatures omitted. See p. 162*]*

Letter of George Washington to the President of Congress

In Convention, September 17, 1787

SIR,

We have now the Honor to submit to the Consideration of the United States in Congress assembled that Constitution which has appeared to us the most advisable.

The Friends of our Country have long seen and desired that the Power of making War Peace and Treaties, that of levying Money & regulating Commerce and the correspondent executive and judicial Authorities should be fully and effectually vested in the general Government of the Union. But the Impropriety of delegating such extensive Trust to one Body of Men is evident—Hence results the Necessity of a different Organization.

It is obviously impracticable in the fœderal Government Of these States to secure all Rights of independent Sovereignty to each and yet provide for the Interest and Safety of all—Individuals entering into Society must give up a Share of Liberty to preserve the Rest. The Magnitude of the Sacrifice must depend as well on Situations and Circumstances as on the Object to be obtained. It is at all Times difficult to draw with Precision the Lines between those Rights which must be surrendered and those which may be reserved. And on the present Occasion this Difficulty was encreased by a Difference among the several States as to their Situation Extent Habits and particular Interests.

In all our Deliberations on this Subject we kept steadily in our View that which appears to us the greatest Interest of every true american the Consolidation of our Union in which is involved our Prosperity Felicity Safety perhaps our national Existence. this important Consideration seriously and deeply impressed on our Minds led each State in the Convention to be less rigid on Points of inferior Magnitude than might have been otherwise expected. And thus the Constitution which we now present is the Result of a Spirit of Amity and of that mutual Deference & Concession which the Peculiarity of our political Situation rendered indispensible.

That it will meet the full and entire Approbation of every State is not perhaps to be expected. But each will doubtless consider that had her Interests been alone consulted the Consequences might have been particularly disagreable or injurious to others. That it is liable to as few Exceptions as could reasonably have been expected we hope and believe That it may promote the lasting Welfare of that Country so dear to us all and secure her Freedom and Happiness is our most ardent wish.

With great respect,

We have the Honor to be, SIR,

Your Excellency's most

Obedient and humble Servants:

George Washington, *President.*

Resolution of the Federal Convention Submitting the Constitution to Congress, September 17, 1787

In Convention, Monday, September 17, 1787

Present

The States of

New Hampshire, Massachusetts, Connecticut, Mr. Hamilton from New York, New Jersey, Pennsylvania, Delaware, Maryland, Virginia, North Carolina, South Carolina and Georgia. Resolved,

That the proceeding Constitution be laid before the United States in Congress assembled, and that it is the Opinion of this Convention, that it should afterwards be submitted to a Convention of Delegates, chosen in each State by the People thereof, under the Recommendation of its Legislature, for their Assent and Ratification; and that each Convention assenting to, and ratifying the Same, should give Notice thereof to the United States in Congress assembled.

Resolved, That it is the Opinion of this Convention, that as soon as the Conventions of nine States shall have ratified this Constitution, the United States in Congress assembled should fix a Day on which Electors should be appointed by the States which shall have ratified the same, and a Day on which the Electors should assemble to vote for the President, and the Time and Place for commencing Proceedings under this Constitution. That after such Publication the Electors should be appointed, and the Senators and Representatives elected: That the Electors should meet on the Day fixed for the Election of the President, and should transmit their Votes certified, signed, sealed and directed, as the Constitution requires, to the Secretary of the United States in Congress assembled, that the Senators and Representatives should convene at the Time and Place assigned; that the Senators should appoint a President of the Senate, for the sole Purpose of receiving, opening and counting the Votes for President; and, that after he shall be chosen, the Congress, together with the President, should, without Delay, proceed to execute this Constitution.

By the Unanimous Order of the Convention

G° WASHINGTON Presid^{t}

W. JACKSON Secretary.

The Amendments

Bill of Rights: Passed by Congress September 25, 1789.
Ratified December 15, 1791.

Amendment I

Congress shall make no law respecting an establishment of religion, or prohibiting the free exercise thereof; or abridging the freedom of speech, or of the press; or the right of the people peaceably to assemble, and to petition the Government for a redress of grievances.

Amendment II

A well regulated Militia, being necessary to the security of a free State, the right of the people to keep and bear Arms, shall not be infringed.

Amendment III

No Soldier shall, in time of peace be quartered in any house, without the consent of the Owner, nor in time of war, but in a manner to be prescribed by law.

Amendment IV

The right of the people to be secure in their persons, houses, papers, and effects, against unreasonable searches and seizures, shall not be violated, and no Warrants shall issue, but upon probable cause, supported by Oath or affirmation, and particularly describing the place to be searched, and the persons or things to be seized.

Amendment V

No person shall be held to answer for a capital, or otherwise infamous crime, unless on a presentment or indictment of a Grand Jury, except in cases arising in the land or naval forces, or in the Militia, when in actual service in time of War or public danger; nor shall any person be subject for the same offence to be twice put in jeopardy of life or limb; nor shall be compelled in any criminal case to be a witness against himself, nor be deprived of life, liberty, or property, without due process of law; nor shall private property be taken for public use, without just compensation.

Amendment VI

In all criminal prosecutions, the accused shall enjoy the right to a speedy and public trial, by an impartial jury of the State and district wherein the crime shall have been committed, which district shall have been previously ascertained by law, and to be informed of the nature and cause of the accusation; to be confronted with the witnesses against him; to have compulsory process for obtaining witnesses in his favor, and to have the Assistance of Counsel for his defence.

Amendment VII

In Suits at common law, where the value in controversy shall exceed twenty dollars, the right of trial by jury shall be preserved, and no fact tried by a jury, shall be otherwise re-examined in any Court of the United States, than according to the rules of the common law.

Amendment VIII

Excessive bail shall not be required, nor excessive fines imposed, nor cruel and unusual punishments inflicted.

Amendment IX

The enumeration in the Constitution, of certain rights, shall not be construed to deny or disparage others retained by the people.

Amendment X

The powers not delegated to the United States by the Constitution, nor prohibited by it to the States, are reserved to the States respectively, or to the people.

Amendment XI

The Judicial power of the United States shall not be construed to extend to any suit in law or equity, commenced or prosecuted against one of the United States by Citizens of another State, or by Citizens or Subjects of any Foreign State.

Passed by Congress March 4, 1794. Ratified February 7, 1795.

Amendment XII

The Electors shall meet in their respective states and vote by ballot for President and Vice-President, one of whom, at least, shall not be an inhabitant of the same state with themselves; they shall name in their ballots the person voted for as President, and in distinct ballots the person voted for as Vice-President, and they shall make distinct lists of all persons voted for as President, and of all persons voted for as Vice-President, and of the number of votes for each, which lists they shall sign and certify, and transmit sealed to the seat of the government of the United States, directed to the President of the Senate;—the President of the Senate shall, in the presence of the Senate and House of Representatives, open all the certificates and the votes shall then be counted;—The person having the greatest number of votes for President, shall be the President, if such number be a majority of the whole number of Electors appointed; and if no person have such majority, then from the persons having the highest numbers not exceeding three on the list of those voted for as President, the House of Representatives shall choose immediately, by ballot, the President. But in choosing the President, the votes shall be taken by states, the representation from each state having one vote; a quorum for this purpose shall consist of a member or members from two-thirds of the states, and a majority of all the states shall be necessary to a choice. [And if the House of Representatives shall not choose a President whenever the right of choice shall devolve upon them, before the fourth day of March next following, then the Vice-President shall act as President, as in case of the death or other constitutional disability of the President.—]* The person having the greatest number of votes as Vice-President, shall be the Vice-President, if such number be a majority of the whole number of Electors appointed, and if no person have a majority, then from the two highest numbers on the list, the Senate shall choose the Vice-President; a quorum for the purpose shall consist of two-thirds of the whole number of Senators, and a majority of the whole number shall be necessary to a choice. But no person constitutionally ineligible to the office of President shall be eligible to that of Vice-President of the United States.
**Superseded by section 3 of the 20th amendment.*

Passed by Congress December 9, 1803. Ratified June 15, 1804.

Amendment XIII

Section 1.

Neither slavery nor involuntary servitude, except as a punishment for crime whereof the party shall have been duly convicted, shall exist within the United States, or any place subject to their jurisdiction.

Section 2.

Congress shall have power to enforce this article by appropriate legislation.

Passed by Congress January 31, 1865. Ratified December 6, 1865.

Amendment XIV

Section 1.

All persons born or naturalized in the United States, and subject to the jurisdiction thereof, are citizens of the United States and of the State wherein they reside. No State shall make or enforce any law which shall abridge the privileges or immunities of citizens of the United States; nor shall any State deprive any person of life, liberty, or property, without due process of law; nor deny to any person within its jurisdiction the equal protection of the laws.

Section 2.

Representatives shall be apportioned among the several States according to their respective numbers, counting the whole number of persons in each State, excluding Indians not taxed. But when the right to vote at any election for the choice of electors for President and Vice-President of the United States, Representatives in Congress, the Executive and Judicial officers of a State, or the members of the Legislature thereof, is denied to any of the male inhabitants of such State, being twenty-one years of age,* and citizens of the United States, or in any way abridged, except for participation in rebellion, or other crime, the basis of representation therein shall be reduced in the proportion which the number of such male citizens shall bear to the whole number of male citizens twenty-one years of age in such State.

Section 3.

No person shall be a Senator or Representative in Congress, or elector of President and Vice-President, or hold any office, civil or military, under the

United States, or under any State, who, having previously taken an oath, as a member of Congress, or as an officer of the United States, or as a member of any State legislature, or as an executive or judicial officer of any State, to support the Constitution of the United States, shall have engaged in insurrection or rebellion against the same, or given aid or comfort to the enemies thereof. But Congress may by a vote of two-thirds of each House, remove such disability.

Section 4.

The validity of the public debt of the United States, authorized by law, including debts incurred for payment of pensions and bounties for services in suppressing insurrection or rebellion, shall not be questioned. But neither the United States nor any State shall assume or pay any debt or obligation incurred in aid of insurrection or rebellion against the United States, or any claim for the loss or emancipation of any slave; but all such debts, obligations and claims shall be held illegal and void.

Section 5.

The Congress shall have power to enforce, by appropriate legislation, the provisions of this article.

**Changed by section 1 of the 26th amendment.*

Passed by Congress June 13, 1866. Ratified July 9, 1868.

Amendment XV

Section 1.

The right of citizens of the United States to vote shall not be denied or abridged by the United States or by any State on account of race, color, or previous condition of servitude—

Section 2.

The Congress shall have power to enforce this article by appropriate legislation.

Passed by Congress February 26, 1869. Ratified February 3, 1870.

Amendment XVI

The Congress shall have power to lay and collect taxes on incomes, from whatever source derived, without apportionment among the several States, and without regard to any census or enumeration.

Passed by Congress July 2, 1909. Ratified February 3, 1913.

Amendment XVII

The Senate of the United States shall be composed of two Senators from each State, elected by the people thereof, for six years; and each Senator shall have one vote. The electors in each State shall have the qualifications requisite for electors of the most numerous branch of the State legislatures.

When vacancies happen in the representation of any State in the Senate, the executive authority of such State shall issue writs of election to fill such vacancies: Provided, That the legislature of any State may empower the executive thereof to make temporary appointments until the people fill the vacancies by election as the legislature may direct.

This amendment shall not be so construed as to affect the election or term of any Senator chosen before it becomes valid as part of the Constitution.

Passed by Congress May 13, 1912. Ratified April 8, 1913.

Amendment XVIII

Section 1.

After one year from the ratification of this article the manufacture, sale, or transportation of intoxicating liquors within, the importation thereof into, or the exportation thereof from the United States and all territory subject to the jurisdiction thereof for beverage purposes is hereby prohibited.

Section 2.

The Congress and the several States shall have concurrent power to enforce this article by appropriate legislation.

Section 3.

This article shall be inoperative unless it shall have been ratified as an amendment to the Constitution by the legislatures of the several States, as provided in the Constitution, within seven years from the date of the submission hereof to the States by the Congress.

Passed by Congress December 18, 1917. Ratified January 16, 1919.
Repealed by amendment 21.

Amendment XIX

The right of citizens of the United States to vote shall not be denied or abridged by the United States or by any State on account of sex.

Congress shall have power to enforce this article by appropriate legislation.

Passed by Congress June 4, 1919. Ratified August 18, 1920.

Amendment XX

Section 1.

The terms of the President and the Vice President shall end at noon on the 20th day of January, and the terms of Senators and Representatives at noon on the 3d day of January, of the years in which such terms would have ended if this article had not been ratified; and the terms of their successors shall then begin.

Section 2.

The Congress shall assemble at least once in every year, and such meeting shall begin at noon on the 3d day of January, unless they shall by law appoint a different day.

Section 3.

If, at the time fixed for the beginning of the term of the President, the President elect shall have died, the Vice President elect shall become President. If a President shall not have been chosen before the time fixed for the beginning of his term, or if the President elect shall have failed to qualify, then the Vice President elect shall act as President until a President shall have qualified; and the Congress may by law provide for the case wherein neither a President elect nor a Vice President elect shall have qualified, declaring who shall then act as President, or the manner in which one who is to act shall be selected, and such person shall act accordingly until a President or Vice President shall have qualified.

Section 4.

The Congress may by law provide for the case of the death of any of the persons from whom the House of Representatives may choose a President whenever the right of choice shall have devolved upon them, and for the case of the death of any of the persons from whom the Senate may choose a Vice President whenever the right of choice shall have devolved upon them.

Section 5.

Sections 1 and 2 shall take effect on the 15th day of October following the ratification of this article.

Section 6.

This article shall be inoperative unless it shall have been ratified as an amendment to the Constitution by the legislatures of three-fourths of the several States within seven years from the date of its submission.

Passed by Congress March 2, 1932. Ratified January 23, 1933.

Amendment XXI

Section 1.

The eighteenth article of amendment to the Constitution of the United States is hereby repealed.

Section 2.

The transportation or importation into any State, Territory, or possession of the United States for delivery or use therein of intoxicating liquors, in violation of the laws thereof, is hereby prohibited.

Section 3.

This article shall be inoperative unless it shall have been ratified as an amendment to the Constitution by conventions in the several States, as provided in the Constitution, within seven years from the date of the submission hereof to the States by the Congress.

Passed by Congress February 20, 1933. Ratified December 5, 1933.

Amendment XXII

Section 1.

No person shall be elected to the office of the President more than twice, and no person who has held the office of President, or acted as President, for more than two years of a term to which some other person was elected President shall be elected to the office of the President more than once. But this Article shall not apply to any person holding the office of President when this Article was proposed by the Congress, and shall not prevent any person who may be holding the office of President, or acting as President, during the term within which this Article becomes operative from holding the office of President or acting as President during the remainder of such term.

Section 2.

This article shall be inoperative unless it shall have been ratified as an amendment to the Constitution by the legislatures of three-fourths of the several States within seven years from the date of its submission to the States by the Congress.

Passed by Congress March 21, 1947. Ratified February 27, 1951.

Amendment XXIII

Section 1.

The District constituting the seat of Government of the United States shall appoint in such manner as the Congress may direct:

A number of electors of President and Vice President equal to the whole number of Senators and Representatives in Congress to which the District would be entitled if it were a State, but in no event more than the least populous State; they shall be in addition to those appointed by the States, but they shall be considered, for the purposes of the election of President and Vice President, to be electors appointed by a State; and they shall meet in the District and perform such duties as provided by the twelfth article of amendment.

Section 2.

The Congress shall have power to enforce this article by appropriate legislation.

Passed by Congress June 16, 1960. Ratified March 29, 1961.

Amendment XXIV

Section 1.

The right of citizens of the United States to vote in any primary or other election for President or Vice President, for electors for President or Vice President, or for Senator or Representative in Congress, shall not be denied or abridged by the United States or any State by reason of failure to pay any poll tax or other tax.

Section 2.

The Congress shall have power to enforce this article by appropriate legislation.

Passed by Congress August 27, 1962. Ratified January 23, 1964.

Amendment XXV

Section 1.

In case of the removal of the President from office or of his death or resignation, the Vice President shall become President.

Section 2.

Whenever there is a vacancy in the office of the Vice President, the President shall nominate a Vice President who shall take office upon confirmation by a majority vote of both Houses of Congress.

Section 3.

Whenever the President transmits to the President pro tempore of the Senate and the Speaker of the House of Representatives his written declaration that he is unable to discharge the powers and duties of his office, and until he transmits to them a written declaration to the contrary, such powers and duties shall be discharged by the Vice President as Acting President.

Section 4.

Whenever the Vice President and a majority of either the principal officers of the executive departments or of such other body as Congress may by law provide, transmit to the President pro tempore of the Senate and the Speaker of the House of Representatives their written declaration that the President is unable to discharge the powers and duties of his office, the Vice President shall immediately assume the powers and duties of the office as Acting President.

Thereafter, when the President transmits to the President pro tempore of the Senate and the Speaker of the House of Representatives his written declaration that no inability exists, he shall resume the powers and duties of his office unless the Vice President and a majority of either the principal officers of the executive department or of such other body as Congress may by law provide, transmit within four days to the President pro tempore of the Senate and the Speaker of the House of Representatives their written declaration that the President is unable to discharge the powers and duties of his office. Thereupon Congress shall decide the issue, assembling within forty-eight hours for that purpose if not in session. If the Congress, within twenty-one days after receipt of the latter written declaration, or, if Congress is not in session, within twenty-one days after Congress is required to assemble, determines by two-thirds vote of both Houses that the President is unable to discharge the powers and duties of his office, the Vice President shall continue to discharge the same as Acting President; otherwise, the President shall resume the powers and duties of his office.

Passed by Congress July 6, 1965. Ratified February 10, 1967.

Amendment XXVI

Section 1.

The right of citizens of the United States, who are eighteen years of age or older, to vote shall not be denied or abridged by the United States or by any State on account of age.

Section 2.

The Congress shall have power to enforce this article by appropriate legislation.

Passed by Congress March 23, 1971. Ratified July 1, 1971.

Amendment XXVII

No law, varying the compensation for the services of the Senators and Representatives, shall take effect, until an election of Representatives shall have intervened.

Originally proposed Sept. 25, 1789. Ratified May 7, 1992.

Transcriptions and Bibliography

Magna Carta

Transcription: National Archives U.K. (translation to modern English by the British Library)

GREAT CHARTER OF LIBERTIES (1215) reprinted in SELECT DOCUMENTS OF ENGLISH CONSTITUTIONAL HISTORY, 42, 47 (George Burton Adams & H. Morse Stephens eds. 1904)

English Declaration of Rights/English Bill of Rights

Transcription: *An Act Declaring the Rights and Liberties of the Subject and Settling the Succession of the Crown*, Lillian Goldman Law Library, Yale University.
See also LOIS G. SCHWOERER, THE DECLARATION OF THE LORDS SPIRITUAL AND TEMPORAL, AND COMMONS, ASSEMBLED AT WESTMINSTER (Baltimore and London, 1981) (transcribing "presentation copy" of the document read to Prince William and Princess Mary on February 13, 1689)

PAUL D. HALLIDAY, HABEAS CORPUS: FROM ENGLAND TO EMPIRE (2010)

AMANDA L. TYLER, HABEAS CORPUS IN WARTIME: FROM THE TOWER OF LONDON TO GUANTANAMO BAY (2017)

Declaration of Rights and Grievances

Transcription: Stamp Act Congress and Lewis Cruger, *Journal of the first Congress of the American Colonies, in opposition to the tyrannical acts of the British Parliament*, New York, E. Winchester, 1845 (retrieved from the Library of Congress)

MICHAEL J. KLARMAN, THE FRAMERS' COUP: THE MAKING OF THE UNITED STATES CONSTITUTION (2016)

Akhil Reed Amar, America's Constitution: A Biography (2006)

Pauline Maier, American Scripture: Making the Declaration of Independence (1997)

Declaratory Act

Transcription: American Colonies Act 1766 (Declaratory Act), 6 Geo. 3. c. 12 (Eng.), Lillian Goldman Law Library, Yale Law School

Declaration of Resolves of the First Continental Congress

Transcription: Documents Illustrative of the Formation of the Union of the American States, Government Printing Office (1927) House Document No. 398 (available via Internet Archive)

Thomas Jefferson, A Summary View of the Rights of British America (1774)

Articles of Association

Transcription: Articles of Association, National Archives

Abraham Lincoln, *First Inaugural Address*, Library of Congress

Petition to King George III

Transcription: Petition of Congress to King George III, Journals of the Continental Congress

Olive Branch Petition to King George III

Transcription: Olive Branch Petition to King George III, Library of Congress

Pauline Maier, American Scripture: Making the Declaration of Independence (1997)

Adam Smith, An Inquiry into the Nature and Causes of the Wealth of Nations (1776)

King George III's Proclamation for Suppressing Rebellion

Transcription: A Proclamation for Suppressing Rebellion and Sedition, Founders' Library

Declaration on the Causes and Necessity of Taking Up Arms

Transcription: Declaration on the Causes and Necessity of Taking Up Arms, National Archives

Samuel Johnson, Taxation No Tyranny (1775)

Declaration of Independence

Transcription (Draft): Jefferson's "Original Rough Draught" of the Declaration of Independence, National Archives

Transcription (Final): Engrossed Declaration of Independence, National Archives

Transcription and Images of 1776 Virginia Constitution and Declaration of Rights, Library of Virginia

CARL L. BECKER, THE DECLARATION OF INDEPENDENCE: A STUDY IN THE HISTORY OF POLITICAL IDEAS (1922)

PAULINE MAIER, AMERICAN SCRIPTURE: MAKING THE DECLARATION OF INDEPENDENCE (1997)

JULIAN P. BOYD, THE DECLARATION OF INDEPENDENCE: THE CREATION OF THE TEXT (1999)

BERNARD BAILYN, THE IDEOLOGICAL ORIGINS OF THE AMERICAN REVOLUTION (1967)

GORDON S. WOOD, THE RADICALISM OF THE AMERICAN REVOLUTION (1991)

JAMES MUNVES, THOMAS JEFFERSON AND THE DECLARATION OF INDEPENDENCE: WRITING AND EDITING THE DOCUMENT THAT MARKED THE BIRTH OF THE UNITED STATES OF AMERICA (1978)

GARRY WILLS, INVENTING AMERICA: JEFFERSON'S DECLARATION OF INDEPENDENCE (1978)

KERMIT ROOSEVELT, III, THE NATION THAT NEVER WAS: RECONSTRUCTING AMERICA'S STORY (2022)

CHRISTOPHER HITCHENS, THOMAS JEFFERSON: AUTHOR OF AMERICA (2009)

ALLEN JAYNE, JEFFERSON'S DECLARATION OF INDEPENDENCE: ORIGINS, PHILOSOPHY, AND THEOLOGY (1998)

THOMAS JEFFERSON, A SUMMARY VIEW OF THE RIGHTS OF BRITISH AMERICA (1774)

JOHN LOCKE, TWO TREATISES OF GOVERNMENT (G. Routledge and Sons 1903)

Article of Confederation

Transcription (Draft): John Dickinson Draft Articles of Confederation (July 12, 1776), Journals of the Continental Congress

Transcription (Final): Engrossed Articles of Confederation (November 15, 1777) National Archives; *see also* Journals of the Continental Congress, Volume 9

MICHAEL J. KLARMAN, THE FRAMERS' COUP: THE MAKING OF THE UNITED STATES CONSTITUTION (2016)

AKHIL REED AMAR, AMERICA'S CONSTITUTION: A BIOGRAPHY (2006)

GORDON S. WOOD, THE RADICALISM OF THE AMERICAN REVOLUTION (1993)

Merrill Jensen , The Articles of Confederation: An Interpretation of the Social-Constitutional History of the American Revolution (1959)

Jane E. Calvert, John Dickinson and the Making of the U.S. Constitution, 1776–1788 (2020)

J. H. Powell, *John Dickinson: Notes and Documents*, The Pennsylvania Magazine of History and Biography 65, no. 4 (1941): 458–81

Northwest Ordinance

Transcription: Miscellaneous Papers of the Continental Congress, 1774–1789, National Archives

Map of the Northwest Territory, World Maps

The Ordinance of 1784 (April 23, 1784)

Andrew C. McLaughlin, The Confederation and the Constitution, 1783–1789 (1905)

Jay Amos Barrett, Evolution Of The Ordinance of 1787: With An Account Of The Earlier Plans For The Government Of The Northwest Territory (1891)

Michael J. Klarman, The Framers' Coup: The Making of the United States Constitution (2016)

Constitution of the United States

Transcription (Draft): Proof Copy of the Committee of Detail Draft, National Archives

Transcription (Final): Engrossed Constitution of United States of America, National Archives

An Act for the Punishment of Certain Crimes Against the United States, 1 Stat. 112, 112–15 (1790)

William Blackstone, Commentaries on the Law of England (Kerr ed. 1876)

James Willard Hurst, The Law of Treason in the United States 5 (1971)

John Locke, Two Treatises of Government (G. Routledge and Sons 1903)

Philip B. Kurland & Ralph Lerner, The Founders' Constitution (1986)

Michael J. Klarman, The Framers' Coup: The Making of the United States Constitution (2016)

John P. Kaminski, et al., The Documentary History of the Ratification of the Constitution (*Multiple Volumes*)

Akhil Reed Amar, America's Constitution: A Biography (2006)

Gordon S. Wood, The Radicalism of the American Revolution (1993)

Eric Foner: Reconstruction: America's Unfinished Revolution, 1863–1877 (2014)

Pauline Maier, Ratification: The People Debate the Constitution, 1787–1788 (2010)

Amanda L. Tyler, Habeas Corpus in Wartime: From the Tower of London to Guantanamo Bay (2014)

Montesquieu, Spirit of the Laws (Colonial Press 1899)

Thomas Hobbes, Leviathan (1651)

Denys P. Myers, *History of the Printed Archetype of The Constitution of the United States of America*, reprinted in 11 Green Bag 2d 217 (2008)

A William Michael Treanor, *The Case of the Dishonest Scrivener: Gouverneur Morris and the Creation of the Federalist Constitution*, 120 Mich. L. Rev. 1 (2021)

Akhil Reed Amar, *Our Forgotten Constitution: A Bicentennial Comment*, 97 Yale L. J. 281 (1987)

David S. Yellin, *The Elements of Constitutional Style: A Comprehensive Analysis of Punctuation in the Constitution*, 79 Tenn. L. Rev. 687 (2012)

William Baude & Michael Stokes Paulsen, *The Sweep and Force of Section Three*, 172 U. Pa. L. Rev. 605 (2024)

Vasan Kesavan & Michael Stokes Paulsen, *Is West Virginia Unconstitutional?*, 90 Cal. L. Rev. 291 (2002)

Frederick Douglass, *The Constitution of the United States: Is It Pro-Slavery or Anti-Slavery?*, Speech, Glasgow, March 26, 1860

Handwritten Voting Records of the Constitutional Convention, National Archives, NAID 301680

Bill of Rights; Amendments

Draft transcriptions provided in text. Final: National Archives

Bernard Schwartz, The Great Rights of Mankind: A History of the American Bill of Rights (1977)

Bernard Schwartz, The Bill of Rights: A Documentary History (1971)

Kurt Lash, The Reconstruction Amendments: The Essential Documents (2021)

Michael J. Klarman, The Framers' Coup: The Making of the United States Constitution (2016)

Akhil Reed Amar, America's Constitution: A Biography (2006)

Akhil Reed Amar, The Bill of Rights (1998)

Pauline Maier, Ratification: The People Debate the Constitution, 1787–1788 (2010)

Kermit Roosevelt, III, The Nation That Never Was: Reconstructing America's Story (2022)

Congress Creates the Bill of Rights, National Archives

Constitution of the United States Compared to the Constitution of the Confederate States of America

Transcription (Confederate Constitution): Engrossed Constitution of the Confederate States of America, The University of Georgia Libraries. *See also* Library of Congress

Transcription (U.S. Constitution): Engrossed Constitution of United States of America, National Archives

Journal of the Congress of the Confederate States of America 1861–1865, Library of Congress

Marshall L. DeRosa, The Confederate Constitution of 1861: An Inquiry into American Constitutionalism (1991)

Henry Putney Beers, The Confederacy: A Guide to the Archives of the Confederate States of America (1986)

Image Credits

George Washington's Annotated Committee of Detail Draft	National Archives, NAID 1501555
William Samuel Johnson's Written *Declaration of Rights and Grievances*	Library of Congress
1215 Magna Carta	British Library
English Bill of Rights	Parliamentary Archives
Journals of the First Continental Congress	Library of Congress
1p Stamp Act Stamp (1765 proof)	Smithsonian National Postal Museum
William Samuel Johnson's Written *Declaration of Rights and Grievances*	Library of Congress
Declaration of Rights and Grievances, Papers of the Continental Congress	House of Representatives
Engrossed Articles of Association	National Archives, NAID 6277397
Benjamin Franklin's "Unite or Die" Political Cartoon	American Philosophical Society
Engrossed Version of Petition to King George III (from the Papers of Benjamin Franklin)	Library of Congress
Olive Branch Petition to King George III	New York Public Library
Thomas Jefferson's Draft Declaration on the Causes and Necessity of Taking Up Arms	Library of Congress

Portsmouth, PA Broadside Printing of Declaration on the Causes and Necessity of Taking Up Arms	Library of Congress
A Proclamation for Suppressing Rebellion and Sedition	National Archives, NAID 44276869
Jefferson's Written Draft Declaration of Independence	Library of Congress
Engrossed Declaration of Independence	National Archives, NAID 1419123
William Stone Engraving of the Declaration of Independence	National Archives, NAID 1656604
Benjamin Franklin's Sketch of Articles of Confederation	National Archives (Microfilm Publication M247, roll 22)
Engrossed Articles of Confederation	National Archives, NAID 301687
George Washington's Annotated Committee of Detail Draft	National Archives, NAID 1501555
George Washington's Annotated Copy of Committee of Style Draft	Library of Congress
Engrossed Constitution of the United States of America	National Archives, NAID 1667751
Bill of Rights	National Archives, NAID
Engrossed Constitution of the Confederate States of America	University of Georgia Libraries
Drafter Portraits	Creative Commons

Index

F

G

H

I

J